Microsoft

T0073284

Exam Ref MS-900:
Microsoft 365
Fundamentals,
Second Edition

Exam Ref MS-900
Microsoft 365
Fundamentals,
Second Edition

Craig Zacker

Exam Ref MS-900 Microsoft 365 Fundamentals, Second Edition

Published with the authorization of Microsoft Corporation by:
Pearson Education, Inc.

ISBN-13: 978-0-13-823711-0
ISBN-10: 0-13-823711-5

Library of Congress Control Number: 2023945794

1 2023

TRADEMARKS

Microsoft and the trademarks listed at *http://www.microsoft.com* on the "Trademarks" webpage are trademarks of the Microsoft group of companies. All other marks are property of their respective owners.

WARNING AND DISCLAIMER

SPECIAL SALES

For information about buying this title in bulk quantities or for special sales opportunities (which may include electronic versions; custom cover designs; and content particular to your business, training goals, marketing focus, or branding interests), please contact our corporate sales department at corpsales@pearsoned.com or (800) 382-3419.

For government sales inquiries, please contact governmentsales@pearsoned.com.

For questions about sales outside the U.S., please contact intlcs@pearson.com.

CREDITS

EDITOR-IN-CHIEF
Brett Bartow

EXECUTIVE EDITOR
Loretta Yates

ASSOCIATE EDITOR
Shourav Bose

DEVELOPMENT EDITOR
Rick Kughen

MANAGING EDITOR
Sandra Schroeder

SENIOR PROJECT EDITOR
Tracey Croom

COPY EDITOR
Rick Kughen

INDEXER
Timothy Wright

PROOFREADER
Charlotte Kughen

TECHNICAL EDITOR
Ed Fisher

EDITORIAL ASSISTANT
Cindy Teeters

COVER DESIGNER
Twist Creative, Seattle

COMPOSITOR
codeMantra

Pearson's commitment to diversity, equity, and inclusion

Pearson is dedicated to creating bias-free content that reflects the diversity of all learners. We embrace the many dimensions of diversity, including but not limited to race, ethnicity, gender, socioeconomic status, ability, age, sexual orientation, and religious or political beliefs.

Education is a powerful force for equity and change in our world. It has the potential to deliver opportunities that improve lives and enable economic mobility. As we work with authors to create content for every product and service, we acknowledge our responsibility to demonstrate inclusivity and incorporate diverse scholarship so that everyone can achieve their potential through learning. As the world's leading learning company, we have a duty to help drive change and live up to our purpose to help more people create a better life for themselves and to create a better world.

Our ambition is to purposefully contribute to a world where:

- Everyone has an equitable and lifelong opportunity to succeed through learning.
- Our educational products and services are inclusive and represent the rich diversity of learners.
- Our educational content accurately reflects the histories and experiences of the learners we serve.
- Our educational content prompts deeper discussions with learners and motivates them to expand their own learning (and worldview).

While we work hard to present unbiased content, we want to hear from you about any concerns or needs with this Pearson product so that we can investigate and address them.

- Please contact us with concerns about any potential bias at
  https://www.pearson.com/report-bias.html.

Contents at a glance

Contents

About the author

CRAIG ZACKER is the author or co-author of dozens of books, manuals, articles, and websites on computing and networking, including *Exam Ref 70-740 Installation, Storage and Compute with Windows Server 2016*, and *Exam Ref 70-744 Securing Windows Server 2016*. He has also been an English professor, editor, network administrator, webmaster, corporate trainer, technical support engineer, minicomputer operator, literature and philosophy student, library clerk, darkroom technician, shipping clerk, and newspaper boy.

Introduction

The Microsoft 365 Certified Fundamentals certification is the initial entry point into a hierarchy of Microsoft 365 certifications. The MS-900 Microsoft 365 Fundamentals exam tests the candidate's knowledge of the components and capabilities of the Microsoft 365 products without delving into specific administrative procedures. With the Fundamentals certification in place, IT pros can then move up to Associate level certifications that concentrate on specific areas of Microsoft 365 administration, such as messaging, security, desktop, and teamwork. The ultimate pinnacle in the hierarchy is the Microsoft 365 Certified: Administrator Expert certification, achievable by passing the MS-102 exam.

This book covers all of the skills measured by the MS-900 exam, with each of the four main areas covered in a separate chapter. Each chapter is broken down into individual skill sections, which cover all of the suggested topics for each skill. It is recommended that you access a trial version of Microsoft 365 as you work your way through this book. Nothing can replace actual hands-on experience, and Microsoft provides a fully functional evaluation platform of Microsoft 365 Enterprise, all the components of which are accessible in the cloud and require no hardware other than a computer with Internet access. Microsoft also provides a wealth of documentation for all of the Microsoft 365 components at *learn.microsoft.com*. With these tools, as well as some time and dedication, you can prepare yourself for the MS-900 exam and the first step toward your Microsoft 365 career.

Organization of this book

This book is organized by the "Skills measured" list published for the exam. The "Skills measured" list is available for each exam on the Microsoft Learn website: *microsoft.com/learn*. Each chapter in this book corresponds to a major topic area in the list, and the technical tasks in each topic area determine a chapter's organization. For example, if an exam covers six major topic areas, the book will contain six chapters.

Preparing for the exam

Microsoft certification exams are a great way to build your resume and let the world know about your level of expertise. Certification exams validate your on-the-job experience and product knowledge. Although there is no substitute for on-the-job experience, preparation through study and hands-on practice can help you prepare for the exam. This book is *not* designed to teach you new skills.

We recommend augmenting your exam preparation plan by using a combination of available study materials and courses. For example, you might use the *Exam Ref* and another study guide for your at-home preparation and take a Microsoft Official Curriculum course for the classroom experience. Choose the combination that you think works best for you. Learn more about available classroom training, online courses, and live events at *microsoft.com/learn*.

Note that this *Exam Ref* is based on publicly available information about the exam and the author's experience. To safeguard the integrity of the exam, authors do not have access to the live exam.

Microsoft certifications

Microsoft certifications distinguish you by proving your command of a broad set of skills and experience with current Microsoft products and technologies. The exams and corresponding certifications are developed to validate your mastery of critical competencies as you design and develop, or implement and support, solutions with Microsoft products and technologies both on-premises and in the cloud. Certification brings a variety of benefits to the individual and to employers and organizations.

> **MORE INFO** **ALL MICROSOFT CERTIFICATIONS**
>
> For information about Microsoft certifications, including a full list of available certifications, go to *microsoft.com/learn*.

Access the Exam Updates chapter and online references

The final chapter of this book, "*MS-900 Microsoft 365 Fundamentals, Second Edition* exam updates," will be used to provide information about new content per new exam topics, content that has been removed from the exam objectives, and revised mapping of exam objectives to chapter content. The chapter will be made available from the link below as exam updates are released.

Throughout this book are addresses to webpages that the author has recommended you visit for more information. Some of these links can be very long and painstaking to type, so we've shortened them for you to make them easier to visit. We've also compiled them into a single list that readers of the print edition can refer to while they read.

The URLs are organized by chapter and heading. Every time you come across a URL in the book, find the hyperlink in the list to go directly to the webpage.

Download the Exam Updates chapter and the URL list at *MicrosoftPressStore.com/ERMS900/downloads*.

Errata, updates & book support

We've made every effort to ensure the accuracy of this book and its companion content. You can access updates to this book—in the form of a list of submitted errata and their related corrections—at

MicrosoftPressStore.com/ERMS900/errata

If you discover an error that is not already listed, please submit it to us at the same page.

For additional book support and information, please visit *MicrosoftPressStore.com/Support*.

Please note that product support for Microsoft software and hardware is not offered through the previous addresses. For help with Microsoft software or hardware, go to *support.microsoft.com*.

Stay in touch

Let's keep the conversation going! We're on Twitter: *twitter.com/MicrosoftPress*.

CHAPTER 1

Describe cloud concepts

The cloud is one of the biggest buzzwords ever to emerge from the IT industry, but it is a word that is difficult to define in any but the most general terms. For a simple definition, you can say that the *cloud* is an Internet-based resource that provides subscribers with various types of IT services on demand. For users, the cloud enables them to run applications, stream video, download music, read email, and perform any number of other tasks, all without having to worry about where the servers are located, what resources they utilize, how much data is involved, and—in most cases—whether the service is operational. Like the electricity or the water in your house, you turn it on, and it is there—most of the time. For IT professionals, however, defining the cloud can be more difficult.

Skills in this chapter:

- Skill 1.1: Describe the different types of cloud services available
- Skill 1.2: Describe the benefits of and considerations for using cloud, hybrid, or on-premises services

Skill 1.1: Describe the different types of cloud services available

System administrators, software developers, database administrators, and user-support personnel all see the cloud in a different light and use it for different purposes. Cloud providers, such as Microsoft, Google, and Amazon, typically offer a wide variety of resources and services. They can provide virtualized hardware, such as servers, storage, and networks; software in the form of back-end server and user applications; and tools for messaging, content management, collaboration, identity management, analytics, and others. Services are provided on an *à la carte* basis, with the subscribers only paying for what they use.

> **This section covers how to:**
> - Describe Microsoft SaaS, IaaS, and PaaS concepts and use cases
> - Describe the differences between Office 365 and Microsoft 365

Understanding cloud services

Different types of IT professionals understand the cloud in different ways. For a system administrator, the cloud can provide virtual machines that function as servers in place of or alongside physical servers in the organization's datacenter. For software developers, the cloud can provide a variety of preconfigured platforms and development environments for application deployment and testing. For a database administrator, the cloud can provide complex storage architectures and preconfigured database management solutions. Cloud services can then organize the data and use artificial intelligence to develop new uses for that data. For user support technicians, the cloud can provide productivity applications and other software, such as Microsoft 365, that are more easily deployed than standalone applications, automatically updated regularly, and accessible on any device platform.

In each of these specializations, cloud services can eliminate the tedious set-up processes that administrators often have to perform before they can get down to work. For example, adding a new physical server to a datacenter can require many separate tasks, including assessing the hardware needs, selecting a vendor, waiting for delivery, assembling the hardware, and installing and configuring the operating system and applications. These tasks can result in days or weeks wasted before the server is even ready for use. With a cloud provider, adding a new virtual server takes only a matter of minutes. A remote management interface, such as the Windows Azure portal shown in Figure 1-1, enables the subscriber to select the desired virtual hardware resources for the server, and within a few minutes, the new server is running and ready for use.

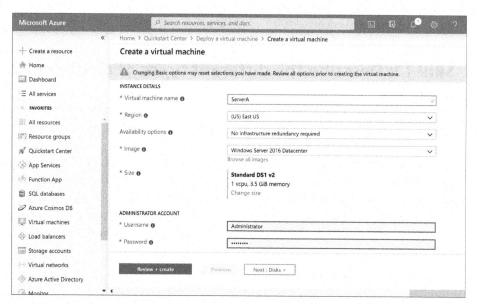

FIGURE 1-1 The Create A Virtual Machine interface in the Microsoft Azure Portal

Describe Microsoft SaaS, IaaS, and PaaS concepts and use cases

The offerings of cloud service providers are typically broken down into service models, which specify what elements of the cloud infrastructure are included with each product. There are three primary cloud service models: Infrastructure as a Service (IaaS), Platform as a Service (PaaS), and Software as a Service (SaaS). Some other products and services use the "as a Service" suffix, such as Desktop as a Service and Data as a Service.

A cloud infrastructure can be broken down into layers forming a stack, as shown in Figure 1-2. The functions of the layers are as follows:

- **People**   The users working with the application
- **Data**   The information that the application creates or utilizes
- **Application**   The top-level software program running on a virtual machine
- **Runtime**   An intermediate software layer, such as .NET or Java, that provides the environment in which applications run
- **Middleware**   A software component that provides intermediate services between an operating system and applications
- **Operating system**   The software that provides the basic functions of a virtual machine
- **Virtual network**   The logical connections between virtual machines running on servers
- **Hypervisor**   The software component on the physical servers that enables virtual machines to share the server's physical resources
- **Servers**   The physical computers that host the virtual machines that provide cloud services
- **Storage**   The hard drives and other physical components that make up the subsystem providing data storage for the physical servers
- **Physical network**   The cables, routers, and other equipment that physically connect the servers to each other and the Internet

In an organization that uses its own on-premises servers for everything, there is no cloud involved, and the organization is obviously responsible for managing all the layers of the stack. However, when an organization uses cloud-based services, the cloud service provider manages some layers of the stack, and the organization manages the rest. This is called a *shared responsibility model*. Which layers the organization or provider manages depends on the service model used to furnish the cloud product. The three basic cloud service models are described in the following sections.

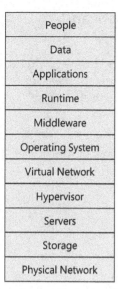

People
Data
Applications
Runtime
Middleware
Operating System
Virtual Network
Hypervisor
Servers
Storage
Physical Network

FIGURE 1-2 The layers of the cloud infrastructure

IaaS

Infrastructure as a Service (IaaS) is a cloud computing model in which a cloud service provider furnishes the client with the physical computing elements: the network, storage subsystem, physical servers, and the hypervisor running on the servers. This gives subscribers everything they need to create and manage their virtual machines. Therefore, all the cloud infrastructure layers above the hypervisor are the subscriber's responsibility, as shown in Figure 1-3.

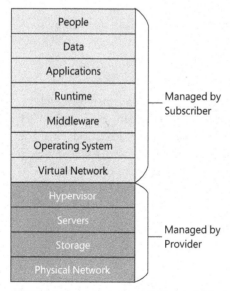

FIGURE 1-3 The shared responsibility model for IaaS

For example, when a subscriber uses Microsoft Azure to create a virtual machine, the provider is furnishing access to a physical server with hypervisor software—presumably Microsoft Hyper-V—running on it. The server has a physical storage subsystem and is connected to a physical network that provides access to the provider's other servers and the Internet. Using the management tools Azure provides, the subscriber can create a virtual machine containing a specific amount of memory, storage, and number of CPUs—all of which are realized virtually.

> **NEED MORE REVIEW?** **CLOUD COMPUTING WITH MICROSOFT AZURE**
>
> For more information on cloud computing as realized in Microsoft Azure, see *https://azure.microsoft.com/en-ca/overview/what-is-cloud-computing*.

The result is a virtual machine that the subscriber can install, configure, and use to run applications like a VM on an on-premises server. The difference is that the subscriber does not have to outfit a datacenter, build a network, procure a physical computer, and install the hypervisor. Instead, the subscriber pays a regular fee for the actual resources that the VM uses. The subscriber can add memory, storage, and CPUs to the VM or remove them as needed, and the subscriber can configure many other settings through a remote management interface. Additional resources incur additional fees, but the process of building a new server takes a matter of minutes instead of days or weeks.

With the IaaS model, the provider is responsible for the physical servers and the physical network, but the subscriber is responsible for managing and maintaining its virtual machines and the virtual network on which they run, as shown earlier in Figure 1-3. Therefore, the provider installs operating system and driver updates on the physical servers, but the subscriber must install any operating system and application updates needed on the virtual machines. The subscriber is responsible for any other VM software, maintenance, and management issues arising.

> **NOTE** **VM UPDATE MANAGEMENT**
>
> For an additional fee, Microsoft Azure can provide an Update Management solution that automates the installation of updates and patches on a subscriber's virtual machines.

Of all the cloud service models, IaaS places the greatest amount of responsibility on the subscriber, and in many instances, this is how administrators want it. By creating and configuring their own virtual machines, administrators can duplicate the environment of their on-premises servers, creating a hybrid cloud-bursting infrastructure that can handle overflow traffic during a busy season.

Organizations with high-traffic websites often run their sites with a dedicated web hosting service provider. However, building the site using virtual machines furnished by a cloud service provider using the IaaS model can often be a far less expensive proposition.

Subscribers can also use IaaS to create a testing and development environment for applications. Rapid deployment and modification of VMs allows administrators to create multiple temporary evaluation and testing platforms and take them down just as easily.

IaaS can also provide subscribers with VMs containing massive amounts of virtual hardware resources impractical to implement in on-premises servers. Large data sets and high-performance computing can require huge amounts of memory and processing power to perform the tasks required for applications such as weather patterning, data mining, and financial modeling. The resources of a high-end cloud service provider make it far less expensive to equip VMs with the necessary virtual hardware than to build physical servers with equivalent resources.

PaaS

In what is sometimes referred to as a *tiered cloud service model* infrastructure, *Platform as a Service (PaaS)* is the second tier in that it builds on the provider's responsibilities from the first (IaaS) tier. PaaS is designed to provide subscribers with a ready-made developmental platform that prevents them from repeatedly building out the virtual hardware and software infrastructure for a test system before they can run a new application.

Because the PaaS platform is accessible through the Internet like all cloud services, an organization with multiple developers working on the same project can provide them all with access to the test environment, even if they are located at different sites.

The PaaS model expands the cloud service provider's responsibility over the IaaS model by adding the virtual network, operating system, middleware, and runtime layers, as shown in Figure 1-4. The greater the responsibility of the provider, the less that of the subscriber.

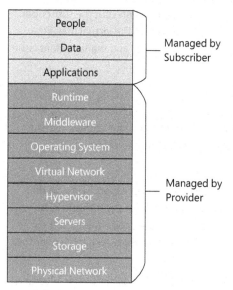

FIGURE 1-4 The shared responsibility model for PaaS

Unlike virtual machines using the IaaS model, the cloud service provider is entirely responsible for the VM operating system, applying updates and patches and performing maintenance as needed. The platform can also include (for an extra fee) additional components specified by the subscriber, such as development tools, middleware, and database management systems. The object of the PaaS model is to eliminate the need for software developers to do anything but actually develop, build, customize, test, and deploy their applications.

Serverless

The fees for PaaS and IaaS virtual machines are typically based on the resources they are configured to use and the amount of time they are running. However, *serverless computing* is another cloud service model for application development related to PaaS. In serverless computing (sometimes known as *Function as a Service* or FaaS), the cloud provider takes on even more server management responsibility by dynamically allocating virtual machine resources in response to application requests or events.

Pricing is based on the resources the VM is actually using. Therefore, this model can be less expensive than a PaaS VM that is incurring charges all the time it is running. In this instance, the term *serverless* does not mean that no server is involved; the name derives from the fact that the cloud subscriber does not have to provision a virtual machine on which the developer's code will run.

SaaS

Software as a Service (SaaS) is the third tier of the cloud service model infrastructure, and in this model, the cloud provider is responsible for nearly all the layers. Only the people and data layers are left to the subscriber, as shown in Figure 1-5. This means the provider is responsible for the applications and all the layers beneath.

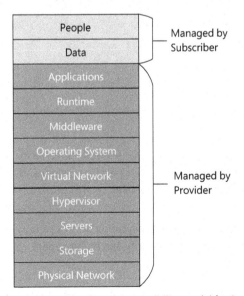

FIGURE 1-5 The shared responsibility model for SaaS

The SaaS model enables users to access cloud-based applications using a web or other thin-client interface without installing the applications first. The Office productivity applications are examples of an SaaS product, as are Microsoft Teams and other Microsoft 365 components. While Microsoft 365 makes it possible to install the Office productivity applications on a client computer, it is unnecessary for the user to do so. The applications are accessible directly through a web browser, with everything but the user's own data files provided through the cloud.

Describe differences between Office 365 and Microsoft 365

In 2020, Microsoft officially changed the name of the Office 365 products to Microsoft 365; at the same time, the distinction between the two products was changed. The Office 365 product was originally a licensing solution that enabled organizations and individuals to subscribe to all standard productivity applications, including Word, Excel, and PowerPoint, with a single license. Various editions of Office 365 also included cloud services, such as email.

For existing Office 365 subscribers, the change is primarily in the software's branding. All Office 365 subscriptions were automatically changed to Microsoft 365 subscriptions in 2020 without altering their terms. Microsoft is also gradually updating the Office 365 websites and apps to reflect the name change and the new Microsoft 365 logo, as shown in Figure 1-6.

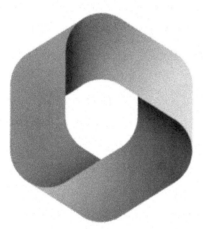

FIGURE 1-6 The Microsoft 365 logo

The Microsoft 365 products include the productivity applications, which are still referred to as Office applications, but the package also includes the latest Windows operating system and a larger selection of cloud-based communication and collaboration services, such as Microsoft Exchange, SharePoint, Teams, and Yammer.

With editions designed for home, business, enterprise, and education subscribers at various price levels, Microsoft 365 can also include a variety of additional security and management tools, such as Microsoft Intune and Azure Information Protection.

Skill 1.2: Describe the benefits of and considerations for using cloud, hybrid, or on-premises services

Flexibility is an important aspect of cloud computing, and Microsoft 365 can accommodate a wide variety of IT environments. While some organizations might be building a Microsoft 365 deployment from scratch, others might have existing infrastructure they want to incorporate into a Microsoft 365 solution. Before it is possible to explore how this can be done, it is important to understand the various types of cloud architectures and service models.

This section covers how to:
- Describe public, private, and hybrid cloud models
- Compare costs and advantages of cloud, hybrid, and on-premises services
- Describe the concept of hybrid work and flexible work

Describe public, private, and hybrid cloud models

Organizations today use cloud resources in different ways and for various reasons. A new business or division might build an entirely new IT infrastructure using only cloud-based resources. Meanwhile, a business already invested in a traditional on-premises IT infrastructure might use the cloud to expand or add selected services. Organizations planning their infrastructures can use any of the three cloud architecture permutations described in the following sections: public, private, and hybrid.

Public cloud

A *public cloud* is a network of servers owned by a third-party service provider at a remote location, which provides subscribers with access to virtual machines or services through the Internet, often for a fee. Prices are based on the resources or services you use. Microsoft Azure, Amazon Web Services, and Google Cloud are all examples of public cloud service providers organizations use to host their virtual machines and access other services.

> **NOTE PUBLIC DOES NOT MEAN UNPROTECTED**
> The term *public cloud* is something of a misnomer; it does not mean that the virtual machines an organization creates in a provider's cloud are public—that is, open to access by anyone. It means only that the provider furnishes services to the public by subscription, accessible from any location at any time via the Internet.

These major players in the public cloud industry maintain thousands of servers in datacenters located around the world. They can accommodate large enterprise clients by providing services on a global scale. There are other, smaller cloud providers offering the same services, which might not be able to function on such a massive scale, but these can also have their advantages. Because the cloud service providers are responsible for managing and maintaining the physical servers, the subscribers save a great deal of time, expense, and human resources.

There are two basic types of public cloud deployment that organizations can use, as follows:

- **Shared public cloud** Subscribers access services that a third-party provider implements on hardware that other subscribers might use simultaneously. For example, a physical host server at a provider site can run virtual machines belonging to different subscribers simultaneously, as shown in Figure 1-7. The VMs are secured individually and functionally isolated from each other. This is what is typically meant by a public cloud.

- **Dedicated public cloud** Subscribers contract with a third-party provider for a hardware infrastructure dedicated to their exclusive use. (See Figure 1-8.) The services provided are the same as those in a shared public cloud; the only difference is the hardware the provider uses to furnish the services. Obviously, this arrangement is more expensive than a shared public cloud, but some organizations need the additional security and fault tolerance provided by having hardware dedicated to their own use.

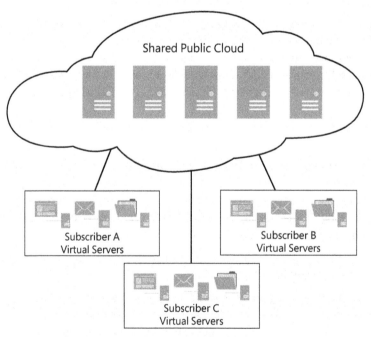

FIGURE 1-7 Virtual servers running in a shared public cloud

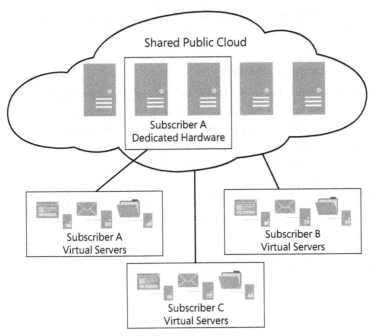

FIGURE 1-8 Virtual servers running in a dedicated public cloud

Therefore, the term *public cloud* can refer to a provider that enables businesses to build their IT networks virtually instead of physically. Microsoft 365 subscribers can use these services to implement all or part of their productivity infrastructure. However, this is not the only function of the public cloud. When people stream movies to their televisions, use web-based banking services, or access their email online, they use public cloud providers. The difference in these cases is that the provider furnishes specific services instead of an IT infrastructure.

Private cloud

A *private cloud* is a network of servers owned and operated by a business solely for its own use. While the services can be the same and appear identical to their end users, the primary difference is that the organization has control over the physical hardware as well.

A public cloud deployment typically works in one of two ways: either the subscriber creates virtual machines on the provider's servers and uses them to install and run specific applications, or the subscriber contracts with the provider for access to services running on the provider's virtual machines. A private cloud deployment usually works in much the same way. In most cases, the organization still creates and utilizes virtual machines to run its applications, but it creates those virtual machines on its physical host servers.

Another variation on the private cloud is the *hosted private cloud*, in which hardware owned or leased by an organization is housed and managed by a third-party provider. The organization has exclusive use of the hardware and avoids the expenses of building and managing a datacenter. They do have to pay ongoing housing fees to the provider, and this arrangement might not satisfy all data storage stipulations, but the overall cost is likely to be less than an on-premises private cloud.

The private cloud architecture can provide a level of security and privacy that a public cloud provider might not be able to meet. An organization might have government contract stipulations or legal requirements that compel them to maintain their own hardware and store sensitive data on-site rather than use third-party hardware not subject to the same stipulations or requirements. For example, the Health Insurance Portability and Accountability Act (HIPAA) dictates how medical data must be secured and protected in the United States. Regardless of whether a third-party cloud provider is involved, a company is legally responsible for all the data stored on its servers. Another example is that an organization might also need to run a legacy application requiring a specific hardware or software configuration that a third-party provider cannot supply.

A private cloud can also provide a greater degree of customization than public cloud resources. Public cloud providers are successful because of the scale of their businesses; their services are configurable, using the options most desired by most of their clients. They are not likely to provide access to obscure software options that only a few of their clients will need. In the case of a private cloud, an organization has access to any and all of the customization options provided by the software they choose to install.

EXAM TIP

The difference between private and dedicated public clouds is who owns and operates the hardware. Exam candidates should be aware that some documentation uses the term *private cloud* instead of *dedicated public cloud* to describe hardware owned and operated by a third-party provider for the exclusive use of one subscriber.

The advantages of a private cloud are its disadvantages as well. The hardware owner is responsible for purchasing, housing, deploying, maintaining, and ultimately retiring that hardware, which can add greatly to the overall expense, as described earlier in this chapter. There are no ongoing subscriber fees for a private cloud, as there are with a public cloud provider, but there are ongoing fees for operating a datacenter, including floor space, power, insurance, and personnel.

The organization is also responsible for purchasing and maintaining licenses for all the software products needed to provide the necessary services. This can include operating system licenses, application server licenses, and user licenses, as well as the cost of additional software utilities. Typically, the overall costs of a private cloud infrastructure are higher than that of a public cloud and can be enormously higher. It is up to the organization to determine whether the advantages of the private cloud are worth the additional expense.

Hybrid cloud

A *hybrid cloud* combines public and private cloud functionality, enabling an organization to enjoy the best of both architectures. There are a variety of scenarios in which an organization might prefer to implement a hybrid cloud architecture.

If an organization has existing services implemented on its own physical hardware, it might want to maintain those services while adding others from a public cloud provider. For example, the organization might have reached the physical capacity of its own datacenter and does not want to invest in a major facility expansion.

An organization might also use public cloud resources to extend the capacity of its private cloud or its in-house network during temporary periods of greater need, such as seasonal business increases. This technique, called *cloudbursting*, eliminates the need for the organization to pay for hardware and other resources that are only required for brief periods. Because it is possible to connect the public and private services, the resources can interact in any necessary way. For example, a business with an e-commerce website implemented in a private cloud can add public cloud-based servers to its web server farm to accommodate the increase in traffic during its busy holiday season.

Another possibility is that an organization might be subject to the type of data storage or other security requirements described in the previous section, but they do not want to build out their entire infrastructure in a private cloud. In this scenario, the organization could conceivably deploy a database containing the sensitive data in a private cloud and use a public cloud provider for a website implementation linked to the database. This way, the network can comply with the storage requirements without having to go to the expense of deploying web servers and other services in the private cloud. The same is true for a variety of other services; organizations can keep their sensitive data and services in the private cloud and use the public cloud for the nonsensitive services. Organizations can also use private cloud resources to run legacy equipment or applications, while all the other services run on a less expensive public cloud.

Some cloud providers supply tools that enable administrators to manage their public and private cloud resources through a single interface. Microsoft Azure provides Azure Active Directory, for example, which enables a subscriber to use the same directory service for public and private cloud resources allowing administrators to access both with a single sign-on. Azure also provides management and security interfaces with built-in support for hybrid cloud architectures.

EXAM TIP

The MS-900 exam requires you to understand the role of the public, private, and hybrid architectures and the IaaS, PaaS, and SaaS service models in cloud computing. However, be sure also to understand how these elements fit in with the Microsoft 365 product.

Compare costs and advantages of cloud, hybrid, and on-premises services

When an organization is building a new IT infrastructure or expanding an existing one, the question of whether to use on-premises resources or subscriber-based cloud services is a critical decision to make these days. Cloud-based services might not be preferable for every computing scenario, but they can provide many advantages over on-premises datacenters. When designing an IT strategy, a business should consider both the practical needs of the organization, including data security and other business factors, and the relative costs of the required services.

Some of the advantages that cloud computing can provide in the various deployment models and their relative costs are discussed in the following sections.

Economy

Cloud services incur regular charges, but they are usually based solely on the subscribers' needs and what they use at a particular time. The monetary savings that result from using cloud services can be significant. Some of the expenses that can be reduced or eliminated by using cloud services include the following:

- **Hardware** The high-end server hardware used by a large enterprise, aside from the standard computer components, can include elaborate storage arrays and other redundant hardware that is an expensive initial outlay before any actual work starts. While the hardware required to construct a datacenter becomes a company financial asset, the leasing fees for equivalent virtualized hardware realized in the cloud are much lower and are amortized over the life of the projects it is used for.

- **Upgrades** In a large enterprise, physical servers and other hardware components have a documented life expectancy, after which they should be retired and replaced. Cloud hardware is virtual, so the subscriber is isolated from the maintenance costs of the provider's physical hardware. Those costs are, of course, factored into the price of the service, but they eliminate another substantial hardware outlay for the subscriber.

- **Software** Software licenses are a significant expense, especially for server-based products. In addition to operating systems and applications, utility software for firewalls, antivirus protection, and backups all add to the expenditure. In the case of cloud-based servers using the IaaS model, the subscriber is still responsible for the software charges. However, in the PaaS and SaaS models, the product's subscription price includes some or all the necessary license fees. As with hardware, software furnished on a subscription basis by a cloud provider requires little or no initial outlay. Typically, cloud-based software also includes updates the provider applies regularly. For example, a Microsoft 365 subscription includes software updates for all of its applications and services and the Windows operating system.

- **Environment** Outfitting a large datacenter on an organization's premises usually involves much more of an expenditure than the cost of the computer hardware alone. In addition to the square footage cost, a datacenter typically needs

  - Special air conditioning and other environmental controls

  - Electricity and power regulation equipment

  - Racks and other mounting hardware

  - Cables and other network connectivity equipment

  - Physical security infrastructure

Depending on the organization's needs, these costs can range from significant to astronomical. None of these expenses are required for cloud-based services, although the provider certainly factors their costs into the fees paid by the subscriber.

- **Network** A datacenter requires an Internet connection and might also require cross-connections between locations within the datacenter. The size and functionality of the datacenter determine how much throughput is required and what technology can best supply it. More speed costs more money, of course. Cloud-based resources eliminate much of this expense because connectivity is part of the service. The subscriber still requires an Internet connection for client and administrator access to the cloud resources, but the amount of data transferred is relatively small. By basing their servers in the cloud, the subscriber does not have to supply the throughput needed for incoming clients to access the servers from the Internet.

- **Redundancy** Depending on the organization's needs, fault tolerance can take the form of backup power supplies and drives, redundant servers, or even redundant datacenters in different cities, which can cause the deployment and operational costs to grow exponentially. Typically, cloud providers can provide these various types of fault tolerance at substantial savings. A contract with a cloud provider usually includes a service-level agreement (SLA) with an uptime availability percentage that insulates the subscriber from the actual fault tolerance mechanisms employed. The SLA simply guarantees that the contracted services will suffer no more than a specified amount of downtime. For example, a contract specifying 99 percent uptime (colloquially called a *two-nines contract*) allows for up to 3.65 days of downtime per year. A 99.9 percent (or *three-nines*) contract allows for up to 8.76 hours of downtime per year. Contract stipulations go up from there, with the cost rising as the allowed downtime decreases. For example, a 99.9999 percent (or *six-nines*) contract allows only 31.5 seconds of downtime per year. If the provider fails to meet the uptime percentage specified in the SLA, the contract typically calls for a credit toward part of the monthly fee or some other sort of reparation.

- **Personnel** A datacenter requires trained people to design, install, configure, and maintain all the equipment. While cloud-based service equivalents require configuration and maintenance, which administrators perform through a remote interface, eliminating the need for hardware installation and maintenance greatly reduces the staffing requirements and the overall cost of a datacenter deployment.

The costs of cloud-based services are not insignificant, but the nature of the financial investment is such that many organizations find them to be more fiscally practical than building and maintaining a physical datacenter. This is because the initial outlay for cloud services is minimal, and the ongoing costs are easily predictable.

Consolidation

Originally, IT departments provided services to users by building and maintaining datacenters containing servers and other equipment. One of the problems with this model is that the servers are often underutilized. To accommodate the increased workload of the "busy season," organizations often build datacenters with resources that far exceed their everyday needs. Therefore, some of those expensive resources remain idle most of the time. Virtual machines (VMs), such as those administrators can create using hypervisor products like Microsoft Hyper-V and VMware ESX, solve this problem. Virtual machines allow the consolidation of multiple logical servers into one physical computer. Administrators can scale VMs by adding or subtracting virtualized resources, such as memory and storage, or they can move the virtual machines from one physical computer to another, as needed.

Cloud providers use this same consolidation technique to provide their subscribers with virtual machines. For example, when a subscriber to Microsoft Azure creates a new server, what actually happens is that the Azure interface creates a new virtual machine on one of Microsoft's physical servers. The subscriber has no administrative access to the underlying physical computer hosting the VM, nor does the subscriber even know where the computer is physically located. The virtual machines on the physical server are also isolated from each other so that two subscribers who are the fiercest of competitors might have VMs running on the same host computer, and they would never know it. The provider can—and probably does—move VMs from one host computer to another when necessary to efficiently utilize the servers' physical resources, but this process is completely invisible to the subscribers.

The end result of this consolidation model is that each VM receives exactly the virtual hardware resources it needs at any particular time. Subscribers pay only for the virtualized resources the VMs are using. Nothing goes to waste.

Scalability

Business requirements change. They might increase or decrease over a matter of years and experience regular seasonal, monthly, weekly, or even daily activity cycles. A physical datacenter must be designed to support the peak activity level for the regular business cycles and also anticipate an expected degree of growth over several years. As mentioned earlier, this can mean purchasing more equipment than the business needs during most of its operational time, leaving that excess capacity often underused.

Cloud-based services avoid these periods of underutilization by being easily scalable. Because the hardware in a virtual machine is itself virtualized, an administrator can modify a VM's resources through a simple configuration change. An on-premises (that is, noncloud) virtual machine is obviously limited by the physical hardware in the computer hosting it and the resources used by other VMs on the same host. In a cloud-based VM, however, these limitations do not apply. The physical hardware resources are invisible to the cloud subscriber, so if the resources the subscriber wants to add to a VM are unavailable on its current host computer, the provider can invisibly move the VM to another host with sufficient resources.

A cloud-based service is scalable in two ways, as shown in Figure 1-9:

- **Vertical scaling**   Also known as *scaling up*, vertical scaling is the addition or subtraction of virtual hardware resources in a VM, such as memory, storage, or CPUs. The scaling process is simply adjusting the VM's parameters in a remote interface; scaling patterns can even be automated to accommodate regular business cycles. Therefore, the subscriber pays only for the resources the VMs used at any given time.

- **Horizontal scaling**   Also known as *scaling out*, horizontal scaling is the addition or subtraction of virtual machines to a cluster of servers running a particular application. For example, in the case of a cloud-based web server farm, incoming user requests can be shared among multiple VMs. Administrators can add or subtract VMs from the cluster if web traffic increases or decreases.

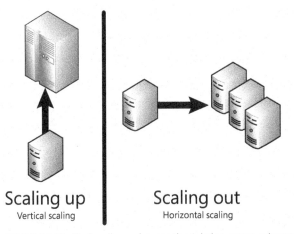

Scaling up
Vertical scaling

Scaling out
Horizontal scaling

FIGURE 1-9 Vertical scaling enhances the existing server, whereas horizontal scaling adds more servers.

For example, suppose an organization's website experiences a sudden increase in traffic that overwhelms the web servers. In that case, network administrators can handle the problem in two ways: either add resources to the existing servers, such as additional memory or storage, or add more servers.

In an on-premises datacenter, both options entail a degree of delay and downtime, which can affect the decision of which scaling to use. In a cloud-based environment, however, the decision is typically a matter of cost. Adding memory to a server or even adding another server are tasks completed in minutes, not days or weeks.

Reliability

In an on-premises datacenter, data backup, disaster recovery, and fault tolerance are expensive services requiring additional hardware, deployment time, and administration. A small business might require only a backup storage medium and software. However, for businesses with highly critical IT requirements, these services can call for more extensive (and more expensive) hardware resources, all the way up to duplicate datacenters in different cities with high-speed connections linking them.

This type of extreme hardware redundancy represents an enormous additional expense for an organization building its IT infrastructure. For large-scale cloud service providers, however, this type of redundancy is exactly what their infrastructure entails. Therefore, cloud providers are in an excellent position to provide these elaborate services without the need for hardware and facility upgrades, and they often can do it for fees that are much less than would be required for businesses to provide them themselves.

For example, Microsoft Azure provides the following reliability mechanisms for its cloud-based services:

- Azure maintains three redundant copies of all data, with one of those copies located in a separate datacenter from the others.
- Azure provides automatic failover to a backup server to minimize downtime during an outage.
- Azure hosts all applications on two separate server instances to minimize downtime caused by hardware failure.

The standard features of other cloud providers might differ, but the scale of their hardware investment usually makes it far easier and more economical for them to provide redundant services than for individual subscribers to purchase the necessary hardware themselves.

Manageability

Because subscribers do not have physical access to the servers hosting their cloud services, they must access them remotely. This is common for organizations with on-premises servers, particularly those with large datacenters. It is often far more convenient for administrators to access servers from their desks than travel to a datacenter on another floor, in another building, or even in another city. Today's remote management typically provides comprehensive and reliable access to server functions.

There are various remote management tools available for both cloud and on-premises resources. Still, the large third-party cloud providers typically provide a secured web-based portal that enables administrators to access all their subscription services using one interface, such as the one for Microsoft Azure shown in Figure 1-10.

FIGURE 1-10 The management interface in the Microsoft Azure Portal

A web-based portal enables administrators to access their services from any location, including from home or while traveling.

Security

Security is a major issue for any datacenter, which administrators typically address by dealing with issues such as data loss and unauthorized access. These are important concerns whether the datacenter is local or virtual. However, in the case of an on-premises datacenter, there is another potential attack vector: the physical. Servers and other equipment can be stolen outright, damaged by fire or other disasters, or physically accessed by intruders. Therefore, additional security measures, such as door locks, surveillance equipment, access credentials, or even manned security checkpoints, might be required.

Cloud-based services eliminate the need for the subscriber to maintain physical security because the provider furnishes it. However, there is still the issue of software-based security, and cloud providers nearly always provide an array of controls and services that enable you to harden the security of your servers and applications to accommodate your business needs.

> **NOTE** **YOU ARE ALWAYS RESPONSIBLE FOR YOUR DATA**
>
> Organizations using cloud resources to implement their servers must be aware that they are still responsible for the security and privacy of their data. For example, if an organization stores patient medical records on a cloud-based file server, the organization remains responsible for any data breaches. Therefore, contracts with cloud providers should stipulate the security policies they must maintain.

Infrastructure

In an on-premises datacenter, the administrators are responsible for all aspects of the servers and other equipment, including environmental control, hardware installation and maintenance, operating system configuration and updates, and application deployment and management. Cloud-based services enable subscribers to specify which infrastructure elements they are responsible for maintaining.

For example, a subscriber can use the IaaS model to contract with a provider for a virtual machine running a server operating system so that the subscriber is responsible for the entire deployment, operation, and maintenance of the virtual server. The subscriber does not have direct access to the physical hardware of the host system, of course, but they do have control over the virtual hardware on which the server is running, as well as all the software running on the server, including the operating system. In some situations, this is desirable or even essential.

In other situations, cloud-based services can take the form of preinstalled server platforms or applications. In this case, the subscriber might have limited access to the server or no access at all. For example, in the case of a subscriber contracting for Microsoft Exchange Online using the SaaS model, the provider grants the subscriber administrative access to the Exchange Server application. Still, it does not provide the subscriber access to the underlying operating system on which the server application is running. For a Microsoft 365 subscriber, the provider only grants access to the Office applications and the various administrative service portals. The subscriber knows nothing about the servers on which the applications run or their operating systems.

These options enable cloud service subscribers to exercise administrative responsibility over specific components only when their business requirements demand it. For the elements administered by the service provider, contracts typically stipulate hardware maintenance requirements and software update policies. The end result can be substantial savings in time and training for the subscriber's in-house IT personnel.

Alleged disadvantages of cloud computing

Some IT professionals persist in saying cloud-based services are inferior to on-premises services. They might say that an on-premises datacenter is more secure and reliable, provides greater equipment access, or suffers less downtime. While one cannot say that the cloud is always a preferable solution, these arguments mostly date from a time when the cloud was a new and immature technology. They have now largely been debunked by years of proven performance.

There are still reasons why businesses can and should maintain on-premises datacenters. For example, they might have special security requirements, or they might have already made a large investment in facilities and equipment. However, each year sees a greater percentage of servers deployed in the cloud and clients accessing cloud-based services. Microsoft 365 is the next step in bringing the cloud to the desktop productivity environment.

Describe the concept of hybrid work and flexible work

One of the primary focuses of Microsoft 365 products is to provide users with a variety of tools that facilitate collaboration. Microsoft Outlook, Teams, and Yammer are all applications that enable users to communicate from different locations and access common information. This capability has become particularly useful in recent years as more employees have been compelled to work from home and other remote locations.

Many organizations have discovered the usefulness of remote networking and collaboration tools—both for employees and employers—and are incorporating them into their standard policies. Two primary models for incorporating offsite work into a job description are hybrid work and flexible work.

Hybrid work

Hybrid work is typically defined as a position that splits employees' work time between the office and their home. In a hybrid work model, the employer establishes the employees' hours and locations using a rotating schedule. For example, one group of employees might be in the office on Mondays and Wednesdays, while another group is there on Tuesdays and Thursdays. All the employees work from home when they are not in the office.

One advantage of this model for the employer is that the demand for office space can be halved. By sharing work areas between the two groups in the office at different times, the employer can save on square footage, furniture, and HVAC costs. A potential disadvantage of this model is the added difficulty in communicating and sharing documents with colleagues at different locations. The Microsoft 365 collaboration tools are designed to make this communication possible, regardless of the users' locations.

The nature of hybrid work is that the employer creates the schedule, and the employees have to abide by it. Working from home might be unsuitable for some employees and impractical for some positions; a hybrid schedule is not likely to please everyone. However, many employees have discovered the advantages of working from home and welcome the continuation of the practice, even when outside circumstances do not require it.

Flexible work

In contrast to hybrid work is *flexible work*, sometimes known as *flex time*. Flexible work is a policy that allows individual employees to choose when and often where they work. As with the hybrid model, employees in a flexible model often divide their work time between the office and their homes. However, the difference is that the employee—not the employer—controls the schedule. Within certain constraints, employees are free to decide when they want to be (or have to be) in the office and when they prefer to work from home.

Flexible work might sound like a recipe for chaos, and it probably would be for some companies and jobs. Maintaining a hybrid schedule and knowing where employees are at any particular time can be a huge problem. However, the Microsoft 365 collaboration tools are designed for precisely those situations. Microsoft Teams, in particular, can provide employees with access to the applications and data they need as well as collaborative communications wherever they happen to be on the Internet.

Summary

- Cloud computing can provide organizations with many benefits, including economy scalability, reliability, manageability, and security.
- There are three cloud service models—IaaS, PaaS, and SaaS, which specify how much of the resource management is the responsibility of the cloud provider and how much is the responsibility of the subscriber.
- There are three basic cloud architectures:
  - **Public** Cloud resources are furnished by a third-party provider on the Internet.
  - **Private** An organization provides its own cloud resources.
  - **Hybrid** The public and private architectures are combined.
- Cloud-based collaboration tools like those in Microsoft 365 facilitate modern workforce models, such as hybrid and flexible work.

Thought experiment

In this thought experiment, demonstrate your skills and knowledge of the topics covered in this chapter. You can find answers to this thought experiment in the next section.

Wingtip Toys has a website on which they sell their products to customers worldwide; it is the company's primary source of sales. The website is hosted on a server farm in the company's datacenter, which is a small room in the building's basement. The incoming traffic is distributed among the servers by a load-balancing switch. Richard, the site administrator, regularly monitors the website traffic, and as the holiday season approaches, he sees the traffic level rise almost to the point at which the servers are overwhelmed.

There is no budget for the purchase of additional web server computers and no room for more servers in the datacenter. Reading about cloud options, Richard thinks that there might be a solution there. How can Richard expand the web server farm to handle the increased traffic for the least expense by using the cloud?

Thought experiment answer

For a minimal expenditure, Richard can create additional web servers using cloud-based virtual machines and add them to his web server farm, forming a hybrid cloud architecture. The cloud-based servers can help to handle the busy season web traffic, and when the traffic levels go down, Richard can remove the VMs from the server farm until they are needed again.

CHAPTER 2

Describe Microsoft 365 apps and services

In its original form, introduced in 2017, the Microsoft 365 product was marketed to enterprise customers and consisted of the following components:

- Office 365 Enterprise
- Windows 10 Enterprise
- Enterprise Mobility + Security

The object of the product is to provide users with a comprehensive workflow that combines cloud-based services, artificial intelligence, and machine learning capabilities. To do this, these three components actually consist of a variety of front-end and back-end applications and services, as described in the sections of this chapter.

In 2020, Microsoft announced the rebranding of the Office 365 consumer and business products to Microsoft 365, so there are now three tiers of Microsoft 365 products: Home, Business, and Enterprise, which can lead to some naming confusion. As of this writing, Microsoft is phasing out the Office brand entirely in favor of Microsoft 365 product names.

Skills in this chapter:

- Skill 2.1: Describe productivity solutions of Microsoft 365
- Skill 2.2: Describe collaboration solutions of Microsoft 365
- Skill 2.3: Describe endpoint modernization, management concepts, and deployment options in Microsoft 365
- Skill 2.4: Describe analytics capabilities of Microsoft 365

Skill 2.1: Describe productivity solutions of Microsoft 365

Microsoft Office is the earliest ancestor of Microsoft 365 and includes Microsoft Word, Excel, and PowerPoint. These became known as productivity applications, which are still at the core of Microsoft 365 products.

However, productivity has changed in the decades since the first Microsoft Office release, and so have the tools that users need to be productive. Microsoft 365 has evolved into a large collection of applications and services that can provide users with the means to be productive.

Describe the core productivity capabilities and benefits of Microsoft 365, including Microsoft Outlook and Microsoft Exchange, Microsoft 365 apps, and OneDrive

Microsoft 365 is not just a collection of workstation applications; it's designed more to be a comprehensive productivity solution for users, as well as a management solution for administrators. For users, the most visible element of Microsoft 365 is the familiar set of Office applications: Outlook, Word, Excel, and PowerPoint, applications they have probably been using for years. However, many Microsoft 365 components operate beneath the immediately visible applications, which help to protect the users and their data and provide them with intelligent communication and collaboration services.

Windows 11 Enterprise

Windows 11 is the operating system that enables users to access both the Office productivity applications and the services provided by the other Microsoft 365 components. The Microsoft 365 E3 and E5 product plans include an upgrade to the Enterprise edition of Windows 11. The Enterprise edition of Windows 11 includes security measures, deployment tools, and manageability functions that go beyond those of Windows 11 Pro, providing administrators of enterprise networks with centralized and automated protection of and control over fleets of workstations.

The Windows 11 Enterprise E3 operating system included in Microsoft 365 E3 is an upgrade to an existing Windows 11 Pro installation. The Microsoft 365 E5 product includes an operating system upgrade to Windows 11 Enterprise E5, which includes all of the E3 features plus Microsoft Defender for Endpoint.

Some of the additional features included in Windows 11 Enterprise are described in the following sections.

SECURITY

All Windows 11 editions include Windows Defender, which protects the operating system from various types of malware attacks. However, compared to Windows 11 Pro, Windows 11 Enterprise includes several enhancements to the Windows Defender software, including the following functions:

- **Windows Defender Application Guard** This enables enterprise administrators to create lists of trusted Internet sites, cloud resources, and intranet networks. When a user accesses an untrusted site using Microsoft Edge or Internet Explorer, Windows 11 automatically creates a Hyper-V-enabled container and opens the untrusted resource within the protected environment that the container provides. If the untrusted resource turns out to be malicious, the attacker is isolated within the container, and the host computer remains protected.

- **Windows Defender Application Control (WDAC)**   This provides defense against malicious applications by reversing the standard trust model in which applications are assumed to be trustworthy until proven otherwise. WDAC prevents a system from running any applications, plug-ins, add-ins, and other software modules that have not been identified as trusted using a policy created with Microsoft Intune or Group Policy. Windows 11 version 22H2 includes Smart App Control, a feature based on WDAC that uses Microsoft's security service to determine whether an app is too dangerous to run.

- **Microsoft Defender for Endpoint**   Windows 11 includes the client-side components of Microsoft Defender, a private cloud-based threat prevention, detection, and response engine. Windows 11 includes endpoint behavioral sensors, which collect behavioral information from the operating system and forward it to the Defender back-end servers in the enterprise's private cloud for analysis. Defender also protects the files in key system folders from unauthorized modification or encryption by ransomware and other attacks, applies exploit mitigation techniques to protect against known threats, enhances the network protection provided by Windows Defender SmartScreen, and performs automated real-time investigation and remediation of security breaches.

UPDATES

Windows 10 and 11 perform system updates differently from previous Windows versions, replacing the major service packs released every few years with semiannual feature updates. The Windows Update process is automated by default for the typical Windows user, but network administrators can still intervene in the process for testing update releases before they are generally deployed.

Microsoft provides the following tools for the administration of updates:

- **Windows Update for Business**   This free cloud-based service enables administrators to defer, schedule, and pause update deployments to specific workstations. Administrators can use the service to allow the installation of updates on designated test systems only and then deploy the updates later if no problems arise. Administrators can pause their deployments indefinitely if there are problems with particular updates.

- **Windows Server Update Service (WSUS)**   This free, downloadable service enables administrators to manage system updates internally by downloading releases to a WSUS server as they become available, testing them as needed, and then deploying them to workstations on a specific schedule. WSUS enables administrators to exercise complete control over the update deployment process. Also, it reduces the update's Internet bandwidth used by downloading releases only once and then distributing them using the internal network. Administrators can install multiple WSUS servers and distribute update preferences and release schedules among them, making the system highly scalable.

While administrators can use these tools to manage updates on workstations running any version of Windows, there are additional enhancements for Windows 11 Enterprise workstations, including its manageability with the Desktop Analytics tool. *Desktop Analytics* is an enhanced service incorporating all the upgrade compatibility and monitoring functionality of Windows Analytics, along with deeper integration into the Microsoft management tools, such as Configuration Manager, and a "single pane of glass" interface that provides administrators with a comprehensive view of the Windows 11 and Microsoft 365 update status.

Some of the update monitoring functions supported by Desktop Analytics are as follows:

- **Upgrade Readiness**   Desktop Analytics collects information about Windows, Microsoft 365, and other applications and drivers and analyzes it to identify any compatibility issues that might interfere with an upgrade.

- **Update Compliance**   Desktop Analytics gathers Windows 11 information about the progress of operating system update deployments, as well as Windows Defender Antivirus signature and result data, Windows Update for Business configuration settings, and Delivery Optimization usage data. After analyzing the information, Desktop Analytics reports any update compliance issues that might need administrative attention.

- **Device Health**   A Desktop Analytics solution that uses the enhanced diagnostic data generated by Windows 11 to identify devices and drivers causing regular crashes. The tool also provides potential remediations, such as alternative driver versions or application replacements.

> **NOTE   WINDOWS ANALYTICS BECOMES DESKTOP ANALYTICS**
>
> Upgrade Readiness, Update Compliance, and Device Health are all part of the Windows Analytics tool in Microsoft Azure, which was retired in 2020. Desktop Analytics is an enhanced version of the tool that integrates with SCCM and provides these same functions for Windows 11 Enterprise workstations.

MANAGEMENT

Microsoft 365 provides many enhancements to the enterprise management environment, enabling administrators to simplify deploying and configuring Windows 11 Enterprise workstations. One of the primary objectives of Microsoft 365 is to automate many of the routine tasks that occupy a great deal of an administrator's time.

- **Windows Autopilot**   This is a cloud-based feature designed to simplify and automate deploying Windows 11 workstations on an enterprise network. Instead of having to create and maintain images and drivers for every computer model, Autopilot uses cloud-based settings and policies to reconfigure the OEM-installed operating system into a user-ready workstation, even installing applications and applying a new product key to transform Windows 11 Pro to the Windows 11 Enterprise edition.

- **Microsoft Application Virtualization (App-V)**   This enables Windows workstations to access Win32 applications that are actually running on servers instead of local disks.

Administrators must install the App-V server components and publish the desired applications. A client component is also necessary, and Windows 11 Enterprise includes the App-V client by default, so no additional installation is necessary. However, the client has to be activated; administrators can activate clients using either Group Policy settings or the *Enable-App* cmdlet in Windows PowerShell.

Windows 10 Upgrade

The Microsoft 365 Business plans do not include the full Windows operating system package because the assumption is that potential deployers already have or will be purchasing computers with a Windows OEM operating system installed. However, Windows 10 or higher is required for the end-user workstations to function with the Microsoft 365 services, so the Microsoft 365 Business plans include upgrade benefits to Windows 10 Pro for computers currently running Windows 7 or Windows 8.1 Pro.

> **NOTE MICROSOFT 365 PLAN COMPONENTS**
>
> For more information about the components included in the various Microsoft 365 plans, see Chapter 4, "Understand Microsoft 365 pricing and support."

Exchange Online

Exchange Online is a cloud-based implementation of Microsoft's flagship messaging and collaboration server product. All Microsoft 365 Enterprise and Microsoft 365 Business plans include Exchange Online access for all users. This eliminates the need for organizations to install and maintain their own on-premises Exchange servers.

As with Microsoft Azure, Exchange Online uses shared servers in Microsoft datacenters to host the mailboxes and other services for multiple subscribers. The Exchange Online services available include the following:

- **Mailboxes**   Each user is provided with mail storage, the amount of which is based on the subscriber's Microsoft 365 plan. An In-Place Archive provides additional storage for mail. Exchange also supports shared mailboxes for groups of users who share responsibility for incoming mail.
- **Calendars**   Users can maintain events and appointments and share them with other users to create a unified scheduling and collaboration environment.
- **Shared calendars**   Users can share their calendars for scheduling, task management, and conference room booking. Exchange Online also provides a global address book, group management, and mailbox delegation.
- **Exchange Online Protection (EOP)**   EOP scans incoming email for spam and malicious code and forwards, deletes, or quarantines potentially dangerous messages based on rules established by administrators.

- **Unified Messaging (UM)** UM enables administrators to combine email messages with voice mail so each user can store both message types in a single mailbox. UM provides standard voice mail features, including call answering, and enables users to listen to their messages from the Outlook Inbox or by using Outlook Voice Access from any telephone.

- **Data Loss Prevention (DLP)** DLP enables administrators to create DLP policies that protect sensitive company information by using deep content analysis to filter messaging traffic based on keywords, regular expressions, dictionary terms, and other criteria and then take specific actions based on the type of information detected. For example, a DLP policy can identify email messages containing credit card numbers and either notify the sender, encrypt them, or block them outright. More complex policies can identify specific types of company documents and use virtual fingerprinting to identify their source.

Microsoft maintains two Exchange Online subscription plans: Plan 1, which is included with Microsoft 365 Business, and Plan 2, which has additional features and is included with Microsoft 365 Enterprise. The features included in each plan are listed in Table 2-1.

TABLE 2-1 Exchange Online plans for Microsoft 365

Exchange Online Plan 1 (Microsoft 365 Business)	Exchange Online Plan 2 (Microsoft 365 Enterprise)
50 GB of mailbox storage per user	100 GB of mailbox storage per user
In-Place Archive	Unlimited additional user storage in In-Place Archive
Access via desktop Outlook, Outlook on the web, and Outlook Mobile	Access via desktop Outlook, Outlook on the web, and Outlook Mobile
Individual user calendars	Individual user calendars
Shared calendars	Shared calendars
Exchange Online Protection	Exchange Online Protection
	Unified Messaging
	Data Loss Prevention

Microsoft 365 administrators do not have direct access to the Exchange Online servers, but they can access the Exchange admin center from a link in the Microsoft 365 admin center to manage Exchange-specific settings using a web-based interface, as shown in Figure 2-1.

In this interface, administrators can perform tasks such as the following:

- Create and manage user accounts
- Grant management role permissions for administrators and users
- Configure mail flow options to integrate on-premises mail servers or third-party mail services into the message-handling solution

- Enable calendar sharing with outside organizations or between users on-premises and in the cloud
- Manage hierarchical and offline address books, address lists, and address book policies
- Create and manage a public folder hierarchy for document sharing and collaboration
- Create and manage client access rules to restrict access to Exchange Online based on client platform, IP address, authentication type, location, and other criteria

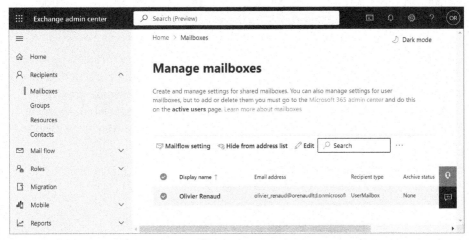

FIGURE 2-1 The Exchange admin center interface

Microsoft Outlook

Users can access Exchange Online services using the Microsoft Outlook application included with the Office productivity tools, as shown in Figure 2-2, the web-based Outlook client, or Outlook Mobile. This enables users to access their mail, calendars, and other services from virtually any device, including smartphones and tablets running iOS, Android, or Windows.

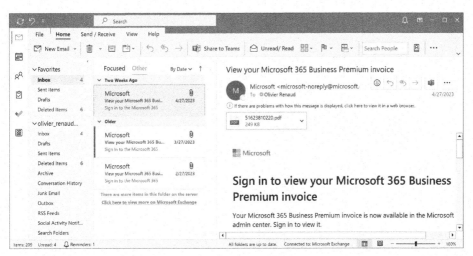

FIGURE 2-2 The Outlook email interface

SharePoint

Microsoft SharePoint is a web-based collaboration tool originally introduced in 2001 as an on-premises server product. SharePoint in Microsoft 365 is the cloud-based equivalent included with nearly all of the Microsoft 365 Business and Enterprise plans.

SharePoint is a service that administrators and workers can use to create document management, distribution, and collaboration websites. At its simplest, SharePoint users can create a document library on the web and upload their files to it. The files are then accessible from any device with access to the site. As SharePoint is part of Microsoft 365, editing a library document opens it in the appropriate Office application, whether online or installed on a desktop.

Users can share their library files with other users with varying degrees of access by assigning permissions to them. A scenario in which an organization or user wants to post documents to a library for many users to access is called a *communication site*. For example, a company could use SharePoint to create a library of human resources documents for all employees to access. SharePoint includes customization capabilities that enable administrators to design websites with modern graphical components, as shown in Figure 2-3.

FIGURE 2-3 A sample SharePoint site

Even more useful, multiple people can edit a single SharePoint document simultaneously, providing a collaborative environment that enables groups to work together. By creating a *team site*, a designated group of users can work simultaneously on documents that only they can access. SharePoint maintains multiple versions of the files in a library so users can review the iterations of a document throughout its history.

Communication and team sites are linked in SharePoint by *hub sites*, which provide centralized navigation to the subordinate sites and downstream searching. The SharePoint service included in Microsoft 365 can host multiple hub, collaboration, and team sites, as shown in Figure 2-4.

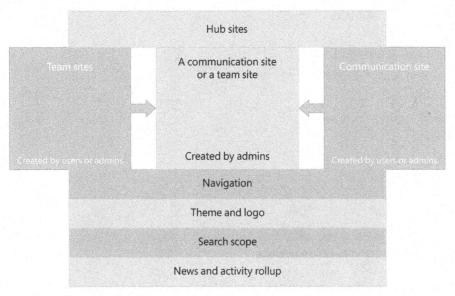

FIGURE 2-4 SharePoint site types

Because SharePoint is integrated with the other Microsoft 365 components, users can take advantage of their security and manageability features. The documents uploaded to Share-Point sites are protected against malicious code by the same antimalware engine used by Exchange Online and Data Loss Prevention. Outlook integration enables users to schedule and deliver team events to members' calendars. SharePoint also can control group memberships and document permissions with user identities taken from Active Directory and Azure Active Directory.

The SharePoint plan included with the Microsoft 365 Enterprise products includes unlimited personal cloud storage. A SharePoint library can have up to 30 million files and folders, although there are limitations when the number goes beyond 100,000. Individual files can be up to 15 GB, and SharePoint can maintain up to 50,000 versions of each file. SharePoint groups can have up to 5,000 users, and users can be members of up to 5,000 groups. Therefore, Share-Point supports enormous installations serving as many as 500,000 users.

OneDrive

OneDrive, shown in Figure 2-5, is Microsoft's cloud-based storage service. All the Microsoft 365 Business subscriptions include one terabyte of cloud storage per user. Microsoft 365 Enterprise subscriptions include 5 TB of cloud storage per user, with up to 25 TB available by administrator request.

FIGURE 2-5 The Microsoft OneDrive online interface

OneDrive is also the default cloud storage location for Microsoft 365 applications. For example, users can save Word, Excel, PowerPoint, and OneNote documents to OneDrive storage and share them with other users. This allows multiple users to access and edit a document simultaneously.

OneDrive support is included with the Windows operating systems 8.1 and later. OneDrive client applications are available for Windows and macOS desktops that provide users with access to their cloud storage and other features, such as file synchronization. Mobile versions of the OneDrive app are also available for Android and iOS, which enable users to access their cloud storage anywhere.

OneDrive is intended to be a personal cloud storage service, while OneDrive in Microsoft 365 is another form of Microsoft cloud storage implemented within SharePoint and provides additional collaboration features intended for business users, such as Content Approval.

Using the Microsoft 365 admin center

Because Microsoft 365 consists mostly of cloud-based services, administrators use web-based controls to manage them, and users can use web-based portals to access them. The individual services included with Microsoft 365, such as Exchange Online and SharePoint, are also available as separate products, so they have their own administrative portals called admin centers.

However, the Microsoft 365 admin center is the main administrative portal for the product, and it provides access to all the individual portals as well.

When you sign on to the Microsoft 365 admin center at *admin.microsoft.com*, you see the Home screen shown in Figure 2-6, with a navigation menu in the left pane and a series of cards containing controls on the right. Administrators can place their most frequently used controls on the Home page by dragging items from the navigation menu to the right pane to add more cards.

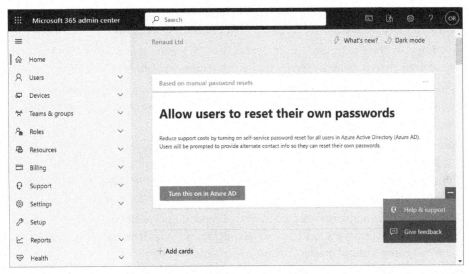

FIGURE 2-6 The Microsoft 365 admin center Home screen

The navigation pane contains menus for control categories, with dropdowns for specific control types. The categories are as follows:

- **Users** Enables administrators to create, manage, and delete user accounts. By assigning licenses to accounts, users will be granted access to Microsoft 365 or other applications and services. Assigning administrative roles to users grants them privileges to access certain additional controls.

- **Devices** Enables administrators to add new devices, individually or in bulk, such as smartphones and tablets, create policies for securing the devices, and manage individual devices by resetting them, removing corporate data, or removing them entirely.

- **Teams & Groups** Enables administrators to create Microsoft Teams teams and various types of groups, including Microsoft 365, security, mail-enabled security, and distribution list groups, assign owners to them, and configure privacy settings. They can also create shared mailboxes for access by all members of a specific group.

- **Roles** Enables administrators to assign built-in Azure Active Directory roles to users to provide them with access to additional admin centers and other resources.

- **Resources** Enables administrators to create and configure rooms and equipment for assignment to meetings and create SharePoint sites and collections.

- **SharePoint** The SharePoint admin center provides full control over SharePoint, but this interface can control site sharing and remove external users.

- **Billing** Enables administrators to purchase additional Microsoft applications and services, manage product subscriptions, monitor available product licenses, and manage invoices and payments.

- **Support** Enables administrators to find solutions to common Microsoft 365 problems and create and view requests for service from Microsoft technicians.

- **Settings** Enables administrators to configure service settings and add-ins for the entire enterprise, configure security settings, and monitor partner relationships.

- **Setup** Enables administrators to monitor their Microsoft products and manage the licenses for those products, purchase or add Internet domains, and migrate data from outside email providers into Microsoft 365 accounts.

- **Reports** Enables administrators to generate various reports, such as email activity, active users, and SharePoint site usage, over intervals ranging from 7 to 180 days. Reports like these can indicate who is using the Microsoft 365 services heavily, who is near to reaching storage quotas, and who might not need a license at all.

- **Health** Enables administrators to monitor the operational health of the various Microsoft 365 services, read any incident and advisory reports that have been generated, and receive messages about product update availability and other topics.

- **Admin Centers** Enables administrators to open new windows containing the admin centers for the other services provided in Microsoft 365, including Security, Compliance, Azure Active Directory, Exchange, SharePoint, and Microsoft Teams.

> **NOTE MICROSOFT 365 ADMIN CENTER**
>
> Because the admin centers for the Microsoft 365 services are web-based, the product developers can easily modify them and add features as they become available without interrupting their users. The figures of the admin center controls in this book are taken from the interface design as it exists at the time of writing. Design and feature changes might have been introduced since the time of publication.

Describe core Microsoft 365 Apps, including Microsoft Word, Excel, PowerPoint, Outlook, and OneNote

Much of the Microsoft 365 infrastructure is invisible to end users; their primary exposure is to the standard Office productivity applications, such as Word and Excel. The selection of productivity applications included with Microsoft 365 depends on the subscription plan the administrators choose for the organization.

Using the Microsoft 365 portal

Once an administrator has given users Microsoft 365 accounts, they can access the Office productivity applications and sign on to the Microsoft 365 user portal at *https://portal.office.com*. After a user signs in with the email address created by the administrator as part of their account, the Microsoft 365 portal appears, as shown in Figure 2-7.

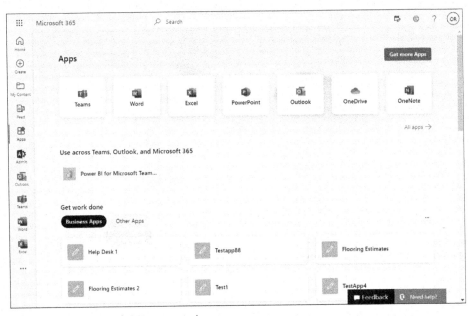

FIGURE 2-7 The Microsoft 365 user portal

The **Apps** tiles on the portal's **Apps** page provide the user access to the web-based versions of the Office productivity applications: Microsoft Teams, Word, Excel, PowerPoint, Outlook, OneDrive, and OneNote. Beneath the icons is a **Get Work Done** area providing the user with access to recently used, pinned, and shared document files stored in the user's OneDrive cloud.

Farther down on the **Apps** page is an **Explore By Category** section that displays tiles for the other Microsoft 365 apps by default, as shown in Figure 2-8.

Clicking one of the application tiles on the **Apps** page opens the online version of the application. All Microsoft 365 subscriptions provide users access to the web and mobile versions of the Office productivity applications. With these versions, users can access the applications on virtually any device from any location with Internet access.

If the users' subscription includes the desktop versions of the applications, the Microsoft 365 portal permits the user to install the Microsoft 365 applications on up to five systems. On the portal's home page, clicking **Install Apps** and selecting **Premium Microsoft 365 Apps** opens the **Get Started With Microsoft 365** page, as shown in Figure 2-9.

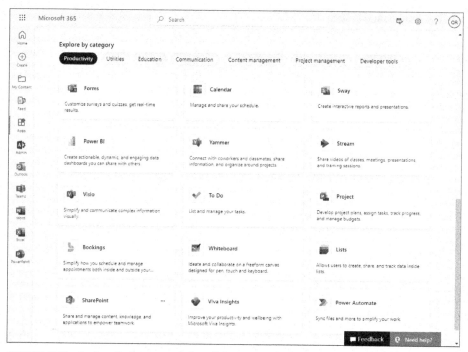

FIGURE 2-8 The Explore By Category section of the Microsoft 365 user portal Apps page

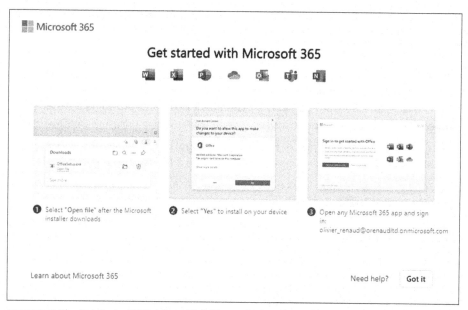

FIGURE 2-9 The Get Started With Microsoft 365 page in the Microsoft 365 user portal

The installation includes all the on-premises Office applications, including Word, Excel, PowerPoint, Outlook, OneNote, Access, Publisher, and OneDrive. This is the only way for a Microsoft 365 user to run the Access and Publisher applications because they don't have web or mobile versions.

Using the Microsoft 365 Applications

The collection of user productivity applications, now known as Microsoft 365 Apps for Business and Microsoft 365 Apps for Enterprise, is one of the core elements of the Microsoft 365 subscription products. Formerly known as Office 365 for Business and Office 365 ProPlus, this element is most visible to users because it provides the applications they probably use every day. For administrators, productivity applications are a crucial part of the Microsoft 365 deployment process because they can use all the cloud-based services included in the Microsoft 365 product.

The various Microsoft 365 subscription products contain application packages that can differ slightly. For example, the Microsoft 365 Business Basic subscription includes only the web and mobile versions of the productivity apps, not the installable desktop versions.

The Office applications for web and mobile use are limited in their advanced features compared to the installed versions, but they enable users with a Microsoft 365 license full access to their documents using any Internet-connected computer or mobile device with a web browser. Users can also save documents in their OneDrive cloud storage for access later.

Most of the other Microsoft 365 packages include the desktop versions, and the core applications are the same; the differences are the additional applications and services that are included in the bundle. Microsoft 365 subscriptions include the following elements:

- **Word** Word processing
- **Excel** Spreadsheets and charting
- **PowerPoint** Presentation graphics
- **Microsoft Teams** Chat, messaging, and collaboration
- **Outlook** Email and scheduling
- **Access** Database management
- **Publisher** Desktop publishing
- **OneDrive** Cloud storage

Other Microsoft 365 business and enterprise packages include various combinations of the Microsoft cloud services discussed earlier in this chapter. The Microsoft 365 E5 package, for example, adds the following:

- **Exchange Online** This cloud-based email and calendaring service provides enterprise users with mailboxes and calendars they can access and share using virtually any device.
- **SharePoint** This cloud-based collaboration tool enables administrators and users to create websites and maintain document libraries.

- **Viva Connections**   This cloud-based employee information feed is built on SharePoint and integrated into Microsoft Teams.
- **Viva Engage**   This is a cloud-based enterprise social networking service that Microsoft is positioning as the successor to Yammer.
- **Power Platform**   This is a low-code end-user development environment that includes Power BI Pro, a data mining and business analytics package; Power Apps, an app development tool; Power Automate, a tool for automating repetitive tasks; and Power Virtual Agents, a tool for creating chatbots.
- **Stream**   This video streaming service enables enterprise users to upload, view, and share video content.
- **Planner**   This cloud-based team management application includes file sharing and communication capabilities.
- **To Do**   This is a cloud-based task management application.

The Microsoft 365 Enterprise E5 package includes all these elements, plus licenses for Windows 11 Enterprise and Enterprise Mobility + Security. The product is designed to enable all these components to work together intelligently and provide users with advanced communication and collaboration capabilities.

EXAM TIP

Microsoft has officially designated the web-based versions of the Office applications as Office on the Web. They were formerly known as Office Web Apps, and some older sources might still refer to them by that name.

Comparing Microsoft 365 with on-premises Office

Microsoft 365 is the subscription-based version of the on-premises Microsoft Office application suite that has been available for decades. Office was originally designed as an on-premises business productivity product consisting of Word, Excel, and PowerPoint applications. All these applications were once standalone products, but by bundling them into the Office package, a single license gives a user unlimited access to all the applications. This simplifies the deployment and licensing process for IT purchasers and administrators.

The most recent release of the on-premises bundle is Microsoft Office 2021, but many corporate IT departments are still using previous versions, such as Microsoft Office 2019 or 2016. The package includes desktop versions of Outlook, Word, Excel, PowerPoint, Publisher, and Access for either Windows or Macintosh. These Office products are purchased outright, so no ongoing subscription fee exists. Office 2021 is available in multiple editions with varying contents. Enterprise administrators typically select Office Professional 2021, which is volume licensed.

Microsoft is clearly attempting to urge the Office market toward its subscription-based products. The list of features and benefits that are not included in the Office 2021 package but available in Microsoft 365 is a long one and includes the following:

- **Automatic feature updates** Microsoft 365 packages all receive regular feature, quality, and security updates at monthly or semiannual intervals determined by the enterprise administrator. By default, Office 2021 automatically downloads quality and security updates monthly from the Microsoft Content Delivery Network (CDN), but it does not receive feature updates. Major upgrades, such as from Office 2019 to Office 2021, require purchasing a new license.

- **Licensed devices** The Microsoft 365 licenses permit each user to install the Office productivity applications on up to five devices, meaning a single license can be used for a user's office, laptop, and home computers—and even two smartphones or tablets. The Office 2021 license only permits the installation of the applications on one Windows or Macintosh computer.

- **Operating system support** While the Microsoft 365 products include Windows 11 Enterprise and require that operating system for many collaboration features, the Office 2021 product can be installed on any Windows 11 or 10 computer (version 1809 or later).

- **OneDrive cloud storage** Any registered user can obtain OneDrive cloud storage, but Microsoft 365 subscribers receive 1 TB of storage. Unlicensed users and Office 2021 licensees are only permitted 5 GB.

- **Technical support** The Microsoft 365 business packages include 24/7 online and telephone support and the FastTrack deployment service. The Office 2021 license has more limited support options.

- **Email hosting and calendaring** Most Microsoft 365 packages include the Exchange Online cloud service, which provides email and calendaring. For Office 2021 users, this service is only available as a separate subscription for an additional fee. There is also an on-premises Exchange Server product that is sold separately.

- **Collaboration tools** Most Microsoft 365 packages include cloud-based collaboration services such as SharePoint and Microsoft Teams. For Office 2021 users, these services are only available as separate subscriptions for additional fees. SharePoint is also sold separately as an on-premises server.

- **Reduced functionality mode** With Microsoft 365, if a user's subscription lapses, if an administrator removes a user's license, or if the computer on which the Office applications are installed does not connect to the Internet at least once every 30 days, the Office productivity applications go into reduced functionality mode and display a message like the one shown in Figure 2-10. In reduced functionality mode, the user can open, view, and print existing documents, but all editing functions are disabled, and the user cannot create new documents. The Office 2021 applications never revert to a reduced functionality mode, and users are not required to connect to the Internet.

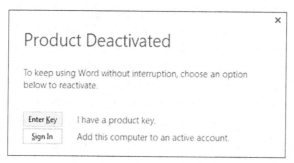

FIGURE 2-10 Microsoft 365 Reduced Functionality Mode warning

While individual users might see these omissions as considerable drawbacks to the Office 2021 product, this is not necessarily so for enterprise administrators. In some cases, administrators might prefer that the Office applications not receive feature updates because of the additional support and training issues they might cause. Every new support issue in the enterprise is multiplied by hundreds or thousands of users, so the sudden appearance of substantial changes or new features in the Office applications can be more trouble than it's worth.

As to the additional cloud services provided in many of the Microsoft 365 packages, such as those providing email and collaboration, many organizations already have solutions for these services in place and do not want to pay for features they do not need or want. Microsoft technical support for individual users might also not be necessary because enterprise administrators typically provide that support themselves. Many large organizations also obtain Office 2021 by purchasing a volume license, which might include incident support, should it be needed.

Compare core services in Microsoft 365 with corresponding on-premises services

Microsoft 365 is based primarily on cloud services, but some of the services are also available as on-premises products. For example, an organization can use Exchange Online for email and scheduling or install its own servers and run an on-premises version of Exchange. The same is true for SharePoint and Azure Active Directory, both of which also have on-premises equivalents. As with any trade-off situation, both sides have advantages and disadvantages.

DEPLOYMENT

A cloud-based service is always simpler to deploy than an on-premises server-based product because the service is provided to the subscriber in an installed and operational state. There is no need to design an infrastructure, obtain hardware, or install server software. An administrator can begin to work with the service immediately after subscribing to it, creating user objects, Exchange mailboxes, or SharePoint sites that are up and running in minutes instead of days or weeks.

UPDATES

One significant advantage to using the cloud-based version of any of these applications or services is that they are regularly and automatically updated with the latest software version. Administrators are relieved of the need to download, evaluate, and deploy updates as they are released. With a cloud-based solution, an organization subscribes to a service, not a software product, so the provider is responsible for maintaining and updating the service's functionality. In many cases, the cloud-based version of a service receives new features sooner, and on-premises software products might not receive certain features at all.

For an on-premises service installation, a responsible update strategy requires testing and evaluation of new software releases and might require service downtime for the actual update deployments.

COST

Costs—both initial and ongoing—are another decisive factor in deploying any of these services. Cloud-based services require the payment of a regular subscription fee, and sometimes there are additional fees for add-on features. A subscription allows organizations to implement a service with a minimal initial outlay because no hardware costs or server licenses are required.

Fees for cloud-based services are predictable and simplify the process of budgeting. Installing the equivalent on-premises service is a more complicated affair. An organization obviously must first purchase the server software license and the computers on which the software will run, as well as an operating system license and client access licenses for all the users. This can be a significant initial outlay.

Depending on the organization's requirements, there might also be additional costs. A large enterprise might require multiple servers to support different physical sites, multiplying the initial outlay cost. Backing up data and storing it also adds to the cost.

There are also fault tolerance and disaster recovery issues to consider. By default, most cloud-based services from Microsoft are supplied with a 99.9 percent service level agreement (SLA), meaning the service will experience no more than 0.1 percent of downtime in a given period. The infrastructure Microsoft uses to maintain that consistent performance is of no concern to the subscriber. Duplicating that performance level with on-premises servers will require redundant hardware and possibly even datacenters. Not every organization requires this same level of consistent performance, but even a more modest uptime guarantee will increase the expenditure for an on-premises solution.

Finally, there is the issue of the people needed to design, install, and maintain on-premises services. For example, deploying Exchange servers is not a simple matter of just installing the software and creating user accounts. Depending on the organization's size, multiple servers might be needed at each location, and the design and configuration process can require administrators with advanced skills. These people will be an ongoing expense throughout the life of the service.

While cloud-based services can provide a great deal of performance for the price, this is not to say that they are always cheaper than on-premises servers. In the long term, cloud-based services can reach a point where they are more expensive. Cloud service fees are ongoing and perpetual, and while expenditures for on-premises servers might begin with a large initial outlay, they can come down to a much lower level once the servers and the software have been purchased and deployed.

A comparison of the relative costs also depends on the organization's requirements and existing infrastructure. For a large enterprise that already maintains datacenters in multiple locations with experienced personnel, deploying a new service in-house might be relatively affordable. The initial outlay for an on-premises service might be unfeasible for a newly formed company with no existing IT infrastructure.

ADMINISTRATION

Compared to on-premises server administrators, who can work directly with server software controls, Microsoft 365 administrators use web-based remote interfaces to work with cloud services. Microsoft 365 admin center provides access to the various tools for all the services included in the product, such as Exchange Online admin center and SharePoint admin center, as shown in Figure 2-11. These tools enable managing configuration settings and creating virtual resources, such as mailboxes and directory service objects.

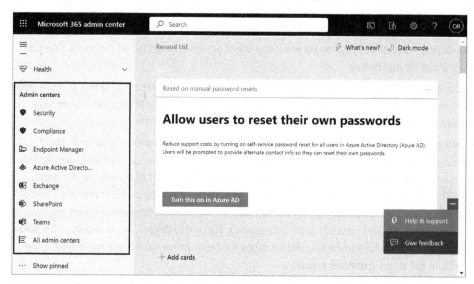

FIGURE 2-11 Admin center access through Microsoft 365

However, administrators of cloud services do not have access to the underlying resources on which the services run. They cannot access the operating system of the computers on which their services are running, nor do they have direct access to the files and databases that form their service environments. For example, while administrators can create mailboxes for users in the Exchange Online admin center, they cannot access the mailbox databases containing the users' messages.

The web-based interfaces are not necessarily a drawback for all administrators. It is entirely possible to manage a cloud-based service without ever requiring access to the service's underlying data structures. In addition, Microsoft maintains responsibility for those data structures, ensuring their availability and security. In an on-premises service deployment, it is up to the local administrators to replicate the data structures for high availability purposes and implement a load-balancing solution to maintain a similar level of performance.

Here again, the differences between the two service environments depend on the experience and preferences of the people responsible for them. Experienced Exchange Server administrators, for example, might be wary of using a cloud-based Exchange implementation that would isolate them from the servers, the operating system, and the traditional Exchange controls. However, an administrator relatively new to Exchange might welcome the simplified access the Exchange Online admin center provides.

SECURITY

One of the most critical factors in the decision to use cloud-based or on-premises services is the location of sensitive data. For many organizations, the security of their data is not just a matter of their own benefit. Sometimes, contractual and regulatory constraints can make cloud-based data storage impossible. For example, a company with a government contract might be required to maintain personal responsibility for its stored data; it cannot pass that responsibility on to a third-party cloud provider.

However, in cases with no legal constraints, storing data in the cloud can provide protection equivalent to several different on-premises security products. Antivirus protection, message encryption, Information Rights Management, and Data Loss Prevention are just some of the security mechanisms that the Microsoft 365 cloud services can provide, all of which would require additional maintenance and expense to implement for on-premises servers.

Service comparisons

Not all the cloud services included in Microsoft 365 are available in on-premises versions. Microsoft Teams and Microsoft Streams, for example, only exist as cloud services. However, some of the core Microsoft 365 services have existed as standalone server software products for years, and organizations planning a Microsoft 365 deployment might want to compare the cloud services to their corresponding on-premises versions, as in the following sections, before committing to one or the other.

OFFICE APPLICATIONS

As noted earlier, the Microsoft Office suite is a collection of productivity applications available as a standalone product for many years. Office 365—and, eventually, Microsoft 365—were introduced as subscription-based products enabling users to access the same applications in several ways. In most of the Microsoft 365 plans, it is still possible to install the applications on a Windows or Macintosh computer for online or offline use, but they are also available in the cloud for access on any device using a web browser. In addition, there are also non-Windows versions of the applications available for use on Android and iOS devices.

With the standalone Office product, currently called Office 2021, you pay only once and receive the productivity applications, such as Word, Excel, PowerPoint, Access, Publisher, and Outlook, but that's all. The Office 2021 license is limited to a single device installation, while Microsoft 365 enables you to install the applications on up to five devices.

Free security updates to the current versions of the applications are released regularly, but not as frequently as the updates for Microsoft 365, which can also include new features. In the event of a major upgrade release, such as from Office 2019 to Office 2021, there is an additional charge for the standalone product. A Microsoft 365 subscription ensures that you always have the latest software version.

Office 2021 is available in several versions for different audiences, with differing price points. Basic versions, such as Office Home & Student 2021, include some of the applications (Word, Excel, and PowerPoint only), while Office Professional 2021 includes the entire suite of productivity applications but none of the Microsoft 365 cloud services. At this point in the life of the Office product, Microsoft is targeting Office 2021 at enterprises that "are not ready for the cloud" and that purchase volume licenses for the entire organization. Because Office 2021 is feature-locked, the applications do not change, which is something that corporate licensees might prefer to avoid interrupting their users' productivity with new feature releases.

Microsoft 365 is available in several different subscription plans that provide cloud services in addition to the productivity applications, such as Exchange-based online email and extra OneDrive storage. The version of the productivity applications included in Microsoft 365, called Microsoft 365 Apps for Business, is integrated with all the cloud services described earlier in this chapter, including Exchange Online, SharePoint, OneDrive for Business, and Microsoft Teams. Integrating the Office applications with these services provides users with advanced intelligence and collaboration features unavailable with Office 2021.

EXCHANGE

All the issues described earlier in this section apply to a comparison of Exchange Online with the on-premises version of Exchange. An Exchange Server deployment can be an elaborate and expensive affair requiring multiple servers and extensive configuration, while administrators can have Exchange Online up and running in less than a day.

Exchange Online provides each user with 50 or 100 GB of storage. In an on-premises exchange installation, the size of users' mailboxes is regulated by the administrators, who often do not want to expend that much storage space, which many users might never need.

Also, unlike Exchange Server, Exchange Online can create Microsoft 365 groups, enabling users to work with shared resources. This can be a valuable resource for administrators. For example, a technical support team can add its members to a Microsoft 365 group. Administrators then grant the group the permissions necessary to access a shared Exchange mailbox, a SharePoint team site, and other resources. When members enter or leave the group, the permissions to access those resources are automatically granted or revoked.

On Exchange Server, by default, user mailboxes exist on one server and are therefore vulnerable to hardware failures, system faults, and other disasters that can render them temporarily unavailable or even lead to data loss. For this reason, an enterprise exchange deployment often requires additional servers to maintain duplicate mailboxes, a reliable backup strategy, and in some cases, duplicate datacenters, all of which add to the cost of the installation. By default, Exchange Online replicates mailbox databases across servers and datacenters, ensuring the continuous availability of the service. This, too, is an issue that some Exchange administrators would prefer to address themselves rather than leave to a service provider, but the market for organizations that like the idea of a turnkey solution and are willing to trust cloud services is growing constantly.

NOTE **HYBRID SERVICE DEPLOYMENTS**

Another possible solution to the availability issues inherent in on-premises Exchange, SharePoint, and Active Directory implementations is for an organization to create a hybrid service deployment using on-premises servers and cloud services together. The cloud service can therefore function as an availability mechanism that might be more economical than creating redundant on-premises servers or datacenters. When you replicate mailboxes, sites, or AD accounts to the cloud, they can take advantage of Microsoft's security mechanisms. A hybrid deployment can also function as a migration mechanism for organizations that want to move from on-premises services to cloud-based ones gradually.

SHAREPOINT

As with Exchange, SharePoint is available as an on-premises server product and as a cloud-based SharePoint service. The main advantages of the cloud version are the same as those of the other services: simplified deployment, automatic updating, data redundancy, web-based administration, and so forth.

Microsoft is presenting its cloud-based products as the next wave in business computing, and SharePoint in Microsoft 365 is now the flagship of the venerable SharePoint product. New features like the Modern experience in site design appear in the cloud version of SharePoint first. However, in the case of SharePoint, this does not mean that SharePoint Server is being left behind.

SharePoint Server 2019 includes features enabling it to work with Microsoft 365 cloud services. For example, administrators can redirect the MySites link in SharePoint Server to OneDrive so that users will be directed to cloud storage rather than to the on-premises server. A hybrid cloud search capability also causes a Microsoft 365 search to incorporate the index from an on-premises server into the standard cloud search.

ACTIVE DIRECTORY

Beginning with the Windows 2000 Server release, Active Directory Domain Services (AD DS) functioned as an identity management solution for enterprise resources. After creating an AD DS domain controller from a Windows server, administrators create a hierarchy of forests and domains and populate them with logical objects representing users, computers, applications, and other resources. With those objects, AD DS functions as an intermediary between users and network resources, providing authentication and authorization services when users attempt to access them. Azure Active Directory (Azure AD or AAD) is an Identity as a Service (IDaaS) mechanism that performs the same basic authentication and authorization functions for the Microsoft 365 cloud services, but it does so in a different way.

There are no forests or domains in Azure AD. After an organization subscribes to Microsoft 365 (or any of the individual Microsoft cloud services), an administrator creates a tenant using the **Create A Tenant** page, as shown in Figure 2-12. In Azure AD, a *tenant* is a logical construct representing an entire organization. Administrators of the tenant can then use the Azure portal to create user accounts and manage their properties, such as permissions and passwords. The accounts provide users with single-sign-on capability for all Microsoft services.

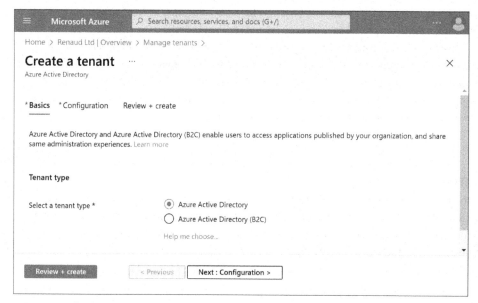

FIGURE 2-12 The Create A Tenant page in the Azure Active Directory portal

AD DS uses protocols such as Kerberos and NT LAN Manager (NTLM) for communication between domain controllers and the other computers involved in authentication or authorization. This is appropriate for its functions because AD DS functions only within the organization's premises; it is not designed to work with users outside of the enterprise or manage cloud-based services like those in Microsoft 365.

Obviously, Azure AD is designed to manage cloud services and can work with users located anywhere, employing different security protocols, such as Security Assertion Markup Language (SAML) and Open Authorization (OAuth). Because they are so different, Azure AD and AD DS are not functionally interchangeable, as are the cloud-based and on-premises versions of services such as Exchange and SharePoint.

Thus, for any organization with an existing on-premises AD DS deployment and considering implementing Microsoft 365, the administrators will have to work with both AD DS and Azure AD. Fortunately, this does not mean that it will be necessary to create duplicate user accounts in each of the directory services. *Azure AD Connect* links the two and provides each user with a *hybrid identity* that spans both on-premises and cloud-based services. This provides the user with single sign-on capability for all applications and services.

Describe work management capabilities of Microsoft 365, including Microsoft Project, Planner, Bookings, Forms, Lists, and To Do

Work management is a software tool class that enables users to organize, schedule, and manage tasks and projects. Most Microsoft 365 packages provide access to several work management tools, whereas others require an additional subscription.

Microsoft's guiding philosophy behind these tools is that more time spent managing work means less time doing work. The work management tools discussed in the following sections streamline the process of organizing projects, assigning tasks, and creating schedules so that team members can devote more time to working.

Microsoft Planner

Microsoft Planner is a simple project management tool that enables users to create plans and populate them with tasks, events, and other elements from various Microsoft 365 services. The default view of a plan consists of vertical columns called *buckets*, each of which consists of tasks, as shown in Figure 2-13. Tasks can contain graphics, links, and files hosted by SharePoint.

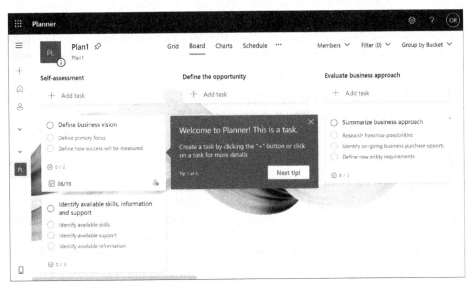

FIGURE 2-13 A plan created in Microsoft Planner

Clicking the **+Add Task** button opens a dialog like that shown in Figure 2-14, in which the user specifies a task name and a due date and assigns it to specific users.

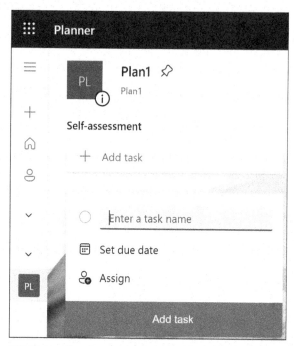

FIGURE 2-14 Creating a task in Microsoft Planner

When a user creates a plan, the tool automatically creates a Microsoft 365 group, the members of which are those to whom the plan applies. The opposite is also true; when a user or administrator creates a Microsoft 365 group, the tool creates a plan for it. As with all Microsoft 365 groups, a group mailbox and calendar are also associated with it; plan users can use them to schedule appointments and events and receive email notifications.

A Planner plan can also be integrated into Microsoft Teams by adding a new tab to a team's General page. Therefore, users can work with planned tasks while contacting other team members via chat or call.

Microsoft Project

While Planner provides basic task management capabilities, administrators requiring more extensive features can run Microsoft Project. Project has existed in various forms (even a DOS version) since 1984, making it one of the oldest Microsoft software products. Today, a desktop version, Microsoft Project 2019, is still available in Standard and Professional versions, and a Microsoft Project Server version is based on SharePoint. However, the primary product is Project for the Web, a cloud-based product available for an additional subscription fee.

While Microsoft Project is considered part of the Office environment, it is not included in any Microsoft 365 subscription products. The cloud-based Project for Web product is available in three subscription plans: Project Plan 1, Project Plan 2, and Project Plan 3. Plan 1 is web-only, whereas Plan 2 and Plan 3 include the desktop version of the application for up to five users.

Project includes a grid view similar to Planner's, in which vertical buckets contain rows of tasks. However, Project also includes a timeline view with an interactive Gantt chart display, as shown in Figure 2-15.

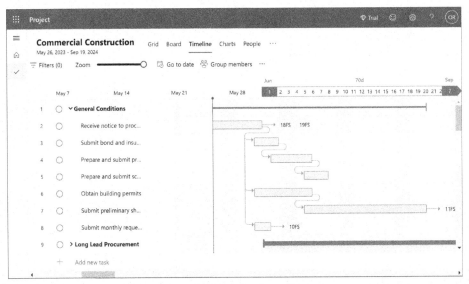

FIGURE 2-15 A sample timeline in Microsoft Project for the web

Project also manages scheduling and budgeting for large-scale projects. Users can establish dependencies between tasks so a scheduling delay added to one task pushes its dependent tasks forward in the schedule by the same amount of time. In the same way, changes in costs for particular tasks are updated in the project's overall budget.

Project allows administrators to assign tasks to specific users or groups and integrates with Microsoft Teams so all involved users can receive updated information about the project. Project is also built on Microsoft Power Platform, enabling users to integrate it with their own Power Apps apps and create Power BI dashboards containing real-time project information.

Microsoft Bookings

Microsoft Bookings is a shared scheduling application enabling users to manage their appointments. The application can integrate with Microsoft Outlook or Microsoft Teams so that users can access their schedules through their already familiar interfaces.

In Bookings, each user has a booking page, as shown in Figure 2-16, containing the user's appointments and availability.

Users can share their booking pages with selected other users or with everyone. Clicking the plus (+) button on the booking page opens an **Edit Meeting Type** interface, as shown in Figure 2-17, where the user can create a new public or private appointment.

FIGURE 2-16 A user's booking page in Microsoft Bookings

FIGURE 2-17 Creating a new meeting in Microsoft Bookings

Microsoft Forms

Microsoft Forms is a relatively simple application that allows users to create surveys, quizzes, questionnaires, and registrations using an interface like that shown in Figure 2-18. Users can share the forms they create in the application with others, who can access them using any web browser.

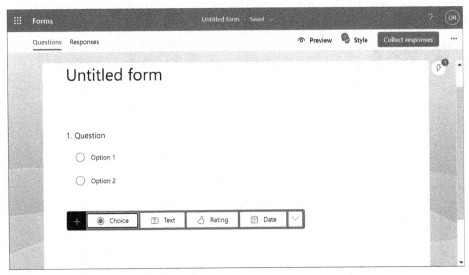

FIGURE 2-18 Creating a new questionnaire in Microsoft Forms

As a form receives replies, the responses appear in the application in real-time. Once all the responses arrive, the application can analyze the results and export them to Microsoft Excel.

Microsoft Lists

As the name implies, Microsoft Lists is a tool for creating lists of various types, such as the itinerary list shown in Figure 2-19, which is based on one of the templates included in the application. As with most work management applications, it is possible to integrate lists into Microsoft Teams or SharePoint.

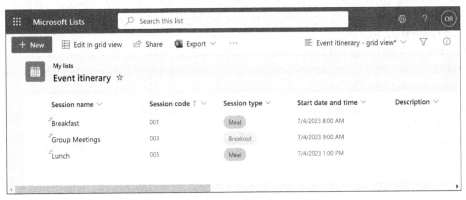

FIGURE 2-19 Creating a list in Microsoft Lists

Microsoft To Do

Microsoft To Do is a cross-platform task management application that allows users to create and manage task lists integrating information from Outlook, Microsoft Teams, and other Microsoft 365 applications and services, as shown in Figure 2-20. Once collated, a user's task list is then available from any platform, including Android and iOS. Users can also share their task lists with colleagues and delegate tasks to other users.

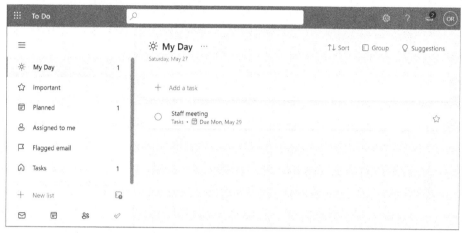

FIGURE 2-20 Creating a task list in Microsoft To Do

Skill 2.2: Describe collaboration solutions of Microsoft 365

At one time, it was common for workplaces to be divided into offices and cubicles. People worked alone, only coming together for meetings held in a separate conference room, away from their workspaces. Then, the open office design became popular; the cubicle walls came down, and workers were compelled to function as a team all day long. Both extremes tended to cause problems. Either it was difficult to get the team together for quality collaboration time because their materials were mostly left back in their workspaces, or people felt cramped and stifled by being stuck together all the time. Achieving a balance between these two extremes can enhance both harmony and productivity. Workers who can collaborate when necessary and still spend some time concentrating on their own can often propel a project toward completion more efficiently.

Microsoft 365 is a product that is designed to provide workers with exactly this kind of flexibility. At first, it might seem to be a simple bundle of applications and services. However, the combination of Microsoft 365 components is designed to be more than the sum of its parts.

Microsoft 365 includes both user applications and cloud services, all of which work together to create an environment that enables people to communicate and collaborate whenever they need to, from wherever they happen to be. Team members can hold group meetings from their own workspaces: in the office, at home, or on the road. Users can exchange messages by whatever medium best suits the team's purposes: chat, email, voice, or video conference. Users can store their documents in the cloud to read, edit, or publish them from anywhere, using any device. Users can work individually, in pairs, or groups of any size, in any combination, anywhere.

Describe the collaboration benefits and capabilities of Microsoft 365, including Microsoft Exchange, Outlook, Yammer, SharePoint, OneDrive, and Stream

This section examines the collaboration capabilities built into the Microsoft 365 components and then discusses how people can use them to enhance their workflows.

Exchange Online

As the Microsoft email messaging server platform, Exchange is the most frequently used collaboration tool for most users, regardless of whether they recognize the name. Email provides rapid cross-platform communication, but it is often not immediate, and while emails can carry information between team members, their asynchronous nature prevents them from being the collaborative equivalent of a face-to-face conversation.

In addition to one-to-one email exchanges, Exchange Online also supports several other means for users to collaborate using email messaging, such as the following:

- **Distribution lists**   Also known as distribution groups, distribution lists enable users to send email messages to multiple recipients simultaneously. This collaboration tool has been available in Exchange for many years, but Microsoft 365 groups now provide a more powerful alternative.

- **Dynamic distribution list**   This is a variation of a standard distribution list in which the membership is calculated each time a message is sent to the list based on rules established by the list administrator. For example, the rules can specify that all users in a specific department or location be included as list members. Each time a message is sent to the list, only the users identified by the rules at that moment are included in the group.

- **Mail-enabled security groups**   Typically, security groups are used to assign permissions to resources, while distribution groups are used for emailing. However, it is possible to enable mail for a security group so that the users possessing permissions to a protected resource can be notified by mail if there are issues pertaining to that resource. For example, if a printer is offline for maintenance or repairs, its users can be notified by email of its unavailability.

- **Shared mailboxes** Typically, shared mailboxes are Exchange mailboxes with attached calendars representing a role rather than an individual, which multiple users can access. For example, a technical support department can create a shared mailbox called *helpdesk@domain.com*, which is monitored by the team members on duty.
- **Public folders** Exchange can maintain a hierarchy of folders that contain documents available to any user. Administrators can link a public folder to a distribution group so that mail sent to the group is automatically added to the folder.

While these mechanisms have their uses, and many administrators have been accustomed to using them for years, Microsoft 365 groups offer a more comprehensive solution for collaboration that works across all Microsoft 365 applications and services.

In addition to mailboxes, Exchange Online provides users with a calendar that provides scheduling, reminder, and sharing capabilities, as shown in Figure 2-21. Users can share their calendars with coworkers, enabling them to see their availability and plan meetings and appointments. Microsoft 365 groups also have their own calendars so group members can share their scheduling information with the team and create meetings that don't conflict with anyone else's obligations.

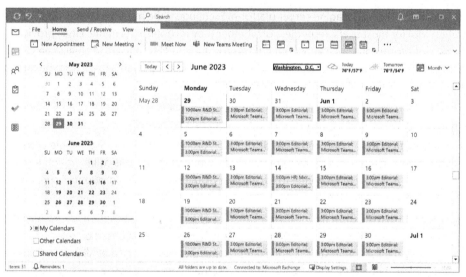

FIGURE 2-21 An Exchange Online calendar as displayed in Outlook

Microsoft Outlook

Microsoft Outlook, shown in Figure 2-22, is the client for the Exchange Online service included in most of the Microsoft 365 subscription plans. Outlook provides email and calendar scheduling functions for connections to Exchange servers and for other types of email services, including Post Office Protocol 3 (POP3) and Internet Message Access Protocol (IMAP).

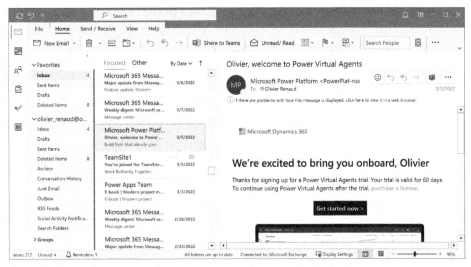

FIGURE 2-22 The Outlook email client

Microsoft 365 groups

Microsoft 365 groups enable administrators to provide group members with access to resources spanning services Microsoft provides. Creating a Microsoft 365 group automatically creates the following resources, which are accessible to all group members:

- **Shared Exchange Online mailbox** This inbox displays all the email messages sent to the group. Unlike a distribution list, the inbox is searchable and maintains a permanent record of the group's email communications. Users can display the contents of the group inbox separately in Outlook, as shown in Figure 2-23, or subscribe to the group so the messages appear in their personal inbox folders.

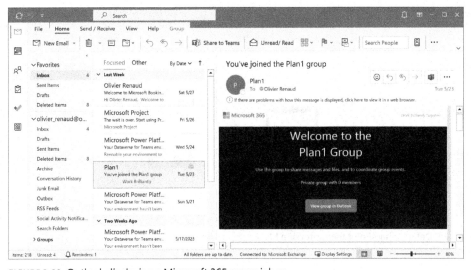

FIGURE 2-23 Outlook displaying a Microsoft 365 group inbox

- **Shared Exchange Online calendar** The group has a shared calendar, so members are invited to all the events posted on that calendar. As with the inbox, users can configure Outlook to add the group calendar events to their personal calendars or view them separately, as shown in Figure 2-24.

- **Shared SharePoint team site** Creating a Microsoft 365 group also creates a dedicated team site for the group in SharePoint, as shown in Figure 2-25, which includes a library where group members can store, share, and collaborate on documents.

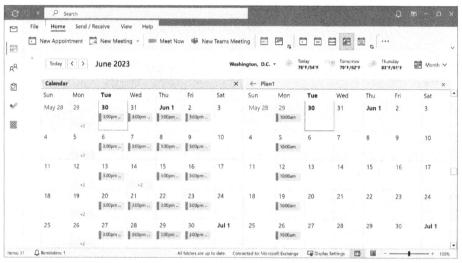

FIGURE 2-24 An Outlook Calendar page with user and group calendars

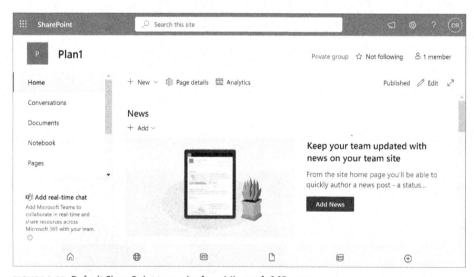

FIGURE 2-25 Default SharePoint team site for a Microsoft 365 group

- **Shared OneNote notebook**   As part of creating the group's team site in SharePoint, a dedicated notebook is created, which members can access through the OneNote web client or the desktop application, as shown in Figure 2-26.

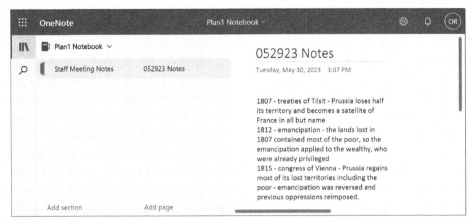

FIGURE 2-26 OneNote client displaying a Microsoft 365 group notebook

Because of their usefulness in so many of the applications and services, there are methods for creating Microsoft 365 groups in many different Microsoft 365 tools, some of which create the group directly and others indirectly, including the following:

- **Microsoft 365 admin center**   On the **Active Teams And Groups** page, clicking **Add A Group** displays the interface shown in Figure 2-27, with which you can create a Microsoft 365 group, as well as a distribution list, security, or mail-enabled security group.

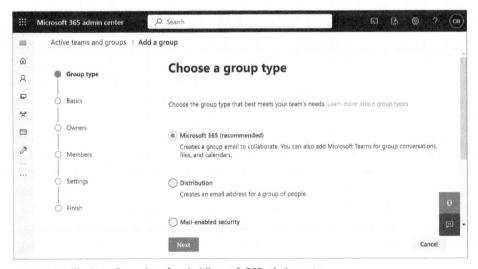

FIGURE 2-27 The New Group interface in Microsoft 365 admin center

- **Azure Active Directory Admin Center** On the **All Groups** page, clicking **New Group** opens an interface in which you can create a Microsoft 365 or a security group.

- **Exchange Online admin center** On the **Groups** page, clicking **Add A Group** opens an interface for creating a new group.

- **SharePoint admin center** When you create a new team site in the SharePoint admin center, using the interface shown in Figure 2-28, a Microsoft 365 group is automatically created, associated with the site and using the same name.

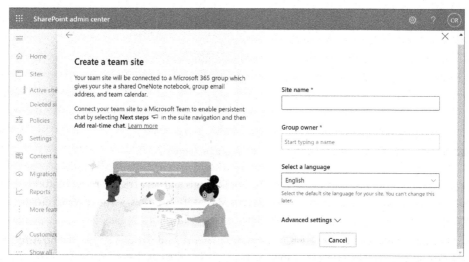

FIGURE 2-28 The team site creation interface in the SharePoint admin center

- **Outlook** Microsoft 365 users and administrators can create groups. The **New Group** button on the home tab enables the Outlook user to create a public or private group and add members to it.

- **Planner** When a user creates a new plan in Planner, the tool creates a Microsoft 365 group for it by default. Users can also opt to create a plan and associate it with an existing Microsoft 365 group.

These interfaces have different appearances, but most of them require the same information, including the following:

- **Group Name** Specifies the name by which the group will be listed in all Microsoft 365 tools.

- **Group Email Address** Specifies an email address in the enterprise domain for the Exchange mailbox created along with the group.

- **Public or Private** This setting specifies whether anyone can see group content or only group members can see group content.

- **Owner Name** Specifies the user who will function as the group's owner and receive full administrative access to its properties.

Microsoft Yammer

Yammer is designed to be a cloud-based social networking service for an enterprise, enabling users all over the organization to communicate and collaborate using the other Microsoft 365 services. Yammer users can communicate much in the way as in other social networking applications, as shown in Figure 2-29, except that the service is local to the enterprise. Administrators can admit outside users, but only on an invitation basis.

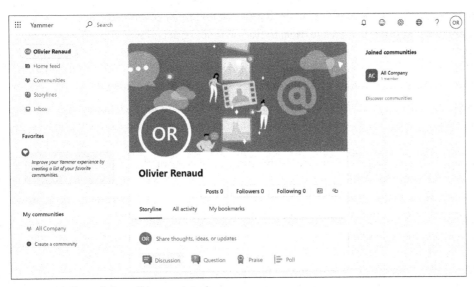

FIGURE 2-29 The web-based Yammer interface

Much like Microsoft Teams, Yammer enables users to access the other Microsoft 365 services available to them within the Yammer interface. For example, users can open a video call, schedule a meeting in Outlook, access files stored in OneDrive, or collaborate on a document from a SharePoint library, all from within a Yammer conversation.

In the Microsoft 365 collaboration model, Yammer is placed in what is referred to as the outer loop, the broader audience within the enterprise. These are people a user might not work with every day. While Yammer can provide group-based collaboration, many organizations use it to provide an alternative, company-wide communications channel, enabling users who rarely see each other because they work in different departments or cities to build a corporate identity.

While Yammer is often referred to as a social networking tool, the fact that its scope is restricted to the enterprise means that its communication need not be strictly social. Yammer users might not all be on the same project team, working toward a definite goal, but they can still exchange valuable information among themselves about best practices or the corporate culture—information that can build a sense of community that can't exist on an Internet service with thousands of utter strangers.

SharePoint

As noted earlier in this chapter, SharePoint is a service that hosts an intranet hub, communication, and team websites that enable users to store libraries of documents and also collaborate on documents by editing them simultaneously. In the Microsoft 365 collection of cloud services, SharePoint occupies an interesting position in that it can function as an end destination for users and provide file storage to other services, such as Microsoft Teams.

Administrators can easily create separate SharePoint team sites for each project a group of users works. Those sites can be populated with libraries containing the documents and files the users will need, including lists, news items, apps, and links to web pages, among other things.

Access to the team site is controlled by the Microsoft 365 group that is automatically created with the team site. Adding users to the group grants them the permissions they need. Users can access a team site from the SharePoint home page using any browser or the SharePoint mobile apps. Users can also access the files on a team site using OneDrive.

SharePoint team sites can also be integrated into a Microsoft Teams interface, along with elements provided by other Microsoft 365 services, such as Exchange Online mailboxes, OneDrive files, Stream videos, and Yammer groups.

OneDrive

Every user registering a personal Microsoft account for use with Windows or other applications receives a free OneDrive account for storing personal files in the cloud. There is also an equivalent OneDrive service provided with Microsoft 365. The personal OneDrive and the Microsoft 365 OneDrive are nearly identical in their functionality. Users can access their OneDrive files from any device with access to the cloud and sync their files to a local disk.

The primary difference between personal OneDrive and Microsoft 365 OneDrive is that the latter is administered as part of Microsoft 365. Office users receive 1 TB of cloud storage space in a personal OneDrive account. However, in Microsoft 365 OneDrive, the amount of space allocated to each user and the access permissions granted to that space are controlled by Microsoft 365 administrators.

OneDrive serves as a storage medium for other Microsoft 365 services. Office uses it for general cloud storage, and Microsoft Teams uses it to store user files and files shared in private chats. However, files shared in a Microsoft Teams channel are stored in a SharePoint library associated with a team site. Users can also access documents stored in SharePoint libraries using the OneDrive client.

Microsoft Stream

Microsoft Stream is a video storage and distribution service that enables browser clients to stream video and provides video content to other Microsoft 365 services, including Office applications, Exchange Online, SharePoint, Microsoft Teams, and Yammer. The Stream service includes its own Azure-based storage and therefore has its own storage quotas.

In addition to accepting preexisting video content uploaded by users, as shown in Figure 2-30, Microsoft Stream can process live events created in Microsoft Teams, Yammer, or Stream itself and provide them as streamed video to real-time users or later as on-demand video content.

Stream can also enhance the video content by generating speech-to-text transcripts and closed captioning, as well as by identifying and indexing the faces of the people speaking in the video. This enables users to locate specific footage in a video by searching for spoken terms or locating a particular speaker. Stream has also introduced a "blur" feature that makes it possible to defocus the background in a video, eliminate distractions and unwanted artifacts, and concentrate the viewer's attention on the speaker.

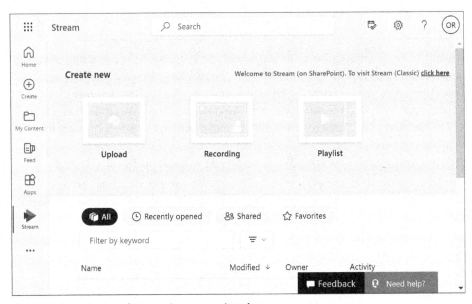

FIGURE 2-30 The Microsoft Stream home page interface

Collaborating in Microsoft 365

As should be clear from the preceding sections, Microsoft 365 provides a wide array of collaboration tools and capabilities. For some administrators, it might even be too wide, requiring a great deal of testing and evaluation even to determine which of the many forms of collaboration available are best suited to their users.

For a worldwide enterprise network with tens or hundreds of thousands of users, there might be sufficient cause to roll out all of the Microsoft 365 components and use them in various ways, but for smaller organizations, a selective deployment might be the better option. So, how can administrators determine which services are most suitable for their users, and how can users determine which of the many forms of collaboration are best for them?

Collaboration in a Microsoft 365 environment depends on the specific needs of the group or team. To determine what collaboration tools are best, consider questions like the following:

- How many people are in the group or team?
- How timely are the team communication requirements?
- Where are the group or team members located?
- Do the team members have to share and edit documents?
- What other media are required for the team's workflow?

Answers to such questions can help administrators determine which components can best benefit the users in their collaboration environment. Take, for example, a project team that at one time would work together in the same room, brainstorming the project and generating reports together. However, the team members are located in several cities, and some travel frequently.

The team's basic communication could conceivably be via email, especially if they use a group mailbox like one supplied by a Microsoft 365 group. This would give everyone access to all the email messages generated by the members. However, in a team environment, it can be difficult to maintain a true conversation via email. Responses can be delayed, and users might not reply to the latest post. A chat environment like that provided by Microsoft Teams might suit the group better.

For the document processing requirements, a SharePoint team site can enable multiple users to work on the same document, emulating the type of collaboration that can occur in a single room. Documents stored in a SharePoint site can easily be integrated into a Microsoft Teams environment.

Microsoft Planner can serve in a project management capacity, allocating tasks to specific users, maintaining a schedule for the group, and generating calendar appointments and email notifications. The Planner information can also be integrated into Microsoft Teams.

As team members are working—whether by themselves or in chat—note-taking can be an important means of maintaining a record of activities. Microsoft OneNote lets users maintain notebooks in the cloud and share them with the other group members. The notebooks can also be integrated into the Microsoft Teams environment.

While chat can provide a steady and immediate conversation stream, video conference calls or presentations might also be necessary at regular intervals. Microsoft Teams can provide calling capability, and Microsoft Streams can maintain a video record of the calls, generating transcripts and facial indexes for future reference. Thus, while an administrator might decide that Microsoft Teams is the preferable tool to create a unified collaboration environment for this particular group, the solution might also involve several other Microsoft 365 services.

This example is based on Microsoft Teams, but many of the same services can be integrated into a SharePoint team site for a group project that doesn't require the chat capabilities that Microsoft Teams provides. Administrators who are familiar with SharePoint might prefer to stick to the tools they know rather than adopt new ones. However, the most efficient use of the Microsoft 365 cloud services would be to think of the overall product as a toolbox and choose the correct ones for each job after familiarizing themselves with all the available tools.

Microsoft thinks of its collaboration tools in terms of the roles they can fulfill in an organization. Much like a solar system diagram, the Microsoft 365 collaboration model consists of outer and inner loops and a central core, as shown in Figure 2-31.

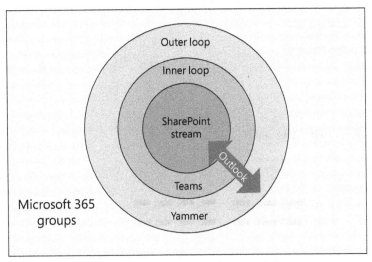

FIGURE 2-31 The Microsoft 365 system of collaboration tools

The outer loop, representing the largest group of users in the enterprise, is serviced by Yammer, which provides a communication medium that spans the enterprise. The inner loop, representing the people users know and work with daily, is serviced by Microsoft Teams. Services like SharePoint and Stream, at the system's center, provide services to both loops, just as Outlook provides communication between both. Underlying the entire model is Microsoft 365 groups, which provides identity services for the entire organization.

The interrelationships between the Microsoft 365 services can be extremely complex, with some components feeding content to many others. For example, Figure 2-32 shows that the Microsoft Stream service can supply video content to SharePoint sites and Yammer groups and send video directly to Exchange Online user or group mailboxes. Microsoft Teams can then receive that same video from the SharePoint team sites. Stream can also record videos of Microsoft Teams meetings and furnish that video to other services, creating a web of content supply and delivery that is further enhanced by exchanging files and email messages.

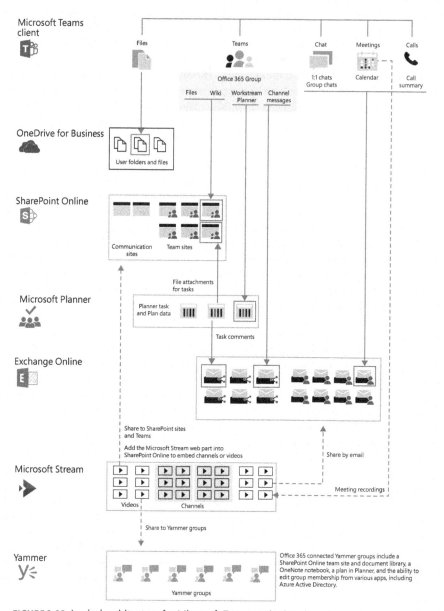

FIGURE 2-32 Logical architecture for Microsoft Teams and related services

Microsoft Graph

Collaboration in Microsoft 365 can therefore be a matter of cloud-based services that provide content to each other, integrating the functions of multiple services into one interface. However, there is more to Microsoft 365 collaboration than simply placing Stream content next to SharePoint content in a Microsoft Teams window. Microsoft Graph is a developer API that enables Microsoft 365 applications to make intelligent suggestions about how users might take advantage of the available content.

For example, when editing a Word document stored on a SharePoint team site, a user can use @*mentions* to communicate with other team members. Pressing the **@** key in a comment causes a list of team members to appear, as shown in Figure 2-33. After selecting a user from the list and typing a message, pressing the **Send** button generates an email containing the message to the selected user.

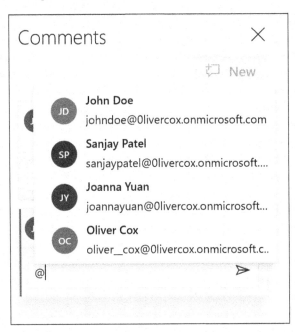

FIGURE 2-33 An @mention insertion list

Another function of the @mention capability is for users to insert notes to themselves by selecting **To-do** from the **@** list. Graph interprets the note's contents and, if there are references to other documents in the SharePoint library, for example, displays an **Insert From File** pane containing suggested files.

Microsoft Graph can also evaluate the data in a document and suggest possible actions. For example, in an Excel spreadsheet that contains a list of countries, clicking the **Geography** button on the **Data** tab adds an information icon to each cell. Clicking the icon in one cell displays information about the country found on the Internet, as shown in Figure 2-34.

Selecting the list of countries and clicking the **Insert Data** button displays a list of statistical properties, as shown in Figure 2-35. Selecting one of the properties, such as **Population**, inserts the appropriate datum for each country in the adjacent cell.

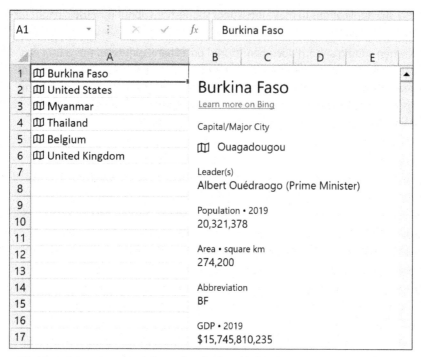

FIGURE 2-34 Internet country information displayed in Excel

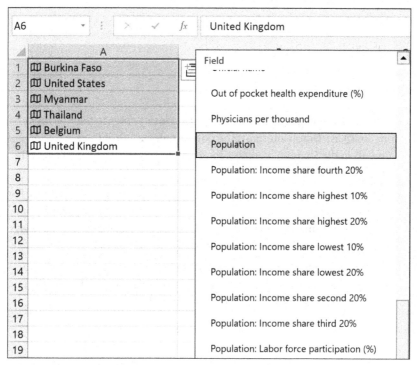

FIGURE 2-35 Insert Data options for selected countries in Excel

Selecting the newly added **Population** figures and clicking the **Quick Analysis** button displays the menu of options shown in Figure 2-36, which enables you to select formatting options and add chart types and totals to the spreadsheet.

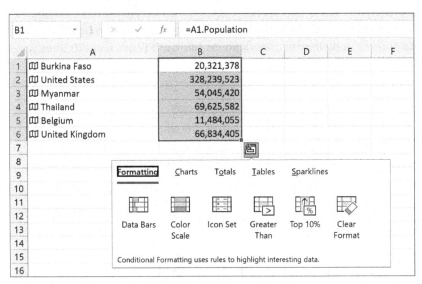

FIGURE 2-36 Quick Analysis options for Excel data

Microsoft 365 administrators and developers can also enhance collaboration processes by using Microsoft Flow to automate workflows that incorporate Graph functions and other services. For example, when users discover a malfunctioning device, they can send a photograph of it to a mailbox associated with a flow. The flow can use Graph to identify the device in the photograph, search for a replacement in an inventory, and generate a shipping order that has the part shipped out to the user that reported the problem. The same type of process can automate technical support services, generate sales leads based on users' Internet presence, and perform any number of other tasks without user intervention.

Describe the collaboration benefits and capabilities of Microsoft Teams and Teams Phone

As shown earlier in Figure 2-31, if Yammer is part of the outer loop in the Microsoft 365 collaboration model, Microsoft Teams is located in the inner loop, close to the people who see each other and work together daily.

Microsoft Teams is a collaboration hub, a single location where users can communicate with colleagues, share files and data, and access specific application instances. The primary organizational paradigms in Microsoft Teams are as follows:

- **Teams** A *team* is a group of people who work together to accomplish a particular goal, plus the documents, applications, and other tools they need to do their work. Only team members are capable of accessing the team's communications and documents.

Microsoft 365 administrators can create up to 500,000 teams with as many as 10,000 members each, so scalability is virtually unlimited.

- **Channels** A *channel* is a subsection within a team with its own conversations and content shared by its members. A channel enables its members to post text, images, and information from outside social media services. Administrators can create channels for specific projects, departments, or workgroups. Microsoft Teams supports three types of channels:
  - **Standard** Accessible by all team members
  - **Private** Accessible only by specified team members
  - **Shared** Accessible to users inside and outside the team

The primary function that is actually built into Microsoft Teams is its real-time chat and voice/video calling capabilities. However, Microsoft Teams is another collaboration tool that can host elements provided by other Microsoft 365 services, as shown in Figure 2-37, and incorporate them into the client. With Microsoft Teams, users can communicate and work together in real-time using document libraries, group and private chats, scheduled and unscheduled meetings, and audio/video calls.

Identity	Storage	Mail/Scheduling	Web Site	Chat	Calls	Video
Microsoft 365 Groups	OneDrive for Business	Exchange Online/ Outlook	SharePoint Online	Teams	Teams	Streams

FIGURE 2-37 Microsoft 365 services used by Microsoft Teams

Microsoft Teams is designed for groups that are actively working in real time and must communicate continuously and immediately, without the latency delays inherent in other media such as email. As noted earlier, this is exactly the kind of collaborative tool that can enable team members to function in their native workspaces and remain in constant communication with their colleagues, even when they are miles apart and using different devices.

EXAM TIP

Office 365 previously relied on Skype for Business for voice calling and video conferencing. These capabilities have now been incorporated into Microsoft Teams. Microsoft is deprecating the Skype for Business product and urging organizations using Skype for Business to migrate to Microsoft Teams. Candidates for the MS-900 exam should know that many older Microsoft 365 and Office 365 sources still reference Skype for Business.

Apart from the chat and calls that provide basic communication in Microsoft Teams, additional components that the group members might need are provided by other Microsoft 365 services, such as the following:

- Microsoft 365 groups

- Exchange user and group mailboxes and calendars
- SharePoint team sites
- OneDrive storage
- Stream meeting recordings and video content
- Planner task lists
- OneNote notebook sharing

One of the primary benefits of Microsoft Teams is that it can combine all of these elements into a single unified collaboration environment using a client interface like that shown in Figure 2-38. This prevents users from running multiple applications and constantly switching between them.

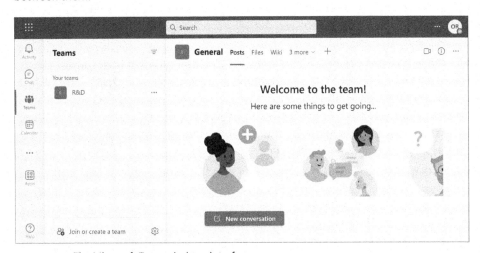

FIGURE 2-38 The Microsoft Teams desktop interface

Teams Chat

The messaging functionality Microsoft Teams provides enables users to create channels—individual chat sessions shared by a team's members. Teams messaging is an independent service that does not rely on email or SMS messaging for communication. Microsoft Teams also supports the transmission of private one-to-one messages between users.

When you create a new team in Microsoft Teams, it consists of a single channel called General. For groups working on multiple projects, you can create additional channels that have their own separate chat conversations, email addresses, and SharePoint folders. For groups whose members span countries or cultures, the chat capability in Microsoft Teams also includes the ability to translate messages into more than forty languages.

Teams Phone

Microsoft Teams includes *Teams Phone* capability, enabling users to place voice and video calls to other Microsoft Teams members over an Internet connection. The Microsoft Teams client applications allow users to easily switch between chat and phone connections to accommodate whatever medium best facilitates communication.

Using Teams Phone to make calls to other team members is built into the base Teams product, but calls to landlines and mobile phones require an additional product. Some Microsoft 365 subscriptions include this capability, but there is an additional charge for others.

Add-on Teams licenses include the following:

- **Microsoft Teams Phone Standard** Provides voice and video calling using an Internet or Public Switched Telephone Network (PSTN)
- **Microsoft Teams Phone with Calling Plan** Provides voice and video calling and includes PSTN service and a phone number furnished by Microsoft.

The enterprise subscriptions, Microsoft 365 E3 and E5, both include Teams Phone Standard and dial-up audio conferencing capabilities, but Microsoft 365 Business subscribers must purchase an additional license for one of the options listed.

Teams Phone Standard includes Phone System, which is a module that functions as a cloud-based Private Branch Exchange (PBX), providing connections to an existing third-party PSTN provider and all of the typical calling functions that users expect, including voice mail, caller ID, call forwarding, and so forth. Phone System also supports a selection of certified hardware telephones that can function as Microsoft Teams clients, allowing users to opt for a standard telephone experience using Teams as its underlying technology.

Phone System enables subscribers to implement their PBX infrastructure in Microsoft's cloud. However, the Teams Calling Plan option enables subscribers to use Microsoft as their PSTN provider, creating a voice-calling solution that is completely implemented in the cloud. Calling Plan coverage is limited to certain metropolitan areas, and subscribers must choose a calling plan that suits them. Some plans provide varying numbers of caller minutes, both domestic and international. The Microsoft Teams product line also includes options to accommodate subscribers with various telephony systems already in place.

Microsoft Teams Administration

Membership and authentication in Microsoft Teams is provided by Microsoft 365 groups, which store their identity information in Azure Active Directory. Microsoft Teams can store members' documents and other files in the cloud using OneDrive. Team websites, implemented using SharePoint, are also accessible through the Microsoft Teams client. Group mailboxes and event and meeting scheduling are provided by Exchange Online and accessed via Outlook. Teams can use the Microsoft Stream service to host and preserve video meetings.

Microsoft Teams is highly scalable and can support collaborative environments ranging from small workgroups to large departments to gigantic presentations, webinars, and conferences. Microsoft Teams is also customizable, enabling administrators to incorporate third-party applications and services into a team's collaborative environment. For example, multiple vendors are working on H.323 video conferencing solutions enabling Teams to collaborate with outside partners.

Describe the Microsoft Viva apps

Microsoft Viva is a set of products that Microsoft refers to as an *employee experience platform (EXP)*. Implemented as apps within Microsoft Teams, Microsoft 365 includes various Viva apps in its subscription levels.

The Viva apps are described in the following sections.

Viva Connections

The proliferation of information sources and applications used to access them sometimes is more difficult for users to find the things they need rather than less difficult. When locating that one essential piece of information requires searches in four or five different applications, the amount of time wasted looking for things can become prohibitive.

Viva Connections is a tool that provides users with a dashboard containing information pushed from a variety of applications, including news items, scheduling reminders, to-do lists, and learning content. The object is to give users access to everything they need to complete their jobs. Based on individual tiles, as shown in Figure 2-39, the Viva Connections display can easily configure itself to accommodate any size screen, from mobile to desktop.

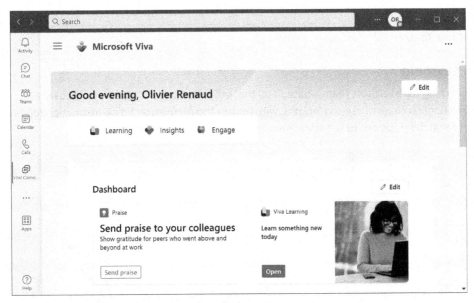

FIGURE 2-39 The Microsoft Viva Connections display

Viva Engage

Viva Engage is an instant messaging application that Microsoft has positioned as the successor to Yammer. Yammer is still an underlying technology in Engage, but it is now part of the Viva brand. Engage enables users to create communities in which they can have conversations, make announcements, ask questions, and conduct virtual events using an interface like the one shown in Figure 2-40. This type of communication can foster a sense of belonging among users separate from their work activities.

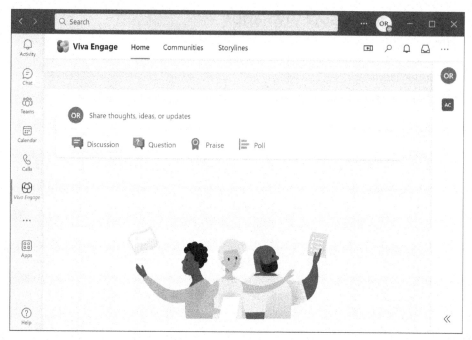

FIGURE 2-40 The Microsoft Viva Engage display

Viva Learning

Viva Learning is a Microsoft Teams–based app that provides users with access to thousands of educational courses of varying lengths, with topics ranging from technical instruction to professional development to self-improvement, as shown in Figure 2-41.

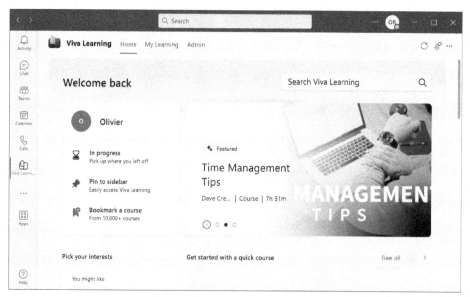

FIGURE 2-41 The Microsoft Viva Learning display

Viva Learning can function as a training hub with connections to multiple content sources, including third-party providers. Organizations can use Viva Learning to publish required training materials for employees or leave it as a voluntary service. The application can also curate content for specific users based on their interests and even fit training time into users' schedules.

Viva Topics

Viva Topics is an artificial intelligence tool that analyzes Microsoft 365 information and finds commonalities that it can link together. For example, Viva Topics can locate all of the available information on a particular project in SharePoint, Exchange, and Microsoft Teams and assemble it into a topic page that can keep everyone up to date.

Topics can identify the users involved in the project by their emails and message posts and make sure that they receive regular updates. Topics can also use the information it curates from the various Microsoft 365 services to enhance the information in other sources by adding linked topic cards, as shown in Figure 2-42.

FIGURE 2-42 A Microsoft Teams display with a Viva Topics card highlighted

Microsoft 365 includes some basic Viva Topics features in most of its subscriptions, but displaying elements such as topic cards and pages requires an add-on license for each Topics user.

Viva Goals

Viva Goals is a tool for establishing objectives and tracking their progress throughout the life of a project. Called an *objectives and key results (OKR)* management tool, Viva Goals enables both users and management to set short- and long-term goals and associate them with schedules and selected users. Figure 2-43 shows that progress toward an objective can be updated manually or by linking it with a data source.

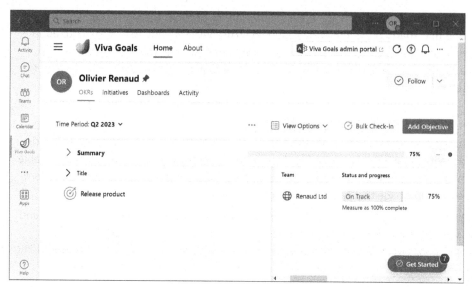

FIGURE 2-43 A Microsoft Viva Goals display

Viva Goals can display objective progress in various ways, some suited to individual users tracking their personal goals and others to management seeking to track the company's overall performance.

Viva Sales

Viva Sales is a tool that is designed to work with existing customer relationship management (CRM) systems and Microsoft 365 tools and services. Like other Viva tools, Viva Sales helps integrate information sources by displaying CRM information as pop-up cards in Microsoft Teams and other applications.

Describe the ways that you can extend Microsoft Teams by using collaborative apps

As noted earlier in this chapter, Microsoft Teams is designed to be a collaboration hub that can integrate information from other Microsoft 365 applications and services into its interfaces. The basis of this expandability is the ability to add apps to Microsoft Teams clients. The Microsoft Teams environment is, of course, stored in the cloud, and users can access it through a web-based interface using a desktop application or apps for all the major mobile platforms.

Adding Microsoft Teams Apps

Clicking the **Apps** button in the Microsoft Teams client menu bar opens a pane like that in Figure 2-44, with a list of apps to choose from. Hundreds of certified apps in the Apps store are available for integration into Microsoft Teams, created by Microsoft and third parties. Most are free, but some might require additional purchases.

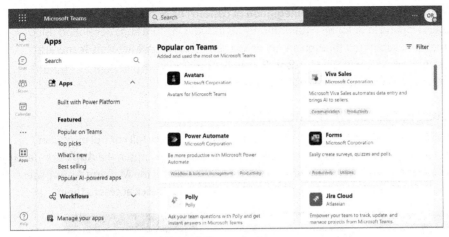

FIGURE 2-44 The Apps page in a Microsoft Teams client

Apps in Microsoft Teams are cloud-based services; selecting and installing them in a Microsoft Teams client does not require downloading binary files. Instead, installing apps just makes them accessible from within the Microsoft Teams client. Users can pin apps to the Microsoft Teams menu bar, or administrators can add tabs to a channel page in the Microsoft Teams client that use connectors to link to other Microsoft 365 applications, such as an Excel spreadsheet or a Planner plan. This is especially advantageous for users working on mobile devices with smaller screens, such as smartphones and tablets. The **Apps** page in Microsoft Teams also includes a **Manage Your Apps** page, as shown in Figure 2-45, which can display information about the currently installed apps.

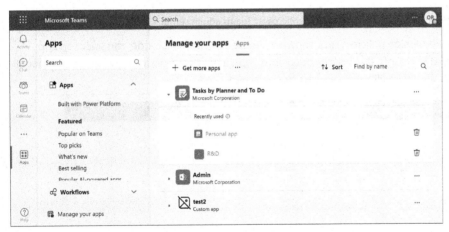

FIGURE 2-45 The Manage Your Apps page in a Microsoft Teams client

By default, Microsoft Teams includes a set of core apps to implement its standard services, such as the Chat, Calls, Teams, and Calendar pages. Many other apps are published by Microsoft on the **Apps** page, as well as apps created by third parties—the security and functionality of which Microsoft has certified.

Microsoft Teams also supports the integration of custom line of business (LOB) apps created by developers working in or for an organization. This includes custom apps developed using standard tools and submitted through an API or as a zipped package. Microsoft Teams also supports content created with the Microsoft Power Platform tools, such as Power BI, Power Apps, Power Automate, and Power Virtual Agents.

Administering Microsoft Teams Apps

Using the Microsoft Teams admin center, administrators can exercise full control over what apps are made available to Microsoft Teams users, who can publish apps in the **Apps** store, and which apps individual users or groups have permission to install. On the **Manage Apps** page shown in Figure 2-46, administrators can select apps and allow or block access to them.

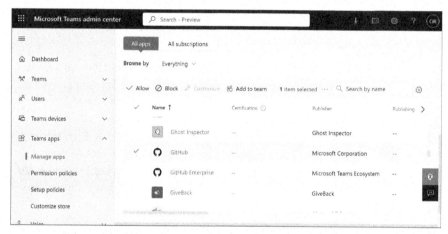

FIGURE 2-46 The Manage Apps page in the Microsoft Teams admin center

On the Permission policies page, shown in Figure 2-47, administrators can select an app type, such as Microsoft, third-party, or custom apps, and use a dropdown to specify whether all those apps should be allowed, blocked, or combined.

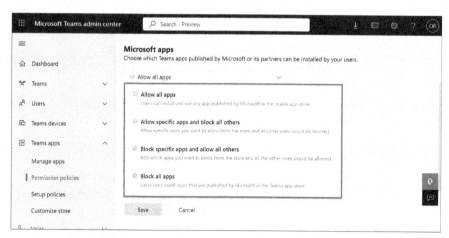

FIGURE 2-47 The Permission Policies page in the Microsoft Teams admin center

Skill 2.3: Describe endpoint modernization, management concepts, and deployment options in Microsoft 365

In IT parlance, an *endpoint* is a physical device that connects to a network to access data. *Endpoint management* is the process of assigning and maintaining access rights and permissions for each endpoint and implementing security policies that protect the company's data, regardless of how it happens to be accessed.

In the early days of local area networking, the network for a typical organization might consist of nearly identical endpoints, such as a fleet of PCs and a file server or two. However, as IT technology advanced, endpoints took many forms. Today, in addition to servers, the endpoints of an enterprise network might consist of client laptops, tablets, smartphones, and traditional desktop computers. There are also virtual machines, embedded devices, and Internet of Things (IoT) devices to consider.

Having all or most of these different technologies on a single network complicates the endpoint management process enormously, but Microsoft 365 includes a variety of tools that make it possible to control and protect different types of endpoints.

Describe the endpoint management capabilities of Microsoft 365, including Microsoft Endpoint Manager (MEM), Intune, AutoPilot, co-management with SCCM, and tenant attach

Modern management was a term that Microsoft coined but rapidly caught on throughout the IT industry. Described by Microsoft using the motto "mobile first; cloud first," it is intended to be a replacement for—or at least an evolution of—the traditional management practices that enterprise IT administrators have been using for years.

The traditional approach to IT device management consists of a paradigm in which all devices are owned, deployed, and managed by the enterprise IT department. This management typically includes the following elements:

- **Deployment** IT administrators create and maintain system image files and deploy them on new computers using a System Center Configuration Manager (SCCM) management tool. Administrators must create and store separate images and drivers for each model of computer purchased and update them whenever the software configuration changes.

- **Updates** Administrators manage operating system and application updates, often using a download, evaluation, and deployment tool, such as Windows Server Update Services (WSUS).

- **Identity** Active Directory is a database of identities and other network resources that provide authentication and authorization services for internal users, services, and applications.

- **Configuration**   Administrators use Group Policy to deploy configuration settings as they connect and log on to the internal network.

This traditional management paradigm has worked for a long time, and many IT professionals are reluctant to abandon it, particularly when adopting a new modern management concept requires them to learn to use new tools and technologies.

The problem, however, is that modern management is not just a fix for something that isn't broken. The idea of users all working on enterprise-owned and managed devices located in a company site is rapidly becoming a relic of the past. Vast numbers of users are working outside the office using their own devices, such as laptops, tablets, and smartphones, which administrators cannot readily deploy, update, and configure to the specifications of the IT department using traditional tools.

The other motivation for modernizing IT management is the enterprise's increased ubiquity of cloud-based applications. As software manufacturers shift their marketing emphasis to cloud-based products, it is becoming increasingly difficult for IT administrators to provide the services their users need with traditional, on-premises applications and services.

Modern management is designed to replace traditional tools with new ones that can work with cloud-based resources, manage users' devices, and simplify the deployment, update, and management processes. The object is to replace traditional reactive management processes with modern proactive processes. Microsoft 365 includes tools that do all these things, such as the following:

- **Deployment**   Windows AutoPilot is a cloud-based service that eliminates the need for separate system images and SCCM and simplifies the process of deploying new computers by automating the process of installing, activating, and configuring Windows.

- **Updates**   The Windows-as-a-Service update program provides Windows 10 and 11 workstations with regularly scheduled feature and quality updates that the computers automatically apply. Microsoft has also implemented technologies to reduce the size of the update downloads, mitigating the burden on networks and Internet connections.

- **Identity**   Azure Active Directory moves user identities from the local network to the cloud, enabling administrators to manage them from anywhere and providing users with single-sign-on capability to all cloud-based services and applications.

- **Configuration**   Microsoft Intune expands an enterprise's management perimeter to include non-Windows devices and devices that are accessible through the cloud. However, Intune can also replace Group Policy for configuring Windows computers because it has been enhanced with hundreds of mobile device management (MDM) APIs enabling Intune and similar tools to control them through the cloud.

Transitioning to modern management

Obviously, new organizations or divisions that choose Microsoft 365 as their initial IT solution can adopt Microsoft's modern management tools and techniques from scratch. Microsoft calls this the "cloud first" option. Even if they have a previous history with traditional management tools, administrators can adapt to the new ones without any conflict between the two models.

However, when an organization has an existing infrastructure based on the traditional model, it must decide whether to change to modern management and how it should do it.

A transition to the modern management model requires new tools and skills for administrators. Microsoft has designed three approaches to a transition from traditional to modern management, as follows:

- **Big switch** In the big switch transition, an organization abandons all the traditional management tools and modalities and begins using modern management tools exclusively. While this might be a feasible option for a relatively small organization, large enterprises will likely find a sudden transition impractical.

- **Group-by-group** In a group-by-group transition, an organization classifies its users by department, location, or workload and converts one group of users at a time to the modern management environment. In many cases, the transition process will be determined by the applications users require and whether they can readily be managed from the cloud.

- **Co-management** The co-management model calls for administrators to maintain both the traditional and modern management paradigms for an extended period. This makes it possible for the organization to transition gradually from traditional applications and procedures to those that support modern management.

Co-management has become a widely accepted solution for enterprises that are reluctant to give up their traditional management model or have applications and services that are not manageable using modern tools. From Microsoft's standpoint, co-management aims to form a bridge from the traditional to the modern management model. Administrators can continue to use elements of their traditional, on-premises infrastructure, such as Active Directory Domain Services and System Center Configuration Manager, and gradually migrate to modern tools, such as Azure Active Directory and Microsoft Intune.

The steps involved in a co-management transition (not necessarily in order) are as follows:

- Begin using the Windows-as-a-Service model for Windows 10 or 11 and the Microsoft 365 productivity apps

- Move from an on-premises Windows update solution, such as Windows Server Update Services, to the cloud-based Windows Update for Business

- Transition from creating, maintaining, and deploying system images for Windows workstations to using Windows AutoPilot for cloud-based, zero-touch deployments

- Stop using Group Policy to configure workstation settings in favor of the Microsoft Intune tool included with some Microsoft 365 subscriptions

Although it is possible to undertake them separately, all these tasks are incorporated into a Microsoft 365 deployment.

Enterprise mobility

As noted earlier in this chapter, the modern workplace is no longer restricted to a single office, building, or even city, and even if it was, typical workers have multiple devices that they have come to expect they can use to access enterprise resources. Mobility has become a critical element of modern management, and Microsoft 365 includes the tools needed to enable users with smartphones, tablets, laptops, and home computers to access the enterprise files, applications, and services they need.

The first obstacle to mobility is access to data, but fortunately, Microsoft 365 enables users, applications, and services to store their data in the cloud, thus making it available to any device with an Internet connection. For this reason, all Microsoft 365 users receive OneDrive cloud storage, and SharePoint also uses cloud storage.

The second issue is access to the various Microsoft 365 applications and services. The traditional Office product required users to install the productivity applications, such as Word, Excel, and PowerPoint, on a desktop computer or laptop. The back-end services, such as Exchange and SharePoint, had to be installed on local servers. On-site users could access their email and SharePoint sites, but special arrangements were needed for users traveling or working from home, such as remote access or virtual private network connections.

With Microsoft 365, users still can install the Office applications on their computers, but the product also includes the Office on the Web applications, which enable users to work with Word, Excel, and PowerPoint documents online, using any device with a web browser and Internet access. The Microsoft 365 back-end services are all installed in the cloud, providing users access to their email and other services without a special connection to the company datacenter. Here again, only an Internet connection is needed.

In addition to the traditional Office productivity applications, new clients such as those for Microsoft Teams and Yammer are available as Web-based apps also, requiring no special preparation. Microsoft 365 also includes downloadable desktop clients for many of its applications, available in versions for all the major mobile platforms, including Android, iOS, MacOS, and Windows.

The third and arguably most critical mobility issue concerns the mobile devices themselves. In the early days of cellular connectivity, organizations provided their users with mobile devices. The devices were relatively limited in their capabilities, and administrators retained full control over them.

However, today's mobile culture is radically different, with smartphones having become ubiquitous and functioning as a personal status symbol as much as a work tool. Some organizations provide mobile devices, but administrators now often accommodate workers who want to use their personal devices to access enterprise resources, which raises complex security and support issues.

Microsoft's task was to develop clients that mobile workers could use to access their enterprise data, applications, and services. However, providing mobile devices with client access is only half the picture. The other half ensures that sensitive enterprise resources are protected against loss, theft, and attack. Microsoft provides tools that make this possible, but it is up to the enterprise administrators to implement them in a manner that is suitable both for the worker's usability needs and the sensitivity of the data.

Enterprise Mobility + Security

The Microsoft 365 components concerned with managing mobile devices and their protection are collectively known as Enterprise Mobility + Security (EMS). The primary tools that compose EMS and the functions they provide for mobile devices are as follows:

- **Azure Active Directory**   Contains the accounts that provide users with single-sign-on capability for all the Microsoft 365 applications and services. Administrators can configure user accounts to require multifactor authentication to enhance the security of mobile devices.

- **Microsoft Intune**   Enrolls mobile devices and associates them with particular users or groups. Using Intune, administrators can specify whether to use Mobile Device Management (MDM) or Mobile Application Management (MAM), specify device compliance policies, and create device configuration policies.

- **Azure Information Protection**   Provides document-level security by applying labels that classify the information files' sensitivity and applying protection to specific documents through encryption, user restrictions, and other means.

- **Microsoft Advanced Threat Analytics**   Gathers information from many Microsoft 365 enterprise sources and analyzes it to anticipate, detect, and react to attacks and other security threats.

The following sections examine some of these components in greater detail.

Microsoft Endpoint Manager

Microsoft Endpoint Manager is a cloud-based portal that works with Microsoft Intune to provide detailed information and administrative access for enrolled devices, such as their hardware properties, serial numbers, installed apps, and other configuration data. However, as of October 2022, the Microsoft Endpoint Manager name has been deprecated, and the product's functionality has been incorporated into the Microsoft Intune admin center. Although the list of admin centers in the Microsoft 365 admin center portal still includes an **Endpoint Manager** link, clicking it opens the Microsoft Intune admin center.

Microsoft Intune

Microsoft Intune is the tool administrators use to enable the enrollment of users' personal devices into Microsoft 365 and regulate their capabilities. Mobile Device Management (MDM) enables administrators to take near-complete control of enrolled devices, even to the point of issuing remote commands that erase all company data on the device.

EXAM TIP

Microsoft has announced that its collection of endpoint management tools will now be known as the Microsoft Intune family of products. Therefore, the name Microsoft Intune can refer to the individual application or the family of products, including Windows Autopilot, Configuration Manager, and Desktop Analytics. Candidates for the MS-900 exam should be cautioned against confusing the individual product with the product family.

For users who do not like the idea of the organization exercising that kind of control over their personal property, Mobile Application Management (MAM) provides devices only with managed applications, leaving the rest of the device unrestricted. Which option administrators choose must depend on the sensitivity of the data that might be stored on the device and any security compliance guidelines the organization must observe.

> **NOTE MDM AND MAM**
>
> For more information on Mobile Device Management and Mobile Application Management, see the "Mobile Device Management" section later in this chapter.

Administrators configure Microsoft Intune settings using the Microsoft Intune admin center, as shown in Figure 2-48. All Intune settings are implemented and stored in the cloud.

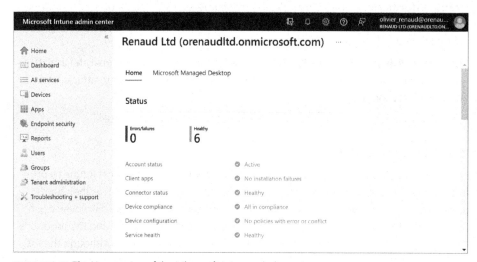

FIGURE 2-48 The Home page of the Microsoft Intune admin center

Microsoft Intune provides settings for a variety of endpoint security features, as shown in Figure 2-49. Administrators can configure these settings to ensure that users' enrolled devices—even their personal devices—provide a safe environment for company data.

One of the most common methods for ensuring client devices are properly secured is assigning device compliance policies to them. Device compliance policies are rules that specify how a device must be configured for it to access Microsoft 365 services.

For example, a policy can require that mobile devices must have a password to unlock it, rather than a simple swipe (as shown in Figure 2-50), that data be stored on the device in encrypted form, and that the operating system on the mobile device updated to a specific level. A device that does not meet the compliance policy settings cannot be enrolled, and even when it is successfully enrolled, it must be checked for compliance at regular intervals to maintain its access to the Microsoft 365 cloud services.

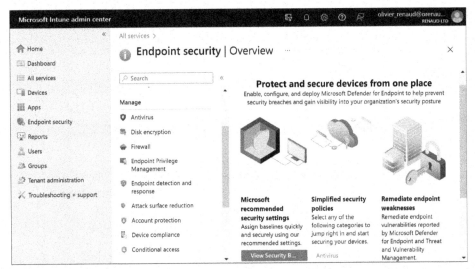

FIGURE 2-49 The Endpoint Security Overview page of the Microsoft Intune admin center

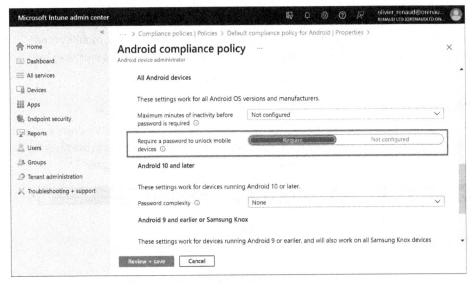

FIGURE 2-50 Device compliance policies in Microsoft Intune

Typically, protecting enterprise data on mobile devices restricts what the device user can do. In some cases, administrators might want to prevent the users from endangering sensitive data. Another major security issue is the possibility of data theft or destruction when a mobile device is lost or stolen. Administrators can control mobile device capabilities by creating configuration profiles in Microsoft Intune for the various platforms and enabling or disabling device functions, as shown in Figure 2-51.

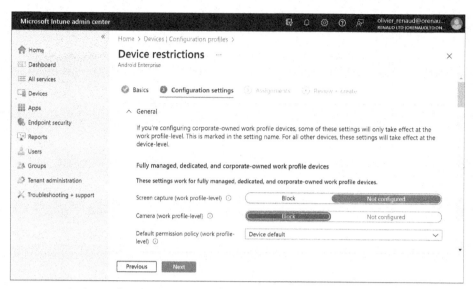

FIGURE 2-51 Device configuration profiles in Microsoft Intune

Administrators can further specify which applications mobile devices are permitted to run and also explicitly block them from running certain applications. Clearly, mobility is not just allowing devices to connect to a Microsoft 365 domain; their capabilities must also be restricted.

Windows Autopilot

Windows Autopilot is a cloud-based tool for automating the deployment of Windows workstations on enterprise networks. Administrators can create Autopilot profiles in the Microsoft Intune admin center, as shown in Figure 2-52, or the Microsoft 365 admin center.

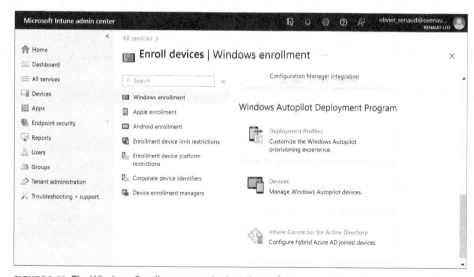

FIGURE 2-52 The Windows Enrollment page in the Microsoft Intune admin center

When an Autopilot profile is properly configured in user-driven mode, IT departments can ship new computers directly to end users from an OEM or dealer. Creating and maintaining image files for each type of computer is no longer necessary. In a typical deployment, IT never touches the machine, and the only tasks required of the end user to set it up are as follows:

1. Open the box.
2. Plug the computer into a power source and turn it on.
3. Choose a language, locale, and keyboard.
4. Connect the computer to a network with Internet access.
5. Supply login credentials for an organization account.

All other prompts that normally appear on a new computer starting for the first time (called the out-of-box experience or OOBE) can be customized or suppressed with Autopilot because the tool can supply the correct responses. For example, a Windows Autopilot deployment profile includes a page like the one in Figure 2-53, which specifies what screens should appear to the user during the OOBE phase of the deployment.

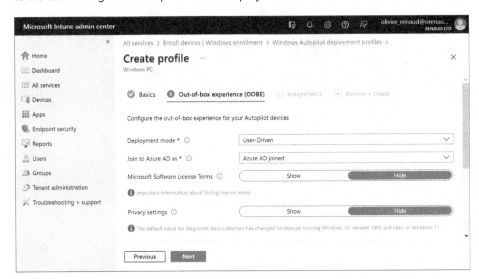

FIGURE 2-53 A Windows Autopilot deployment profile in Microsoft Intune

In addition to handling the OOBE settings, Autopilot can do any or all of the following:

- Upgrade Windows to a new edition, such as Windows 11 Enterprise
- Enroll devices into mobile device management (MDM) in Microsoft Intune
- Join the computer to an Azure Active Directory or Active Directory Domain Services domain
- Add the computer to selected groups
- Install applications
- Apply policies and configuration settings

Co-management with Configuration Manager

The Configuration Manager product, formerly known as System Center Configuration Manager, is now part of the Microsoft Intune family of products. Originally designed as a management tool for on-premises devices, Configuration Manager can perform many of the same functions as Intune, including deploying new workstations, distributing software updates, installing applications, and so forth.

Microsoft Intune can handle all the endpoint management needed for a new enterprise network based on cloud technologies. However, for a hybrid network with existing on-premises devices already managed by Configuration Manager, it is possible to create a co-management arrangement between Intune and Configuration Manager. This can be a permanent arrangement or part of a gradual transition from the datacenter to the cloud.

Co-management is the process of connecting a Configuration Manager installation to the cloud so administrators can manage their devices with both Intune and Configuration Manager, as shown in Figure 2-54.

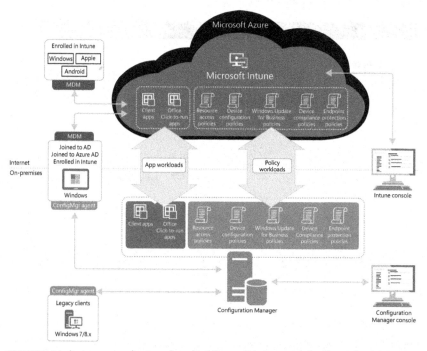

FIGURE 2-54 A co-managed enterprise with Microsoft Intune and Configuration Manager

Microsoft 365 uses the cloud-based Azure Active Directory (Azure AD) directory service to manage the identities of its users. An on-premises Configuration Manager installation typically uses Active Directory Domain Services (AD DS), hosted on a local server functioning as a domain controller. By default, these two directory services are completely separate. All the identities must be in one place to create a co-management environment. Therefore, administrators must create a hybrid Azure AD service by installing Azure AD Connect, a tool that runs on the AD DS domain controller and synchronizes its user accounts with the Azure AD directory. This ensures that both directories contain all the user accounts and are regularly updated. Once the directory services are synchronized, for co-management of a client device to occur, it must have both the Configuration Manager client installed and be enrolled in Microsoft Intune. Therefore, for administrators attempting to connect a cloud-based Microsoft 365 network to an on-premises Configuration Manager installation, they will have to upgrade the client devices in one of two ways:

- For devices already enrolled in Microsoft Intune, install the Configuration Manager client.
- For existing Configuration Manager clients, join the device to the Azure AD directory and enroll it in Microsoft Intune.

Once the co-management environment is established, administrators can manage clients from either the Microsoft Intune admin center or the Configuration Manager console. For administrators accustomed to working with Configuration Manager clients and consoles, their existing practices will change as a result of co-management. However, once co-managed, those clients will have access to Microsoft Intune features that Configuration Manager cannot provide, such as conditional access and remote restart.

Tenant attach

Tenant attach is a process of synchronizing the devices in a Configuration Manager installation with those of a Microsoft Intune tenancy by uploading them. Once the two directories are synchronized, administrators can manage all the network's devices from the Microsoft Intune admin center Devices page—even the Configuration Manager devices.

For a network that is already co-managed, administrators can configure tenant attach by modifying the CoMgmtSettingsProd co-management properties settings to enable device uploads, as shown in Figure 2-55.

FIGURE 2-55 CoMgmtSettingsProd properties settings in Configuration Manager

For networks that are not yet co-managed (and are running at least version 2111 of Configuration Manager), administrators can complete the entire process of enabling co-management and tenant attach by running the Cloud Attach Configuration Wizard, as shown in Figure 2-56.

FIGURE 2-56 The Cloud Attach Configuration Wizard

Cloud attach is a Microsoft term that refers to the entire process of integrating Configuration Manager devices into the Microsoft 365 cloud. Running the Cloud Attach Configuration Wizard completes all of the following tasks:

- Enable co-management
- Enroll devices into Microsoft Intune
- Enable Endpoint Analytics
- Upload devices to Microsoft Intune

Compare the differences between Windows 365 and Azure Virtual Desktop

Windows 365 and Azure Virtual Desktop (formerly Windows Virtual Desktop) are both virtual desktop solutions that enable organizations to deploy a cloud-based Windows desktop environment to any user device with Internet access. Sometimes called Desktop as a Service (DaaS), these technologies are fundamentally similar in delivering a fully configured Windows desktop to client users. That desktop is running on a Microsoft Azure virtual machine.

However, despite their similarity, IT personnel should carefully compare the Windows 365 and Azure Virtual Desktop (AVD) products before committing to either one. The operational and cost differences can be substantial. Generally speaking, Windows 365 is simpler to purchase and deploy but lacks flexibility. Azure Virtual Desktop is much more flexible than Windows 365 but is also more complex and requires more of an existing Azure infrastructure.

Windows 365

Windows 365 is the simpler of the two virtual desktop options, with fewer elements configurable by the subscriber. The product is sold on a tiered monthly subscription basis, much like Microsoft 365 and many other Microsoft products. This makes Windows 365 a familiar purchasing experience for existing Microsoft customers.

Windows 365 delivers what Microsoft calls a *cloud PC*. A cloud PC is essentially a virtual machine running on a server in a Microsoft datacenter. Customers purchase cloud PCs in much the same way as a physical PC from an online retailer. They select a model with a specific processor, a certain amount of RAM and storage, and other hardware characteristics, paying more for tiers with more RAM, for example. The decision as to which pricing scheme is preferable must be based on the size and requirements of the individual organization.

Once subscribed, users can access their cloud PCs through the Windows 365 website (*windows365.microsoft.com*), the Windows 365 app, or a Microsoft Remote Desktop client.

NOTE **KEY DIFFERENCE**

Windows 365 is a flat-rate monthly subscription service with specified limits in virtual hardware, storage, and bandwidth. Subscribers pay the entire monthly fee however much the desktop is actually used. By contrast, AVD pricing is usage-based. Customers pay only for the services they actually consume.

The Windows 365 products are divided into two types: Business and Enterprise. The Business plans are intended for small and medium businesses, whereas the Enterprise plans are designed for large businesses with existing IT infrastructures. In addition, both the Business and Enterprise cloud PCs are available in three tiers: Basic, Standard, and Premium, which define three virtual hardware configurations for the cloud PC, as shown in Table 2-2.

TABLE 2-2 Windows 365 Product Tiers

	Basic	Standard	Premium
Processors	2 vCPU	2 vCPU	4 vCPU
RAM	4 GB	8 GB	16 GB
Storage	128 GB	128 GB	128 GB

	Basic	Standard	Premium
Apps	Microsoft 365 apps	Microsoft 365 apps	Microsoft 365 apps, Microsoft Visual Studio, Power BI, Dynamics 365
Microsoft Teams	Voice and chat only	Desktop version	Desktop version
Maximum users	Business: 300 Enterprise: unlimited	Business: 300 Enterprise: unlimited	Business: 300 Enterprise: unlimited

The primary difference between Business and Enterprise cloud PCs is in their respective manageability. Business cloud PCs run in a Microsoft Managed Azure subscription, not the customer's own Azure subscription (if they have one). Therefore, the subscriber has no administrative access to the underlying Azure technology.

Business Cloud PCs are also provisioned with a standard Windows image and use many default settings. They have no means of remote management or configuration. All modifications must be performed through the user interface. The experience is essentially that of a small business owner with no IT infrastructure purchasing individual PCs for their business.

Enterprise cloud PCs support remote management through enrollment in Microsoft Intune, but users must have an Intune license, and the organization must have an existing Azure subscription that supports Azure AD Hybrid Join. The customer's Azure subscription is also responsible for the network communication to and from the cloud PC virtual machine.

As with Business cloud PCs, the VM for an Enterprise cloud PC runs in a Microsoft Managed Azure subscription. However, the virtual network interface card in the VM is connected to a vNet in the customer's Azure subscription. Therefore, while the customer does not have to pay the Azure costs incurred by the cloud PC's VM, they do have to pay whatever costs arise from the VM's network traffic, all of which passes through the customer's Azure account.

In addition to the distinctions already mentioned, Enterprise cloud PCs also provide administrators with more flexibility in deployment. The subscriber can supply a customized image file for the cloud PCs and specify configuration settings, such as group memberships, security permissions, and group policies. None of these things are possible on a Business cloud PC.

Therefore, obtaining a Business cloud PC is no more difficult than ordering a physical computer from an online retailer. The only prerequisite (besides the monthly fee) is an Internet-connected device that can access the cloud PC. Enterprise cloud PCs are a bit more complicated, since Microsoft assumes that their target audience is larger businesses with an established IT infrastructure and a commitment to Microsoft management tools, such as Microsoft 365 Enterprise subscribers.

Azure Virtual Desktop

If Windows 365 Business is the simplest virtual desktop solution to deploy, and Windows 365 Enterprise is a small step up in complexity, Azure Virtual Desktop is a larger step up, both in complexity and flexibility. AVD is a virtual desktop solution based on the Azure components needed to provision virtual PCs, as shown in Figure 2-57.

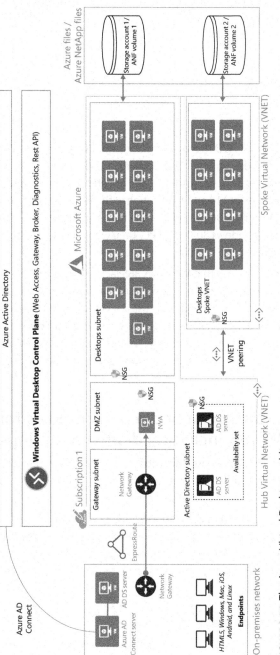

FIGURE 2-57 The Azure Virtual Desktop architecture

Customers must have an Azure subscription and will have to obtain the following Azure components for a typical AVD deployment:

- Virtual machines
- System storage
- User personal storage
- User profile storage
- Networking

Administrators perform all AVD management through the Azure portal. AVD requires no special operating system licensing other than a Microsoft 365 or Windows license, and its pricing model is consumption-based, so customers pay only for the actual services they use. This can be a major economic benefit to an organization with fluctuating compute requirements that would leave some Windows 365 cloud PCs idle for part of the time. Subscribers must still pay the monthly fee for a Windows 365 cloud PC, even when it is not in use, but shutting down an AVD VM stops all charges from accruing.

AVD includes some capabilities that Windows 365 lacks, such as multi-session desktops and app virtualization, which might be why some customers opt for AVD over Windows 365. However, the most common factor that draws customers toward AVD is experience with Azure administration. For customers with experience with the various services provided by Azure and linking them into a workable infrastructure, AVD should be a familiar deployment experience. For those without a lot of Azure experience, Windows 365 is probably a better virtual desktop alternative.

Describe the deployment and release models for Windows-as-a-Service (WaaS), including deployment rings

Beginning with the Windows 10 release, Microsoft changed how it generates and releases operating system updates. Dubbing the new system *Windows-as-a-Service (WaaS)*, it is designed to reduce the burden on users and administrators.

In the past, Microsoft released major version Windows upgrades every three to five years, large service packs between those upgrades, and small monthly updates. The version upgrades were a major undertaking both for administrators and users. Administrators had to reinstall the operating system on all their workstations, and users were faced with a different interface and new features.

Windows-as-a-Service update releases

The Windows-as-a-Service update model eliminates major Windows version upgrades. Instead, there are two basic Windows update types:

- **Feature updates** Released semi-annually (in approximately March and September), feature updates provide new or revised operating system functions. Because the feature updates are more frequent than the previous major version upgrades, they spread out the update deployment process for administrators and do not represent as profound an interface and feature change to the users.

- **Quality updates** Released monthly, quality updates can contain nonsecurity or security + nonsecurity releases. Microsoft releases quality updates in a cumulative release package, ensuring all systems remain current.

The monthly quality updates in the old Windows servicing model took the form of many individual patches, which enterprise administrators had to evaluate and deploy individually. Many administrators chose to deploy only essential security fixes, leaving their workstations in a fragmented state. Only the infrequent service packs incorporated all the previous patches and fully updated the workstations. Platform fragmentation made it difficult or impossible for Microsoft to predict future updates' results accurately.

The WaaS quality updates take the form of cumulative monthly releases, including the latest security and reliability fixes. This leaves workstations in a fully patched state each month. Therefore, Microsoft can test subsequent updates on a consistent platform rather than being concerned whether all the previous patches have been applied.

Windows-as-a-Service servicing channels

Servicing channels are options that administrators can select to specify when their Windows clients should receive updates. Microsoft offers three servicing channels in Windows-as-a-Service, as follows:

- **General Availability Channel** By default, Windows-as-a-Service client installations use the General Availability Channel, which applies all updates as soon as Microsoft releases them. Therefore, the clients receive feature updates twice annually and quality updates monthly.

- **Windows Insider Channel** For users or organizations that want early access to updates for compatibility testing and the ability to provide feedback to Microsoft, the Windows Insider channel releases all updates before they are made available to the General Availability Channel.

- **Long Term Servicing Channel** For devices with specialized functions in which continuity is essential, such as medical equipment, point-of-sale systems, and kiosks, there is the Long Term Servicing Channel (LTSC), which receives feature updates only every two to three years. LTSC systems still receive quality updates monthly.

The General Availability feature update cycle begins with a development phase in which the update is first run by Microsoft engineers and then by a larger group of Microsoft internal users for six months, a process that Microsoft calls "dogfooding." Then, Microsoft releases the feature update to the Windows Insider program members for testing and feedback. Finally, the update goes into general release, which typically consists of a pilot or test deployment in a large enterprise, followed by a general production deployment to all workstations, as shown in Figure 2-58.

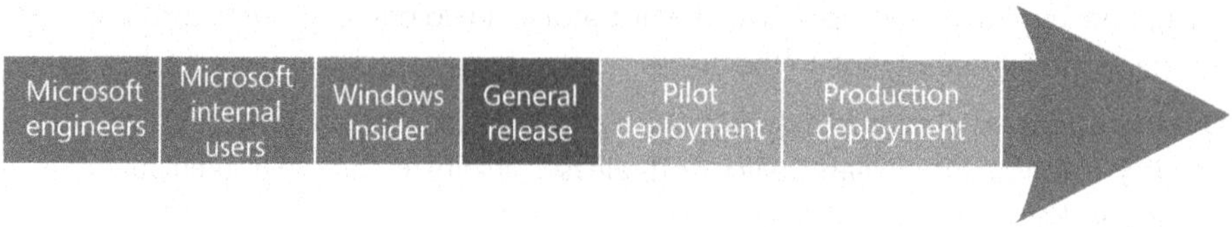

FIGURE 2-58 Phases of a Windows 10 feature update release

Windows deployment rings

In a responsible enterprise, deploying an operating system—or any software—is a rigorously planned process executed in phases. One of the common plans used in Windows deployments calls for three phases, which Microsoft refers to as rings, as shown in Figure 2-59.

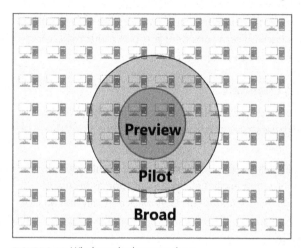

FIGURE 2-59 Windows deployment rings

The rings represent the growing size of the deployment groups. While the names assigned to the rings might differ, the phases of the deployment are often as follows:

- **Preview** A small group that receives the software before the general release for basic functionality and feature testing, such as Windows Insider users.
- **Pilot** A larger, but still relatively small, group that receives the software immediately upon general release to validate its functionality on a larger variety of devices.
- **Broad** Sometime after the general release, barring problems experienced by the previous groups, the software goes into wide release to the entire organization.

Microsoft 365 deployment

As noted earlier, Microsoft 365 consists of multiple products. However, the process of deploying Microsoft 365 is not just a matter of obtaining licenses for these products and installing them. How the Microsoft 365 components work together to provide intelligent management, security, and collaboration requires that the deployment be undertaken as an integrated process.

The complexity of a Microsoft 365 enterprise deployment depends on the size of the existing enterprise, its needs, and the applications already running on it. Microsoft has defined three Microsoft 365 deployment strategies:

- **FastTrack for Microsoft 365** FastTrack is a benefit included as part of a Microsoft 365 Enterprise subscription that provides ongoing support from Microsoft personnel, including a FastTrack manager, an engineer, and a migration engineer. These specialists divide the subscriber's Microsoft 365 deployment into three stages, called Envision, Onboard, and Drive Value, enabling them to plan and deploy Microsoft 365 into the existing enterprise infrastructure and then help the organization's people adapt their roles to the Microsoft 365 environment.

- **Third-party services** Microsoft partners and consulting services can provide help with a Microsoft 365 deployment at many levels, ranging from complete control of the operation to occasional support.

- **Self-deployment** The Microsoft 365 Enterprise deployment documentation defines a process in multiple phases for creating a viable Microsoft 365 installation, including Windows 10 or 11 Enterprise and the Office productivity applications. After that, the administrators can create workloads and scenarios specific to the organization, including Exchange Online, SharePoint, and Microsoft Teams.

The Microsoft 365 Enterprise deployment documentation breaks the foundation infrastructure—sometimes called a *core deployment*—into phases, as described in the following sections. Each phase is divided into steps or tasks that must be completed before the phase can be considered complete.

For a deployment in a relatively small or new organization that is just beginning to use Microsoft's cloud-based products, following the phases of the deployment process in order will create a reliable structure for the workloads and scenarios to be deployed later. For an existing enterprise already using some of the Microsoft 365 components, some of the required tasks might already have been completed, and the phases do not have to be followed in an unbroken sequence. Administrators can approach the phases in any order they find practical if they meet the requirements for each phase.

> **NEED MORE REVIEW**
>
> For more detailed coverage of the steps in each phase of the Microsoft 365 deployment process, as well as procedures for deploying Microsoft 365 workloads and scenarios, see the Deploy Microsoft 365 Enterprise documentation at *https://learn.microsoft.com/en-us/microsoft-365/enterprise/?view=o365-worldwide.*

NETWORKING PHASE

The Networking phase of a Microsoft 365 deployment is intended to ensure that all clients have sufficient Internet connectivity to access the cloud resources they will require regularly. This is not just a matter of bandwidth, however. The Microsoft Global Network provides endpoints to its cloud services worldwide, and for Microsoft 365 clients to function efficiently, they should have access to the closest possible endpoint.

Many enterprise networks were designed and constructed at a time when the proximity of the Internet connection was not a priority. It was common for Internet traffic at remote sites to be routed over a backbone network to a central location that provided the actual Internet access. This can result in a significant amount of network latency (that is, transmission delays), which can have a negative effect on Microsoft 365 performance.

Microsoft's Domain Name System (DNS) servers direct client traffic to the nearest endpoint based on their initial connection request. The clients should therefore also utilize a geographically local DNS server for their outbound Internet traffic.

For an enterprise that has a centralized Internet access infrastructure, the organization should take the steps necessary to reroute the Internet traffic so that each client is directed to the Microsoft endpoint that is geographically closest to its location. In a large enterprise with many remote sites, this can be a substantial undertaking that might play a role in deciding whether to adopt Microsoft 365 in the first place.

Microsoft also recommends that enterprise networks avoid using protection mechanisms, such as proxy servers and packet inspection, for Microsoft 365 traffic. The DNS names and IP addresses used by the Microsoft 365 cloud services are well-known, and Microsoft's own mechanisms already protect the services. Duplicating this protection at the enterprise end can also have a negative effect on Microsoft 365 performance. Bypassing these local protection mechanisms requires browsers, firewalls, and other components to identify Microsoft 365 traffic and process it differently from other types of Internet traffic.

IDENTITY PHASE

In the Identity phase of a deployment, administrators create the Azure AD accounts that will be needed for users to access Microsoft cloud services and applications. These accounts can be for the organization's internal users or for partners, vendors, and consultants outside the organization. For organizations without an on-premises infrastructure or for users who only require cloud services, administrators can create accounts directly in Azure AD. If the organization has an internal infrastructure based on Active Directory Domain Services, the administrators can synchronize the existing AD DS accounts to Azure AD.

Administrators should also plan how they will group users in the organization and how they will use Microsoft 365 groups for network administration. For example, Microsoft 365 supports group-based licensing, in which group members are automatically granted licenses for specific products. As with AD DS, assigning permissions to groups is possible, allowing the members access to SharePoint team sites and other resources. Azure AD also supports dynamic group membership, in which user accounts with specific properties, such as a department or country name, are automatically added to a group.

In this phase, administrators also configure protection for administrative accounts. Global administrator accounts, the most privileged in Microsoft 365, should be configured with the strongest passwords that are practical and also use multifactor authentication (MFA). In addition to the password, MFA can call for a biometric attribute, such as a fingerprint, or a verification code sent to a smartphone. Other administrator accounts, such as those for specific services, and even standard user accounts, might require a similar level of MFA protection.

When an organization has an existing AD DS infrastructure, administrators can conceivably create duplicate accounts in Azure AD, but they would have to manually make any future changes to both directories. A more streamlined solution is available in the creation of hybrid accounts. *Hybrid accounts* are AD DS accounts that are synchronized with Azure AD accounts, using a tool called Azure AD Connect. Running on an internal server, Azure AD Connect polls AD DS for changes in accounts and groups and replicates them to Azure AD, as shown in Figure 2-60.

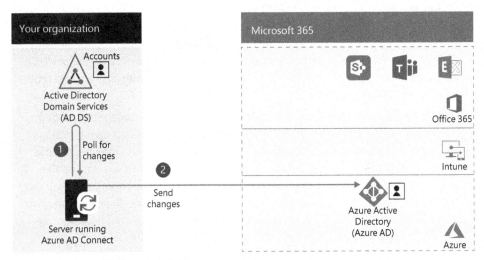

FIGURE 2-60 Azure AD Connect hybrid account maintenance

WINDOWS DEPLOYMENT PHASE

The process of deploying Windows 10 or 11 Enterprise can vary depending on the current condition of the network and the tools administrators use to manage the workstations. For an enterprise that has workstations already running Windows 7 or Windows 8.1, it is possible to perform an in-place upgrade to Windows 10 or 11 Enterprise and automate the process using Microsoft Configuration Manager.

Administrators can use Windows AutoPilot to customize the workstation configuration for new Windows workstations, including changing the Windows 10 or 11 edition from Pro to Enterprise.

To begin the process, administrators must first configure AutoPilot by creating a deployment profile and registering the workstations to be deployed. This can include modifying the Out of Box Experience (OOBE) with company branding and other specific installation settings and configuring enrollment of the workstations in Windows Intune. As noted earlier in this chapter, once AutoPilot is properly configured, workstation users have to sign on using only their Microsoft 365 account credentials. AutoPilot then completes the rest of the deployment process.

MOBILE DEVICE MANAGEMENT

One of the most important features of Microsoft 365 is the capability to support mobile devices, such as laptops, smartphones, and tablets, even those running non-Microsoft operating systems, such as Android, iOS, and MacOS. Microsoft Intune is the tool administrators use to manage mobile devices in Microsoft 365. Microsoft Intune is included as part of Microsoft 365 Enterprise subscriptions.

Microsoft Intune provides two basic approaches to the management of mobile devices, as shown in Figure 2-61:

- **Mobile Device Management (MDM)**   In MDM, devices are enrolled in Intune and become managed devices. Administrators can install applications, assign password policies, encrypt or remove any data on managed devices, and apply policies, rules, and settings. MDM essentially grants the organization complete control over the device, allowing administrators to ensure that the device is compliant with any required regulatory or other company policies.

- **Mobile Application Management (MAM)**   In MAM, Intune manages specific applications but not the entire device. Administrators can impose policies on the managed applications, such as requiring a password to access Exchange, and they can remove corporate data from the applications, but they cannot remove just any data on the system. MAM is more commonly used for organizations that support a Bring Your Own Device (BYOD) policy, in which users might not want to grant the organization full control over their personal property and when the company does not have rigorous security compliance policies to maintain.

As part of the Intune planning process, administrators must decide whether to use MDM, MAM, or both, and if the latter is chosen, which devices should use which management model. Using Intune in a hybrid management environment and another product, such as Configuration Manager, is also possible.

Enrollment is the process by which a device is added to Microsoft Intune for *management*. Before devices can be enrolled in Intune, administrators must create Microsoft 365 users and groups and assign Intune licenses to them. Administrators can create users and groups manually or synchronize the existing users from Azure AD or an on-premises AD DS installation. It might also be necessary to create additional groups specifically for Intune. For example, administrators might want to create individual groups for specific device types.

The enrollment process can take many forms, depending on the device platform and whether an administrator or user is enrolling the device. For BYOD devices, for example, users can download a portal app and perform the enrollment themselves. For devices owned by the organization, administrators can set up autoenrollment protocols and use the device enrollment manager (DEM), a special user account that enables the enrollment of up to 1,000 devices.

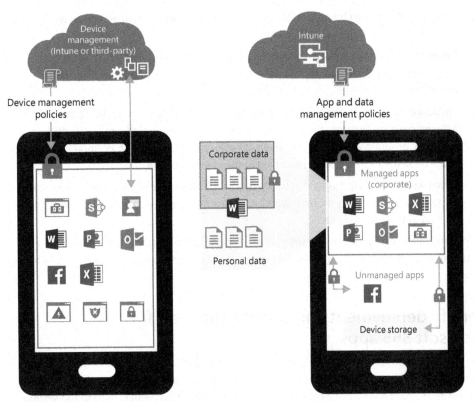

FIGURE 2-61 Microsoft Intune MDM or MAM

Once devices are enrolled, administrators can add applications through the **All Apps** page in the Microsoft Intune portal. The procedures for adding applications and the possible management tasks after the applications are added vary depending on the device platform and the type of application.

The most critical aspect of managing mobile devices with Microsoft Intune is protecting the organization's resources. One of the most powerful ways of doing this is by creating *compliance policies* that specify the security conditions a device must meet. For example, administrators can create and assign policies requiring a minimum operating system version, specify a required password length, or prevent the use of devices that have been rooted or jailbroken. Administrators can restrict access to specific applications or the entire device based on a device's compliance with the assigned policies. This is called *conditional access*.

One of the most powerful management tools for mobile devices is the device profiles that you can create in Microsoft Intune, which enable administrators to apply a wide variety of features and settings that can enhance or restrict a device's capabilities.

Workloads and scenarios

Once the Microsoft 365 infrastructure is in place, administrators can implement the workloads and scenarios that utilize its services. The workloads of Microsoft 365 typically involve

Microsoft Teams, Exchange Online, and SharePoint. The deployment process for each workload consists of three phases, as follows:

- **Envision** Assemble a team representing the enterprise's business, IT, and user interests. Then, brainstorm and prioritize the scenarios in which the organization will make use of the capabilities the service provides.

- **Onboard** Prepare a detailed plan for the service rollout, including any necessary account creation and data migration planning and whether help from Microsoft's FastTrack program will be needed. Then, create a pilot deployment, preferably including some or all the representatives involved in the envision phase.

- **Drive value** Deploy the service to the rest of the enterprise, encourage its adoption as needed, and carefully monitor activity reports and user feedback to determine the success of the deployment.

Once the Microsoft 365 workload services are in place, administrators can develop scenarios that utilize them, such as implementing data protection technologies and building team websites.

Identify deployment and update channels for Microsoft 365 apps

There are several ways to install the Microsoft 365 productivity applications in a Microsoft 365 deployment, but they all should be preceded by a preliminary assessment and planning process. The assessment consists of a review of the target workstations with regard to the system requirements for Microsoft 365, languages, licenses, and compatibility with other applications.

In the planning stage of the deployment, administrators must make decisions such as the following:

- What deployment tool to use
- What installation packages will be needed
- Where the source files will be located (cloud or local source)
- Which update channel the workstations should use

In some cases, these decisions will vary for different parts of the enterprise, depending on the workstation equipment used, the availability of Internet connectivity, and the administrative personnel available.

> **NOTE** **CREATING A PILOT DEPLOYMENT**
>
> Whichever deployment method an organization uses, Microsoft's best practices recommendations call for creating at least two separate Microsoft 365 deployment groups, such as a pilot group and a broad group. Depending on the deployment method, this will call for creating two or more collections or ODT scripts. Administrators should deploy the pilot group first and test it for compatibility before deploying the broad group.

Deployment methods

With the deployment plan in place, administrators can proceed to use any of the following Microsoft 365 deployment methods:

- **Microsoft Intune** For exclusively cloud-based organizations, administrators can deploy the Microsoft 365 apps using Microsoft Intune, as shown in Figure 2-62. Intune makes it possible to select the apps to install and configure all of their settings, including the update channel. Then, the administrator selects the users or groups to receive the apps.

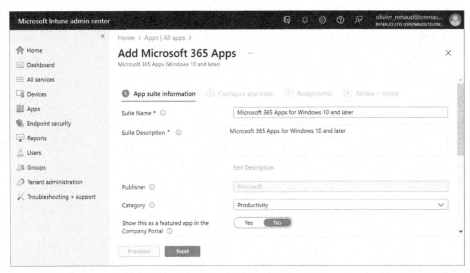

FIGURE 2-62 The Add Microsoft 365 Apps page in Microsoft Intune

- **Configuration Manager** For organizations that already use Microsoft Configuration Manager, administrators can deploy the Microsoft 365 applications as they would other apps, with no special modifications to the procedure. Administrators create collections representing groups of workstations with different installation requirements, then configure the Microsoft 365 Installer with settings such as the update channel to use and whether to add language packs. Once the application is configured, administrators can schedule the deployment to occur at a specific time.

- **Office Deployment Tool (ODT) with cloud source** The ODT is a command-line tool that uses an XML script file to specify installation settings for Microsoft 365 applications. Administrators can modify the XML script manually, but Microsoft also provides an Office Customization Tool website, which uses a graphical interface to generate the XML code. The default **Installation Options** setting—**Office Content Delivery Network (CDN)**—causes the ODT to use source files in the cloud to install the applications, as shown in Figure 2-63. Cloud-based installations perform delta updates, which download only the data each system needs, and can use delivery optimization to share source data among peers, both of which minimize the amount of data downloaded from the Internet. Then, to perform the installation, run the ODT executable, naming the script file on the command line as follows: `setup.exe /configure scriptfile.xml`.

FIGURE 2-63 Office Customization Tool

- **Office Deployment Tool with local source**   The process for installing the Microsoft 365 applications using the ODT with a local source calls for administrators to create an XML script with the **Local Source** value in the **Installation Options** setting and a path name to a network share. Running the ODT with the `/download` switch—as in `setup.exe /download scriptfile .xml`—causes the program to download the Microsoft 365 installation files to the path specified in the script. Microsoft recommends using cloud-based source files rather than local ones because they need regular local source file downloading and maintenance and cannot perform delta updates or use delivery optimization. Once the download is complete, administrators can deploy Microsoft 365 by running the ODT with the `/configure` switch using the same script.

- **Self-install using the Microsoft 365 portal**   The self-install method is typically used for workstations that are not connected to the internal network and do not have access to installation tools, such as Configuration Manager and ODT. Users install Microsoft 365 themselves by signing on to the Micrsoft365.com website using their Microsoft 365 accounts and clicking **Install Apps**, as shown in Figure 2-64.

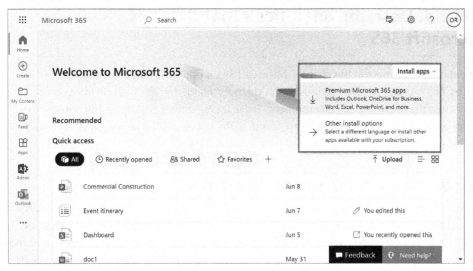

FIGURE 2-64 Microsoft 365 portal installation controls

Update channels

An important element of the Microsoft 365 application deployment process is the selection of the update channel the installed workstations will use. The update channel specifies how often the workstations will receive feature updates. Microsoft 365 supports the following application update channels:

- **Current Channel** Provides Microsoft 365 workstations with monthly security updates (on the second Tuesday of the month) and feature and cumulative nonsecurity updates whenever they are released (with no set schedule, usually several times per month).

- **Current Channel (Preview)** Provides Microsoft 365 workstations with Current Channel updates approximately a week (or more) before the general Current Channel release, allowing administrators time to evaluate the updates in a pilot deployment before the general release.

- **Monthly Channel** Provides Microsoft 365 workstations with new features, security, and nonsecurity updates only once per month on the second Tuesday of the month.

- **Semi-annual Channel** Provides Microsoft 365 workstations with feature updates twice yearly, in January and July. The channel provides security and nonsecurity updates once per month on the second Tuesday.

- **Semi-annual Channel (Preview)** Provides Microsoft 365 workstations with Semi-annual Channel updates in March and September, four months before the general Semi-annual Channel release, allowing administrators time to evaluate the updates in a pilot deployment before the general release. The channel also provides security and nonsecurity updates once per month on the second Tuesday.

Skill 2.4: Describe analytics capabilities of Microsoft 365

As mentioned elsewhere in this chapter, Microsoft 365 is not just a bundle of applications and services. The product includes various analytical tools that gather information from components across the Microsoft 365 environment. These tools—called analytics—can detect existing and potential security breaches, track usage of the Microsoft 365 applications, and even examine user and group production and collaboration patterns.

Describe the capabilities of Viva Insights

Viva Insights is an information hub similar to some of the other Viva tools in that it can insert pop-up content into the displays of other applications, such as Microsoft Teams and Outlook. Viva can display information about the patterns of Microsoft 365 usage for individual users and groups, such as the amount of time they spend collaborating with co-workers using Microsoft Teams, Outlook, Yammer, or other Microsoft 365 apps.

In addition, Insights can also generate recommendations based on those usage patterns. The tool also attempts to engage users in wellness activities by adding meditation sessions to their calendars, tracking their moods, and suggesting other activities, as shown in Figure 2-65. Insights might suggest, for example, that a user take a break after working several consecutive hours.

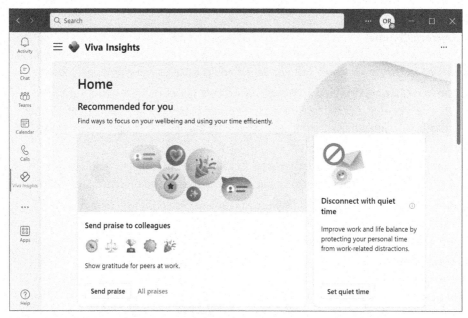

FIGURE 2-65 The Microsoft Viva Insights display

When incorporating the functionality of MyAnalytics and Workplace Analytics—both have now been deprecated—Insights can be integrated into Microsoft Teams like the other Viva apps, but it can also be displayed in Outlook. The application also tracks users' activities and provides them with advice in the form of personal insights, which can help them be more productive.

Viva Insights is included in the Microsoft 365 Enterprise E3 and E5 subscriptions but is limited to displaying personal insights about the user. There is also an additional Insights subscription that expands the tool's functionality. In addition to personal recommendations, the full Insights product can evaluate a team's performance by tracking collaboration time, as shown in Figure 2-66, sending regular briefing emails, and popping up reminders of milestones that must be met.

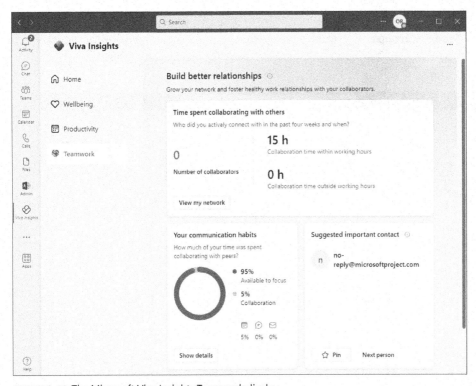

FIGURE 2-66 The Microsoft Viva Insights Teamwork display

In addition to personal and team information, the full Insights product also includes organizational insights that notify managers of the online progress of their teams.

Describe the capabilities of the Microsoft 365 admin center and Microsoft 365 user portal

Microsoft 365 provides access to most of its features through cloud-based portals, including the Microsoft 365 admin center and the Microsoft 365 user portal, as described in the following sections.

Microsoft 365 admin center

The Microsoft 365 admin center—available at *admin.microsoft.com*—is the primary tool for administrators to manage the configuration of their Microsoft 365 tenancies. The admin center's Home screen contains tiles that administrators can configure with frequently used functions. On its first appearance, the menu bar contains items providing many of the primary functions Microsoft 365 administrators need, including the following:

- **Users** Create and manage Alexa AD user accounts
- **Devices** Perform emergency functions on devices enrolled in Microsoft Intune, including removing company data and performing a factory reset on the device
- **Teams & Groups** Create and manage groups, as shown in Figure 2-67, including Microsoft 365, Distribution, Mail-Enabled Security, and Security groups

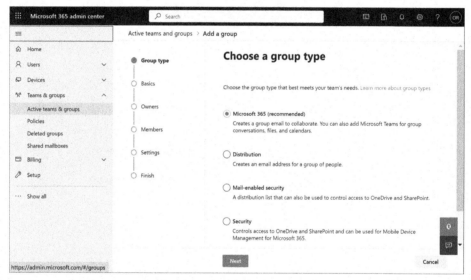

FIGURE 2-67 Creating a group in the Microsoft 365 admin center

- **Billing** Purchase and manage Microsoft product subscriptions and assign product licenses to users, as shown in Figure 2-68.
- **Setup** Display the current status and provide explanations and configuration settings for important Microsoft 365 subscription options

The Microsoft 365 admin center home screen also includes a **Show All** button, which expands the menu bar to show additional functions, as shown in Figure 2-69. Expand the menu bar to show links to all the other admin centers included with Microsoft 365.

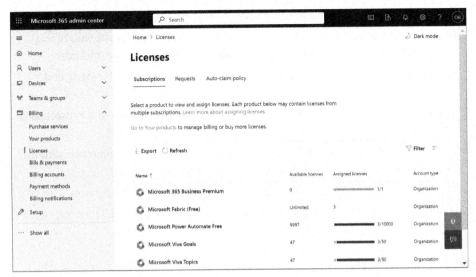

FIGURE 2-68 The Microsoft Viva Insights page for managing subscriptions

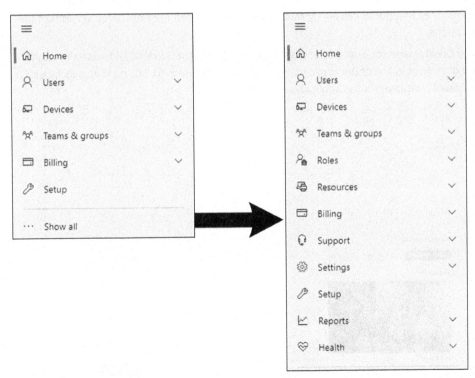

FIGURE 2-69 The Microsoft 365 admin center menu bar, in its basic form and with Show all selected

The additional menu items displayed in the admin center are as follows:

- **Roles**   Create and assign roles to users for Azure AD, Exchange, Intune, and billing, granting the users access to the appropriate admin centers and other resources

- **Resources**   Create mailboxes for resources representing rooms, equipment, and SharePoint sites

- **Support**   Display help content and service request history, and access Microsoft hardware support

- **Settings**   Provide access to a large collection of Microsoft 365 configuration settings, as well as purchase, install, and deploy third-party apps

- **Reports**   Provide access to usage reports for specific Microsoft 365 services

- **Health**   Display information about the performance of Microsoft 365 services, including incidents and advisories

Microsoft 365 user portal

The Microsoft 365 user portal—available at *microsoft365.com*—is a cloud-based portal shown earlier to allow users to download and install the Microsoft 365 productivity applications. However, the same portal can also provide users with access to the web-based versions of the applications.

The **Create** page, for example, contains a row of document tiles that allow users to create a new document in any of the applications, as shown in Figure 2-70. The page also includes a selection of templates for the applications.

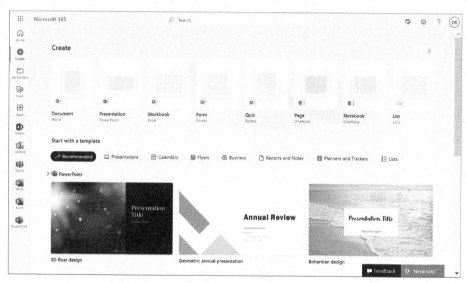

FIGURE 2-70 The Create page in the Microsoft 365 user portal

The web-based versions of the Microsoft 365 applications are also accessible from the menu bar, which contains all the applications the user is licensed to access, and from the **Apps** page, which provides tiles for the applications and links for apps created using **Power Apps**, as shown in Figure 2-71.

FIGURE 2-71 The Apps page in the Microsoft 365 user portal

Describe the reports available in the Microsoft 365 admin center and other admin centers

Virtually all the admin centers for the Microsoft 365 apps and services have a **Reports** menu that provides information about the ongoing usage of the products. The following sections describe some of the reports that are available to administrators.

Microsoft 365 Adoption Score

The **Reports/Adoption Score** page in Microsoft 365 admin center provides ratings and charts tracking how well the tenant organization utilized the Microsoft 365 technologies in the most recent 28 days, as shown in Figure 2-72.

The tool gathers information from various Microsoft 365 applications and services, including Exchange, SharePoint, Microsoft Teams, OneDrive, Word, Excel, PowerPoint, OneNote, and Outlook, to calculate the adoption score. The tool scores the organization in two areas:

- **People experiences**   A score based on the degree of communication and collaboration among users, as well as the modes of communication they employ
- **Technology experiences**   A score reflecting the performance and efficient use of the organization's network hardware and software, based on Endpoint Analytics in

Microsoft Intune and connectivity statistics for the Microsoft 365 services, including Exchange, SharePoint, and Microsoft Teams

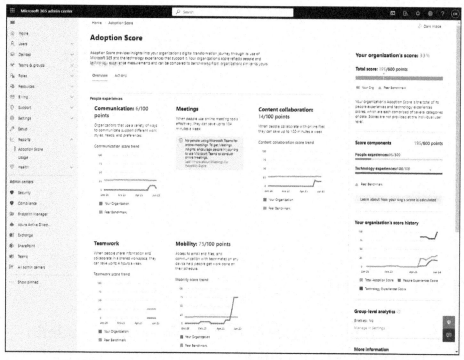

FIGURE 2-72 The Adoption Score page in the Microsoft 365 admin center

The **Adoption Score** tool evaluates the organization by assigning scores of up to 100 points in each of the following eight categories for a maximum possible score of 800:

- Communication (100 points)
- Meetings (100 points)
- Content collaboration (100 points)
- Teamwork (100 points)
- Mobility (100 points)
- Endpoint analytics (100 points)
- Network connectivity (100 points)
- Microsoft 365 Apps Health (100 points)

In addition to the score, the **Adoption Score** page also provides insights and recommendations for improving collaboration and productivity, as shown in Figure 2-73.

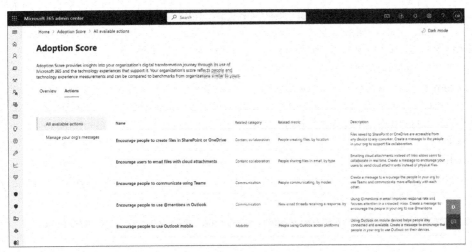

FIGURE 2-73 The Actions tab on the Adoption Score page in the Microsoft 365 admin center

Microsoft 365 usage

The **Reports/Usage** page in Microsoft 365 admin center can display information about activity levels in the various Microsoft 365 services in chart form, as shown in Figure 2-74. Administrators can modify the charts to display 7, 30, 90, or 180 days of information. Microsoft 365 Usage Analytics is a service within the Power BI business analytics tool to track how workers use the various Microsoft 365 components over the previous 12 months in much greater detail.

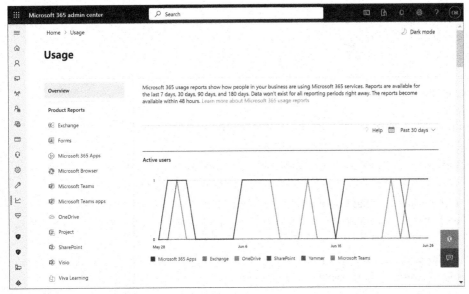

FIGURE 2-74 A service usage chart in Microsoft 365 admin center

Administrators can use the Power BI–based service to determine what tools workers use to perform specific types of tasks, which Microsoft 365 components are over- or underused, and which might be seldom adopted. This type of information can enable administrators to determine whether workers might need training to better use specific tools available to them.

For example, some users might complain that it is difficult for them to communicate company-wide because they usually spend most of their time with their immediate team members. These users might not be aware that Viva Engage exists or know how to use it. A brief tutorial might resolve these users' problem and increase cross-communication within the enterprise.

With the information that Microsoft 365 gathers, the administrator can add the Microsoft 365 Usage Analytics connection to the Power BI application, authenticate the enterprise's tenancy, and generate a dashboard of chart-based data, as shown in Figure 2-75.

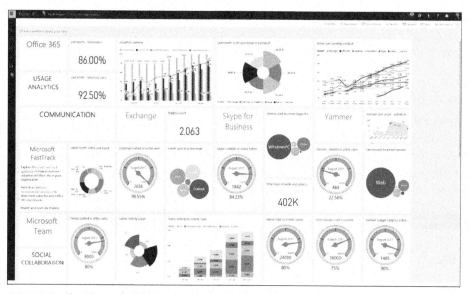

FIGURE 2-75 The Microsoft 365 Usage Analytics dashboard in Power BI

By clicking individual charts, administrators can see more detailed information about specific usage factors, including the following:

- **Office activation** Specifies the number and types of devices on which users have installed their five copies of Microsoft 365, as permitted by their license

- **Adoption** Specifies how many Microsoft 365 licenses have been assigned to users each month, how many are actually in use, and how many people are using Microsoft 365 for the first time

- **Collaboration** Indicates how often users collaborate by accessing other users' documents stored in SharePoint libraries or OneDrive

- **Communication** Specifies which Microsoft 365 tools workers prefer to use to communicate with each other in the enterprise, such as Exchange email, Microsoft Teams, or Viva Engage

- **Product usage**   Tracks the usage of specific activities within each Microsoft 365 service
- **Storage use**   Tracks per-user cloud storage for SharePoint sites, OneDrive, and Exchange mailboxes
- **Access from anywhere**   Specifies which clients and devices workers are using to connect to email, Microsoft Teams, and Viva Engage
- **Individual service usage**   Provides activity reports for individual Microsoft 365 services, including Exchange, SharePoint, and Microsoft Teams

Power BI is also customizable, enabling administrators to create their own reports and even add their own additional data sources.

Other admin center reports

Many of the other admin centers for the Microsoft 365 services have reporting capabilities, including the following:

- **Exchange**   The Exchange admin center provides a collection of reports on various aspects of the server's mail flow, as shown in Figure 2-76.

FIGURE 2-76 Mail flow reports in the Exchange admin center

- **Teams**   The **Analytics & Reports** menu in the Microsoft Teams admin center provides access to usage reports for many specific user activities, as shown in Figure 2-77.
- **Intune**   The **Reports** page in the Microsoft Intune admin center provides access to dozens of reports on device management, security, endpoint analytics, and other topics, as shown in Figure 2-78.

FIGURE 2-77 The Microsoft Teams Usage reports page

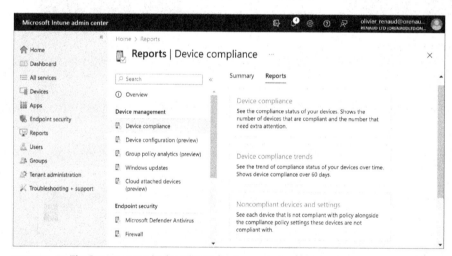

FIGURE 2-78 The Reports page in the Microsoft Intune admin center

Summary

- Microsoft 365 consists of many components, with various combinations provided in the different subscription levels. In addition to Windows 10 or 11 and the Office productivity applications, Microsoft 365 includes additional services, including Exchange Online, SharePoint, and Microsoft Teams. Enterprise subscriptions also include Azure Active Directory Premium, Microsoft Intune, Azure Information Protection, and Advanced Threat Analytics.

- Some of the Microsoft 365 components are available as on-premises applications and services. The incentives to use cloud-based rather than on-premises software include reduced initial cost outlays, more frequent feature updates, and high availability.

- Collaboration is one of the primary focuses of Microsoft 365 products, which are designed to work together to provide a variety of communication channels. Microsoft Teams can function as an information hub for many of the other Microsoft 365 applications.

- Microsoft Viva is a collection of applications that form what Microsoft calls an employee experience platform (EXP), which is an environment that fosters improved connection, insight, purpose, and growth among an organization's users.

- Modern management is an evolution of the traditional IT deployment and support models to emphasize client mobility and cloud-based services and administration.

- Microsoft 365 includes traditional, installable Office productivity applications, including Word, Excel, PowerPoint, and Outlook, as well as cloud-based services, such as Exchange Online, SharePoint, and Microsoft Teams. Compared to the on-premises products, Office 2016 and Office 2019, Microsoft 365 offers many advantages, including more frequent updates, licenses for up to five devices, mobile device support, and cloud-based email and collaboration services.

- Microsoft 365 is designed to allow users to work anywhere, using any device. By supplying cloud-based collaboration tools and enabling administrators to manage users' Bring Your Own Device hardware, Microsoft 365 supports a more modern productivity model.

- The Microsoft 365 Enterprise subscriptions include additional endpoint management and deployment tools, including Microsoft Intune, Windows Autopilot, and Azure AD Connect, which enables on-premises Configuration Manager installations to coexist with the Microsoft 365 cloud services.

- Microsoft 365 includes analytics tools that can gather information from applications and services across the enterprise and use it to anticipate threats and improve worker productivity.

Thought experiment

In this thought experiment, demonstrate your skills and knowledge of the topics covered in this chapter. You can find answers to this thought experiment in the next section.

Alice is planning a software deployment for her company's new branch office in Chicago and is comparing the advantages and disadvantages of Microsoft 365 and Office 2019. The branch office is expected to ramp up to a maximum of 120 new users within a year, and Alice is trying both to anticipate users' needs and stay within her initial outlay budget, which is relatively limited.

Alice wants to create as stable a working user environment as possible, to minimize technical support and training issues. She is concerned about the possibility of monthly feature updates in Microsoft 365, which might generate too many support issues and require additional training for both users and support personnel. She knows that Office 2019 does not receive feature updates.

The branch office is connected to the Internet through a local Internet service provider. The company's main office has on-premises Exchange and SharePoint servers accessible through the Internet. Alice is wondering whether it would be more efficient for the users to access their mail and document libraries on the main office servers or for her to use the cloud-based Exchange Online and SharePoint services. A third option would be for her to install on-premises Exchange and SharePoint servers at the branch office. She is also concerned about Exchange and SharePoint administration because she would prefer that her onsite staff manage the new user onboarding and maintenance processes.

Alice is also concerned about identity management for the branch office users and the Active Directory authentication traffic they will generate. The New York office has Active Directory Domain Services domain controllers installed, but Alice has not as yet planned to install domain controllers in the branch office. She is aware that Azure Active Directory can provide cloud-based identity management, but she is concerned that the branch office users might sometimes require access to resources stored on New York servers.

After carefully considering all these factors, Alice chose Microsoft 365 and its cloud services for the branch office deployment. List five reasons why her selection is justified.

Thought experiment answers

Alice can address all her concerns by deploying Microsoft 365 and using cloud-based Exchange Online and SharePoint services for the following reasons:

- Microsoft 365 can be configured to receive feature updates only twice a year, reducing the potential training and support issues compared to monthly updates.

- Because it is subscription-based, Microsoft 365 has a much smaller initial cost outlay than Office 2019, which must be paid for in full during the initial deployment.

- Microsoft 365's cloud-based services provide users access to Exchange and Share-Point through a nearby Microsoft Global Network endpoint. Requiring users to access Exchange and SharePoint servers in New York would likely generate additional network latency and reduce user efficiency.

- Exchange Online and SharePoint are administered through web-based tools that can be accessed directly by the branch office support staff. Onboarding new users on the New York servers would require remote access or participation of the New York staff to complete the onboarding processes.

- Azure Active Directory would enable the branch office support staff to manage the user accounts themselves and lessen the network latency that authenticating through the New York domain controllers would cause. Azure AD can also be configured to synchronize with the New York domain controllers, enabling branch office users to receive authenticated access to resources on New York servers.

CHAPTER 3

Describe security, compliance, privacy, and trust in Microsoft 365

Microsoft 365 was originally conceived as a product that would present users with familiar tools—such as the Office productivity applications—enabling them to collaborate in new ways more easily, more efficiently, and using any device at any location. This is a wonderful aspiration, but the product's designers soon realized that this idea of universal collaboration raised security, compliance, privacy, and trust issues that had to be addressed before the ideal could be realized.

Typically, these issues are the main impediment to the full adoption of Microsoft 365 for many IT professionals. The idea of storing sensitive data in the cloud and allowing workers to use their own devices to access that data is terrifying to administrators for whom security is becoming a greater issue every day. However, Microsoft 365 designers have taken great pains to address these issues, and they have created a product that, when used correctly, should satisfy the concerns of even the most skittish IT directors.

Skills in this chapter:

- Skill 3.1: Describe Zero Trust security principles for Microsoft 365
- Skill 3.2: Describe identity and access management solutions of Microsoft 365
- Skill 3.3: Describe threat protection solutions of Microsoft 365
- Skill 3.4: Describe trust, privacy, risk, and compliance solutions of Microsoft 365

Skill 3.1: Describe identity and access management solutions of Microsoft 365

Identities are the fundamental security issue in Microsoft 365 or any network environment. Identities are the doors and windows that provide ingress and egress to the enterprise network environment. They are essential if anyone is going to be able to actually use the information stored by the enterprise services. Therefore, protecting those identities from improper use is a major priority in designing, implementing, and maintaining an enterprise network.

Describe the identity and access management capabilities of Microsoft Entra ID

An *identity* is a logical representation of a user in a network environment. To users, an identity is a name they type to sign in to the network, along with a password or other means of authentication. To administrators, an identity is a collection of attributes associated with a particular individual, as shown in Figure 3-1. The sign-in name is one of those attributes, but there can be many others, including personal information, such as a home address, telephone number, job title, and so on.

An identity also typically includes a list of the groups to which the individual is a member. Administrators use groups to assign rights and permissions to individuals. When a group is assigned rights and permissions to access network resources, all the group's members automatically inherit those rights and permissions. This is an efficient alternative to assigning multiple rights and permissions to each user identity individually.

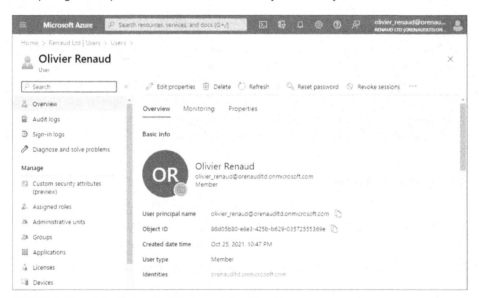

FIGURE 3-1 User attributes in Microsoft Azure Active Directory

Microsoft 365 and Directory Services

A directory service is a service or software product that stores information about network resources to unify them into a single, manageable entity. For example, the Domain Name System (DNS) is a directory service that associates the names of network resources with their corresponding IP addresses.

Entra ID and Active Directory Domain Services (AD DS) are the directory services that store and manage user identities for the various Microsoft 365 components. Entra ID stores its directory information in the Microsoft Azure cloud, and AD DS is stored on Windows servers configured to operate as domain controllers.

> **NOTE AZURE AD NAME CHANGE**
>
> As of this writing, Microsoft is currently in the process of changing the product name of Azure Active Directory to Microsoft Entra ID. Microsoft Entra is a new product family that includes all of Microsoft's identity management tools. The MS-900 objectives mention that Azure AD is part of Microsoft Entra, but the name Entra ID will eventually replace Azure AD entirely.

Entra ID is available in three plans, as shown in Table 3-1. All Microsoft 365 products include either the Premium P1 or Premium P2 plan.

TABLE 3-1 Azure Active Directory licenses

Azure Active Directory License	Included with
Azure Active Directory Free	Office 365 or Microsoft Azure, Dynamics 365, Intune, and Power Platform subscriptions
Office 365 Apps	Office 365 E1, E3, E5, F1, and F3
Azure Active Directory Premium P1(Microsoft Entra ID P1)	Microsoft 365 Enterprise E3 and Microsoft 365 Business Premium
Azure Active Directory Premium P2(Microsoft Entra ID P1)	Microsoft 365 Enterprise E5

The Azure Active Directory Premium P1 plan supports the following features and services:

- **Unlimited directory objects**   Enables administrators to create cloud identities for unlimited users.

- **User and group management**   Enables administrators to create and manage user and group identities using cloud-based tools, such as the Entra admin center and the Microsoft 365 admin center.

- **Cloud authentication**   Enables users to sign on to the network using hybrid identities stored in the cloud and with password hash synchronization or pass-through authentication.

- **Synchronization with AD DS using Azure AD Connect**   After installing the Azure AD Connect tool on an AD DS domain controller or on-premises server, on-premises identities can be replicated to the Entra ID directory in the cloud. This creates hybrid identities enabling users to access cloud-based and on-premises resources with a single sign-on.

- **Seamless single sign-on**   Enables users with hybrid identities connected to the on-premises network to sign in with no interactive authentication procedure.

- **Support for federated authentication** Enables administrators to offload the Entra ID authentication process to a federated service, such as Active Directory Federation Services.

- **Multifactor authentication using phone, SMS, or app** Enables administrators to require that users supply two or more forms of identification when signing in with an Entra ID identity, such as a password plus a biometric scan or a one-time code sent to the user's smartphone.

- **Support for hybrid user access to cloud and on-premises resources** Enables users with hybrid identities to access both cloud-based and on-premises resources after a single Entra ID authentication.

- **Self-Service Password Reset** Enables users with cloud-based identities to modify their passwords without administrator assistance.

- **Device write-back from Entra ID to AD DS identities** Enables devices registered in Entra ID and modified cloud identity passwords to be copied to an AD DS container. Ordinarily, Azure AD Connect synchronizes data only from AD DS to Entra ID.

- **Application proxy** Enables cloud-based remote users to access internal web applications by forwarding their requests to a connector running on an on-premises server.

- **Dynamic groups** Enables administrators to create rules specifying the attributes a user account must possess to be automatically added to a group.

- **Group naming policies** Enables administrators to create policies that specify a format for group names. For example, group names can be required to specify a function, a department, or a geographic location.

- **Conditional access** Enables administrators to specify conditions that mobile devices must meet before they are granted access to cloud-based resources, such as sign-in risk, client app in use, the state of the mobile device, and the device's location.

- **Microsoft Identity Manager** Provides identity and access management, including synchronization of users, groups, and other objects for AD DS and Entra ID, as well as third-party directory services.

- **Azure Information Protection Premium P1** Enables users and administrators to classify and label documents based on the sensitivity of the data they contain.

- **Security and activity reporting** Provides administrators with reports that list potential threats, including risky sign-ins and audit logs that document user activities.

With these features and services, the Azure Active Directory Premium P1 plan enables administrators to manage an organization's cloud-based resources and identify, predict, detect, and remediate a wide variety of security threats. However, the Azure Active Directory Premium P2 plan supports everything included in the P1 plan and also provides the following additional security features:

- **Microsoft Defender for Identity (Azure AD Identity Protection)** Evaluates users' sign-in activities, quantifies their risk levels, and takes action based on those levels.

- **Privileged Identity Management**   Enables administrators to regulate access to sensitive resources by granting temporary privileges to specific users, requiring additional security measures, and receiving notifications when the resources are accessed. The objective is to prevent users with administrative privileges from using them unnecessarily.

- **Microsoft Defender for Cloud Apps (Cloud App Security)**   A cloud-based service that analyzes traffic logs and proxy scripts to identify and monitor the apps that users are accessing.

- **Azure Information Protection Premium P2**   Expands on the capabilities of the Premium P1 plan by automating the process of identifying, classifying, and labeling documents.

Active Directory Domain Services

Active Directory Domain Services (AD DS) is an object-oriented, hierarchical directory service that functions as an internal authentication and authorization provider for Windows networks. Because it is not located in the cloud like Entra ID, the primary source of protection for AD DS is the firewall and other perimeter protection surrounding the on-premises network. AD DS domain controllers are Windows servers located inside the network perimeter; they must not be deployed in a DMZ or any other way that leaves them open to access from the Internet.

Also, unlike Entra ID, network administrators must design, deploy, and maintain an AD DS directory. The service takes the form of a role in the Windows Server operating system, which administrators must add after installing the operating system itself. An AD DS directory does not include Microsoft's cloud services' built-in maintenance and fault tolerance.

Typically, servers that function as AD DS domain controllers do not perform any other services except for acting as DNS servers. For example, using domain controllers as application or file servers is not considered secure. Administrators must install multiple domain controllers to ensure fault tolerance and high availability, preferably at different sites. The domain controllers replicate the contents of the directory among each other regularly.

Unlike Entra ID, AD DS is a hierarchical directory service that enables administrators to create a directory that emulates their organization's departmental or geographical infrastructure, as shown in Figure 3-2.

Forests, trees, domains, and organizational units are AD DS objects that contain other objects, such as users, groups, and computers, as shown in Figure 3-3. As with a file system, permissions flow downward through the hierarchy. Permissions granted to a container object are inherited by all the objects in that container and all subordinate containers beneath it. Administrators can design the AD DS hierarchy however they want.

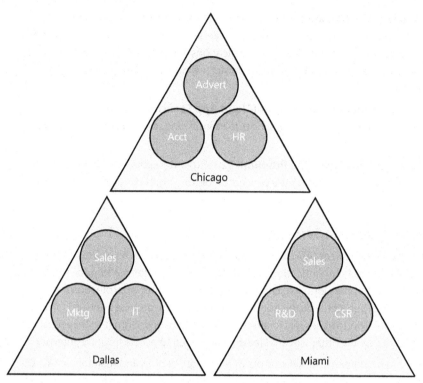

FIGURE 3-2 An Active Directory Domain Services container hierarchy

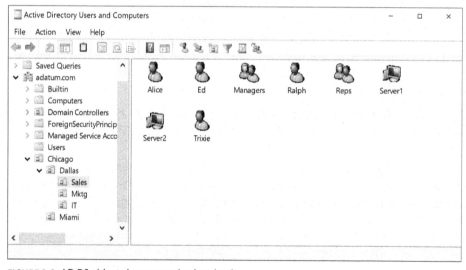

FIGURE 3-3 AD DS objects in an organizational unit

In AD DS administration, much more work is left to the network administrator than in Entra ID. In Entra ID, you can begin creating users and groups immediately after establishing a tenancy without installing and maintaining domain controllers or designing an infrastructure. There are also no concerns about physical security with Entra ID because Microsoft is responsible for its datacenters and for maintaining the computers that provide the services. The initial cost outlay for an Entra ID directory is also minimal. AD DS requires the purchase of server computers and the Windows Server operating system, but there are no ongoing subscription fees.

Although AD DS uses a substantially different infrastructure than Entra ID, it performs the same basic services by authenticating users and authorizing access to network resources. However, AD DS does not support many of Entra ID's advanced security features. For example, AD DS has no internal support for multifactor authentication, although it is possible to use an external authentication service for some additional authentication factors. AD DS also does not include Azure AD Identity Protection, Conditional Access, and Azure Information Protection.

Because domain controllers are often connected to the same network as workstations and other less sensitive systems, they can be vulnerable to a lateral attack from an intruder who has gained access to another computer on the network. As a result, even though the domain controllers themselves might be protected, any typical attack vectors to which on-premises computers are susceptible can threaten the AD DS implementation. For example, any computer on the network that is not current in its operating system and application updates or lacks virus or malware protection can be a target for attack and a launch point for a further invasion of the AD DS directory.

AD DS is also more vulnerable to credential theft than Entra ID because of the unsafe use of privileged credentials. Administrators of an on-premises network can sometimes be careless about using their privileged identities to perform everyday tasks, such as browsing the Internet or signing on to computers that are not fully secured. In Azure Active Directory Premium P1, these practices can be addressed with the Privileged Identity Management feature, but Microsoft has not integrated the Entra ID security tools into AD DS.

EXAM TIP

For MS-900 examination candidates new to these technologies, it can be easy to confuse the capabilities of the cloud-based Entra ID and the on-premises Active Directory Domain Services (AD DS). It is important to know that AD DS is a hierarchical directory service provided with the Windows Server operating system that requires a fairly extensive design and implementation process. Entra ID, by contrast, is subscription-based, is not hierarchical, and requires virtually no setup. Candidates should also know which features are provided in the Azure Active Directory Premium P1 and Azure Active Directory Premium P2 plans.

Describe cloud identity, on-premises identity, and hybrid identity concepts

Every computer or mobile device can maintain a user's identity and employ it to protect the device from being accessed by anyone else. However, when the user wants to access applications, services, or data from the company network, they need another identity; this identity is created and maintained by the network's administrators and stored on the network, not on the user's computer or another device.

On-premises identities

Beginning with the Windows 2000 Server release, enterprise identities were stored in Active Directory, an on-premises directory service still a part of the Windows 2019 Server product, although it is now called Active Directory Domain Services (AD DS). Installing the AD DS role on a Windows Server computer enables it to function as a domain controller, which contains an object-oriented database of user identities and other network resources, including groups, computers, and applications. AD DS is a domain-based hierarchical database that uses container and organizational unit objects to separate users and other resources into logical collections, which usually represent the departmental or geographic divisions of the company.

Typically, enterprise networks have multiple domain controllers, which administrators configure to synchronize the contents of their AD DS databases with each other for fault tolerance and high availability purposes. AD DS uses multiple master replication, meaning administrators can create or modify users and other objects on any domain controller, and the changes will be replicated to all of the other domain controllers, as shown in Figure 3-4.

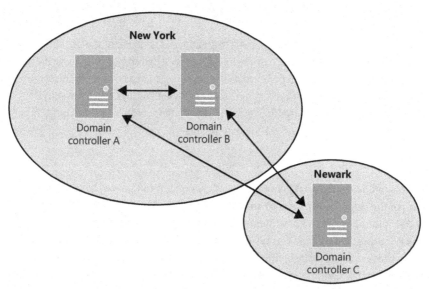

FIGURE 3-4 Active Directory Domain Services multiple master replication

Administrators can create AD DS user objects using graphical tools, such as Active Directory Users and Computers, as shown in Figure 3-5, or command-line tools, such as the New-ADUser cmdlet in Windows PowerShell.

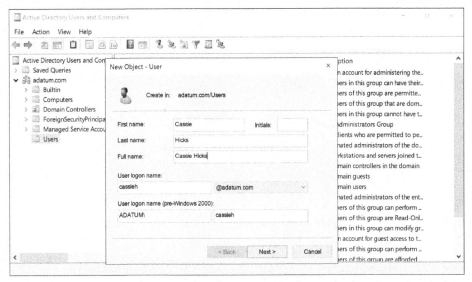

FIGURE 3-5 The New Object – User dialog box in the Active Directory Users And Computers console

The user objects in AD DS are strictly *on-premises identities*. Domain controllers must be located within the network perimeter and not directly accessible from the Internet. When users access on-premises resources, their identities are authenticated and authorized by the nearest domain controller, which uses a protocol called Kerberos to perform a complicated ticket-based authentication procedure. Users outside the network perimeter can only perform an AD DS sign-in to the network by establishing a VPN connection to a remote access server. This gives users a presence on the internal network, enabling them to access internal resources.

Cloud identities

Because AD DS can perform its functions only when both the user and the resources to be accessed are located on-premises, it is not a viable solution for cloud-based applications and services. Therefore, Microsoft had to devise an alternative authentication and authorization solution for its cloud-based products, such as Microsoft 365. This solution is Entra ID, a cloud-based directory service alternative (or companion) to AD DS in which administrators create *cloud identities*. Azure AD is currently undergoing a name change. All Microsoft identity management tools are being added to the new Microsoft Entra product family. Azure Active Directory will soon be known as Microsoft Entra ID.

Microsoft 365 relies on the Entra ID service for its identity management, and all Microsoft 365 services use Entra ID for authentication and authorization. Microsoft 365 subscribers (as well as Office 365 and Windows Azure subscribers) become Entra ID tenants automatically. When a user accesses a Microsoft 365 application in the cloud, as shown in Figure 3-6, Entra ID is the invisible intermediary that confirms the user's identity with the authentication mechanisms the Microsoft 365 administrators have selected. In the same way, Entra ID authorizes the user's access to the application and to the files the user opens in the application.

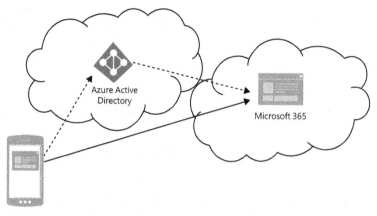

FIGURE 3-6 Azure Active Directory provides authentication and authorization services for Microsoft 365 applications and services

Unlike AD DS, administrators don't need to install multiple domain controllers for Entra ID or configure directory replication. An Entra ID tenancy is automatically replicated to multiple datacenters in the Microsoft Global Network. Also, unlike AD DS, Entra ID uses a single master replication model. There is only one primary replica of an Entra ID tenant, and all new users and account modifications are written to that primary replica. The changes are then automatically replicated to multiple secondary replicas at different datacenters, as shown in Figure 3-7. The secondary replicas handle all incoming read requests using the replica closest to the requesting user, application, or service. Because there are many secondary replicas, the Entra ID service is always available. Because there is only one primary replica, it works differently by using a deterministic failover procedure.

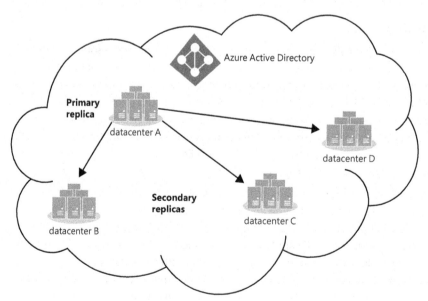

FIGURE 3-7 Azure Active Directory single master replication

Administrators can use several tools to create users in Entra ID, including the Microsoft 365 admin center and the Azure Active Directory admin center. Azure ID's authentication and authorization are also token-based, but the protocols and procedures used by Entra ID differ from those used by AD DS. Instead of Kerberos, Entra ID uses OAuth 2.0 or OpenID Connect.

Hybrid identities

It is important to understand that Azure Active Directory is not intended to replace Active Directory Domain Services, nor are the two interchangeable. If an organization has internal servers and an on-premises AD DS implementation, they should not expect to be able to migrate their user identities from AD DS to Entra ID and then deprecate their AD DS domain controllers. It is equally important to understand that Microsoft 365 requires Entra ID; it is not possible to use AD DS identities to authenticate and authorize users for Microsoft 365 applications and services. The converse is also true; using Entra ID identities to provide authentication and authorization services for on-premises resources is impossible.

It is, however, possible to use Entra ID and AD DS together, creating what are known as hybrid identities. A *hybrid identity* is a user account in both the Entra ID and AD DS directories with the same set of attributes. The usual scenario for hybrid identities is an organization with an existing AD DS infrastructure but considering expanding into the cloud by using Software as a Service (SaaS) products, such as Microsoft 365. The organization might have hundreds or thousands of on-premises identities, but the prospect of re-creating them in Entra ID and then maintaining two identities for each user could be a deciding factor in the organization choosing not to use cloud services.

Hybrid identities are a solution to this problem. Because the assumption is that the AD DS identities already exist, creating hybrid identities is a matter of synchronizing them from AD DS to Entra ID. To do this, administrators must install Azure AD Connect on the on-premises network, which accesses the AD DS directory on a domain controller and replicates all the user accounts it finds to Entra ID (along with their passwords and other attributes).

> **NOTE FIRST SYNCHRONIZATION**
>
> When Azure AD Connect synchronizes on-premises AD DS identities to Entra ID for the first time, new cloud identities for the users are created, but product licenses are not automatically assigned to them. Therefore, in a new Microsoft 365 hybrid identity deployment, administrators must add Microsoft 365 licenses to the Entra ID users after the first synchronization is complete, using the Microsoft 365 admin center or another tool. The administrators can add licenses to Entra ID users individually, but the process can also be performed dynamically by making the license assignment a result of group membership.

HYBRID IDENTITY PASSWORDS

Passwords in AD DS are stored as a hash (a one-way mathematical algorithm that cannot be reversed to extract the password), and by default, Azure AD Connect applies another hash algorithm to the AD DS hash. Thus, the password transmitted by Azure AD Connect to the cloud is secured by it being a hash of a hash. The passwords in Entra ID are never stored in plain text or encrypted using a reversible algorithm.

After the initial synchronization, Azure AD Connect continues to detect changes made to the AD DS identities and replicates those changes to the corresponding Entra ID identities in the cloud, as shown in Figure 3-8. Therefore, administrators managing hybrid identities must use the AD DS tools—such as Active Directory Users and Computers—to make changes to the on-premises user accounts. Because the identity replication flows in only one direction—from AD DS to Entra ID—no one should make changes directly to the cloud identities using the Microsoft 365 tools.

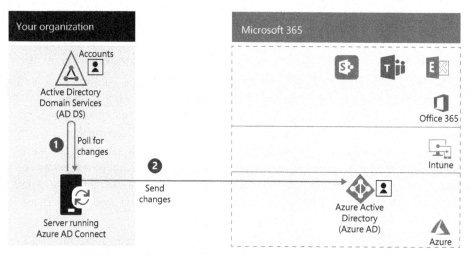

FIGURE 3-8 Azure AD Connect identity synchronization

NOTE ENTRA ID APPLICATION PROXY

While Entra ID is not a replacement for AD DS, it can provide remote users with access to internal web applications using a feature called Application Proxy. Application Proxy consists of a service that runs in the cloud and a connector that administrators install on an on-premises server. When remote clients attempt to access the internal web application with a URL, they are directed to an Entra ID sign-in page, where they authenticate using an Entra ID identity. The clients then pass the token they received as a result of the sign-in to the Application Proxy Service, which forwards it to the Application Proxy Connector on the internal network. The connector then forwards the user's request to the internal web application, which returns its response to the client through the connector and the Application Proxy Service.

Hybrid identities can simplify the identity management process for administrators, but they can also simplify the user experience as well. For administrators adding cloud services to an existing on-premises infrastructure, the main objective should be to make user access to the cloud applications as invisible as possible. One way to do this is to implement *single sign-on*

(SSO) so that users can authenticate with their familiar AD DS credentials and receive access to the cloud services without signing in again, either at the Entra ID level or in the individual applications. Another seamless single sign-on option enables users connected to the enterprise network to automatically sign in without any interactive authentication. Seamless sign-on is compatible with password hash synchronization and pass-through authentication methods but incompatible with the federated authentication method.

HYBRID IDENTITY AUTHENTICATION

While installing Azure AD Connect, an administrator must select the authentication method that Entra ID will use to provide users access to cloud resources. There are three options to choose from:

- **Azure AD Password Hash Synchronization** The simplest Azure AD Connect authentication method requires no additional infrastructure to implement. Azure AD Connect creates a hash of each user's AD DS password hash and applies it to the corresponding Azure ID identity, allowing users to access both on-premises and cloud resources using the same password, as shown in Figure 3-9. Azure AD Connect updates the cloud identity passwords every two minutes without interrupting a session in progress when a password change occurs. Because the password hash synchronization model is fully implemented in the cloud, it shares the high availability of the other Microsoft cloud services. To ensure continuous operation, Microsoft recommends the installation of Azure AD Connect on two or more servers as a standby, preferably at different locations.

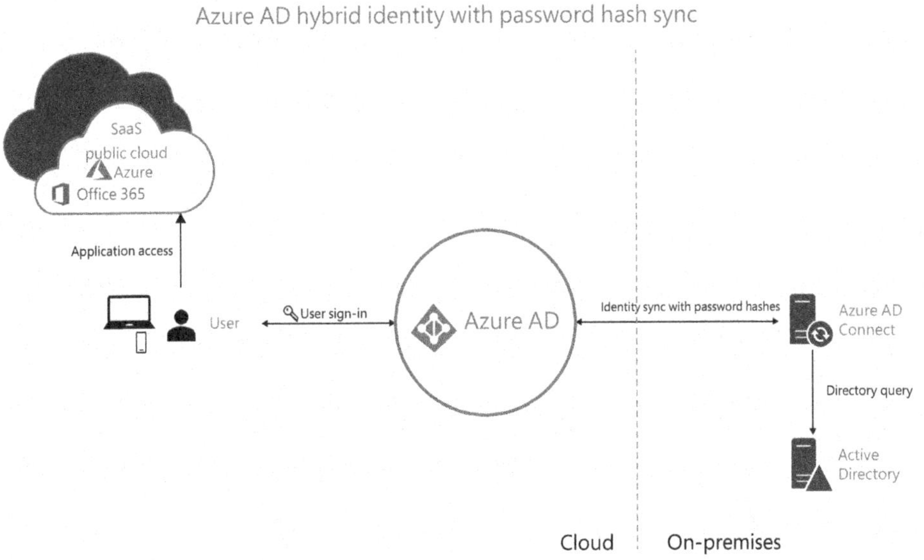

FIGURE 3-9 Entra ID password hash synchronization

- **Entra ID Pass-Through Authentication** Avoids all cloud-based password validation by using a lightweight pass-through authentication agent installed on-premises servers. (Microsoft recommends three.) When users sign in to Entra ID, their requests are forwarded to the agent, which forwards them (in encrypted form) to a domain controller to validate the users against their on-premises identities in AD DS, as shown in Figure 3-10. The agents require only outbound Internet access and an AD DS domain controller, so they cannot be located on a perimeter network. The end result is the same user experience as password hash synchronization. Still, this method avoids storing user passwords in the cloud in any form and enables administrators to enforce on-premises Active Directory security policies, such as disabled or expired accounts. It allows sign-in hours and complies with contracted security requirements. It is also possible to deploy password hash synchronization and pass-through authentication to function as a backup in the event of an on-premises failure that prevents the agents from functioning.

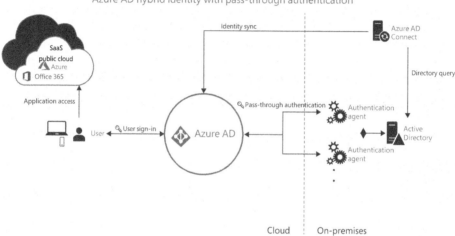

FIGURE 3-10 Entra ID pass-through authentication

- **Federated Authentication** Offloads the authentication process to an external solution that the organization trusts, such as Microsoft Active Directory Federation Services (AD FS). The configuration and management of the authentication process—as well as the user experience—are the responsibility of the federated system; Entra ID is not involved. Depending on the organization's security requirements, the sign-in process with the federated system might be simpler or more complicated than that of Entra ID. The federated system typically consists of a load-balanced cluster of servers—called a farm—for high availability and fault-tolerance purposes. Because the federation servers require access to Entra ID and AD DS domain controllers, the servers (or proxy intermediaries) must be located in a screened subnet of an on-premises perimeter network, as shown in Figure 3-11. Organizations typically opt for the federated authentication option because they want to (or are compelled to) use an authentication method that

Entra ID does not support, such as certificates or smart cards. The additional hardware, software, and administrative infrastructure the federated authentication method requires can be a significant extra expense. Organizations that choose this option often do so because they have already invested in the infrastructure. It is also possible to deploy password hash synchronization in addition to federated authentication to function as a backup in the event of an on-premises failure that prevents federation servers or their proxies from functioning.

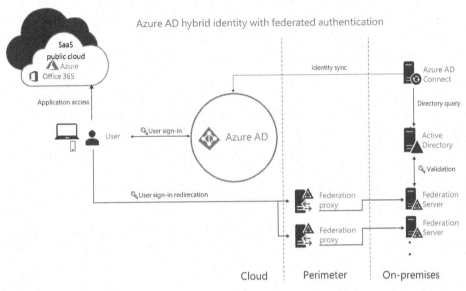

FIGURE 3-11 Federated authentication

Describe how Microsoft uses methods such as multi-factor authentication (MFA), self-service password reset (SSPR), and conditional access to keep identities, access, and data secure

The traditional means of authenticating a user's identity is for the individual to supply an account name and a password. In Microsoft 365, administrators can create password policies that compel users to create long and complex passwords and change them frequently.

However, passwords are always subject to potential weaknesses that make them an unwieldy authentication mechanism, including the following:

- Users might struggle remembering long or complex passwords and write them down in unsecured locations.

- Users might share their passwords with coworkers for the sake of convenience.

- Users with dedicated accounts with elevated privileges might overuse their administrative passwords for everyday tasks.

- Users might supply the same passwords for multiple services or resources, compounding the damage if a password on one server is compromised.

- Users might be tricked into supplying their passwords by phishing or social engineering attacks.

- Users' identities might be compromised when their passwords are subjected to replay attacks, in which an intruder retransmits a captured password to gain access to a protected resource.

- Users' passwords might be compromised by malware that captures keystrokes and transmits them to an intruder.

- Some users can be relentlessly clever in discovering ways to evade the password policies imposed on them.

Because human failings, rather than technological failings, cause some of the weaknesses of password-based authentication, strengthening user passwords is often an educational process. Administrators can devise policies to mitigate some password weaknesses, though urging users to abide by them can be difficult.

For example, a 20-character, randomly generated, administrator-assigned password would be extremely difficult for attackers to compromise, but it might be equally difficult to put down the outright insurrection that could result from the users forced to use them. Because of the complications inherent in using passwords, Microsoft 365 supports other types of authentication mechanisms that administrators can use instead of (or along with) passwords.

Windows Hello for Business is a desktop authentication mechanism that can replace passwords with a certificate or key-pair authentication using a PIN or a biometric credential, such as a fingerprint scan or an infrared facial recognition process. Microsoft Authenticator is a mobile device app that enables users to sign in to a Microsoft account using a combination of authentication mechanisms, including PINs, biometrics, and one-time-passcodes (OTPs).

> **NOTE IDENTITY PROTECTION**
>
> For more information on protecting identities, see "Describe how Microsoft 365 addresses the most common threats" later in this chapter.

Authentication types

If identities are the doors and windows in the enterprise network environment, authentications are the locks that keep them secure. An administrator can grant a specific user the permissions needed to access a file, an application, or a service, but this means nothing unless there is some way to ensure that the individual using those permissions is really the person to whom they were assigned. Authentication is how individuals actually prove their identities.

There are three basic means of authenticating an individual's identity. The individual must supply one or more of the following:

- **Something you know** A piece of information that only the individual possesses, such as a password or PIN
- **Something you are** A characteristic that is unique to the individual, such as a fingerprint or a facial scan
- **Something you have** A unique item that the individual possesses, such as an ID card or a smart phone

Password authentication

A password is *something you know*, and this has been the standard means of authenticating users' identities for many years. Password authentication costs nothing to implement, and it can be relatively secure. However, there are many possible flaws in the password authentication model. For example, passwords can be forgotten, shared, written down, easily guessed, or overly simple.

Administrators can create policies that specify rules for creating and maintaining passwords to prevent users from creating passwords that provide too little security. Operating systems and directory services, such as Entra ID and AD DS, include tools that administrators can use to create and enforce such policies.

In Entra ID, user accounts are subject to the following password policies:

- **Characters allowed** Specifies the characters that users may use when creating passwords, including upper- and lowercase alphabetical characters, numbers, blank spaces, and most symbols.
- **Password restrictions** Specifies that passwords must have from 8 to 256 characters and contain three of the following four character types: uppercase, lowercase, number, and symbol.
- **Password expiry duration** Specifies that passwords expire in 90 days by default. The value can be modified using the `Set-MsolUser` PowerShell cmdlet.
- **Password expiry notification** Specifies that the user will receive a password expiration notification 14 days before the password is set to expire. The value can be modified using the `Set-MsolPasswordPolicy` PowerShell cmdlet.
- **Password expiry** Specifies a default value of False, indicating that the password will expire after the Passwords expiry duration interval. The value can be modified using the `Set-MsolUser` PowerShell cmdlet.
- **Password change history** Specifies that users cannot reuse the same password when changing passwords.

- **Password reset history** Specifies that users can reuse the same password when resetting a forgotten password.
- **Account lockout** Causes users to be locked out of their accounts for one minute after 10 unsuccessful but unique sign-in attempts. Additional unsuccessful attempts result in longer lockout intervals.

In AD DS, administrators can configure password settings using Group Policy. The available settings have slightly different names, but their functions are essentially the same.

These password policies are designed to prevent users from creating overly simple passwords for convenience, but password security is difficult for administrators to enforce. Users can still create passwords that would be easy for attackers to guess by using their children's names and birthdays, for example. There is also no software setting that can prevent users from writing their passwords down or sharing them with their coworkers.

As threats to network security become ever more severe, administrators have sought ways to enhance the security of the authentication process. Alternative authentication methods have been available for many years, which could conceivably augment or replace passwords, but until recently, these technologies were too expensive or inconvenient to be practical for the average user base. The increased need for identity protection has brought these authentication technologies to a wider market, resulting in lower prices. And the need is constantly increasing. Microsoft 365 includes the ability to enhance the authentication process's security in various ways.

Multifactor authentication

Multifactor authentication is a procedure in which users prove their identities in two or more ways. Typically, in addition to a password—*something you know*—users must supply a different authentication factor: *something you are* or *something you have*.

SOMETHING YOU ARE

The *something you are* is usually some type of biometric scan. The Windows Hello for Business feature in Windows 10 and 11 supports multifactor authentication with biometric scans as one of the factors. It is also possible to use the Microsoft Authenticator app for mobile devices as a biometric scanner that enables users to access Microsoft 365 resources with no password.

Fingerprint readers are inexpensive and an increasingly common feature on laptops and other mobile devices. There are also aftermarket keyboards for desktop computers with integrated fingerprint readers as well. Fingerprint scans do not provide impenetrable security; fingerprints can conceivably be duplicated, and a scan of a finger would presumably still work, even if it was not attached to its owner. However, in combination with a password, fingerprint scans provide a multifactor authentication solution that usually cannot be penetrated casually.

Facial recognition is another type of biometric scan that Windows Hello can use for multifactor authentication. Cameras are all but ubiquitous in modern society, so it would seem that the hardware costs of a facial recognition system are minimal. This is not the case, however, at least with Microsoft's facial recognition products. Facial recognition raises questions both of security and of privacy. If a computer can recognize a person's face as a security factor, what would stop an intruder from holding up a picture of the person to the camera? And where is the image of the user's face being sent to accomplish the authentication?

Microsoft has answers to both questions. Windows Hello for Business supports the use of facial recognition for user authentication, but it requires a camera with a separate infrared light source and a near-infrared sensor. The main problem with facial recognition systems on personal devices is that people can conceivably use them in any kind of lighting. Near-infrared imaging provides a consistent image regardless of the visible light conditions. Windows Hello also does not store images of the user's face and never transmits them to other locations for authentication. When a user enrolls in Windows Hello, the Windows Biometric Framework processes a facial image within the device and stores it as an enrollment profile. The system performs the same process in subsequent authentication attempts and compares the results to the profile.

SOMETHING YOU HAVE

While the *something you have* in multifactor authentication can be a smart card or some other form of identification, in Microsoft 365, it is usually a cell phone. This is a more practical option because most people today carry cell phones with them, whereas card readers are far less common.

Internet websites commonly require a secondary authentication factor, usually in the form of a code (called a one-time password or OTP) sent to the user's cell phone as a call or SMS text. The user supplies the code from the website, and authorization is granted. Microsoft 365 supports this method for multifactor authentication of users' Entra ID identities, among others.

The cellphone-based options for Entra ID Multifactor Authentication (MFA) are as follows:

- **SMS Text Of OTP Code To Mobile Phone** After the user completes a standard password authentication, Entra ID sends a text message containing an OTP code to the user's preconfigured telephone number. The user types the code into the sign-in screen to complete the authentication.

- **Automated Voice Call To Mobile Phone** After the user completes the password authentication, Entra ID generates an automated voice call to the user's preconfigured telephone number. The user answers the call and presses the phone's # key to complete the authentication.

- **Notification To Mobile App** After the user completes the password authentication, Entra ID sends a notification to the Microsoft Authenticator app on the user's smartphone. The user taps the Verify button in the app to complete the authentication.

- **Verification Code In Mobile App** The Microsoft Authenticator app generates a new open authentication (OATH) verification code every 30 seconds. After the user completes the password authentication, the user types the current verification code from the Microsoft Authenticator app into the sign-in screen to complete the authentication.

Of course, cell phones can be lost, stolen, or destroyed, so any authentication method that relies on them will not be completely secure, but in combination with a password, they provide a significant barrier against the standard attacker. Multifactor authentication is not required for Microsoft 365, but it is a *de facto* standard for network security today, largely because many administrators are finding that they have reached the limits of their password authentication policy effectiveness as far as users' tolerance is concerned.

Administrators can enable multifactor authentication for specific users using the multifactor authentication screen in the Microsoft Entra admin center, as shown in Figure 3-12.

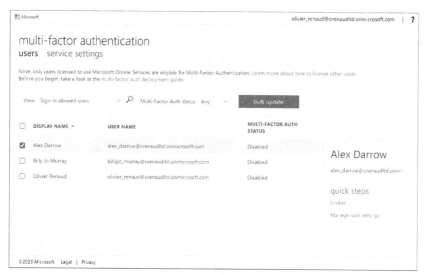

FIGURE 3-12 The Multi-factor Authentication screen in the Microsoft Entra admin center

The next time users sign in, a screen like that shown in Figure 3-13 enables them to enter a phone number and specify whether the initial contact to a user should be through a code sent to the user's cell phone or a mobile app, such as Microsoft Authenticator.

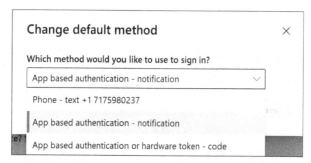

FIGURE 3-13 The Change Default Method dialog box

Self-service password reset

Self-service password reset (SSPR) is a feature in Azure Active Directory that enables users to reset their own forgotten passwords, change their existing passwords, and unlock their accounts when they have been frozen. This can significantly reduce routine trouble calls without sacrificing identity security.

Before users can reset their own passwords, administrators must enable SSPR in the Microsoft Entra admin center, as shown in Figure 3-14. The interface allows administrators to enable self-service password reset for all users or selected ones.

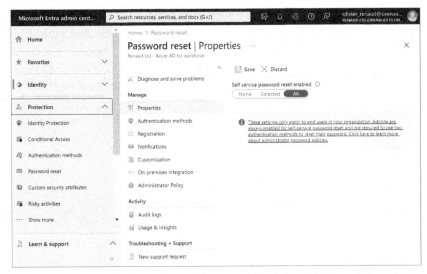

FIGURE 3-14 The Password Reset | Properties screen in the Microsoft Entra admin center

The next time users log on after SSPR is enabled, a screen appears, prompting them to register by selecting the authentication methods they will use during the password reset or downloading the Microsoft Authenticator app, as shown in Figure 3-15.

FIGURE 3-15 The Action Required pop-up window

Conditional access

Conditional access is an Entra ID feature that enables administrators to create policies that control user access to applications and data based on a variety of conditions. Entra ID processes conditional access policies after the user's first authentication factor.

When processing conditional access policies, Entra ID analyzes information about the user, the user's device, the device's location, the applications on the device, and the degree of risk associated with the protected resources, as shown in Figure 3-16. Based on this information, Entra ID might allow or deny the user access to the resource, require the user to complete additional authentication factors or even switch to a more compliant device.

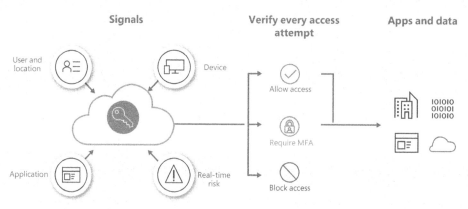

FIGURE 3-16 The conditional access verification procedure

The conditional access assessment is essentially an if/then statement that balances the incoming signals with a series of possible outcomes. For example, when a user attempts to access a particular application, a conditional access policy might evaluate signals such as the following:

- If the user is connected to the on-premises network
- If the user completes their first authentication successfully
- If the user is a member of a group granting permissions for the application
- If the user is working on a device with adequate malware protection

If the user meets all of these requirements, the conditional access policy processes the Then parts of the statement:

- Then the user must complete the second factor of a multifactor authentication
- Then the user is granted access to the application

Administrators can use the Microsoft Entra admin center to create conditional access policies, as shown in Figure 3-17. The **Conditional Access** page includes templates for creating policies, such as **Require Multifactor Authentication For A dmins**, or it is possible to create an entirely new policy.

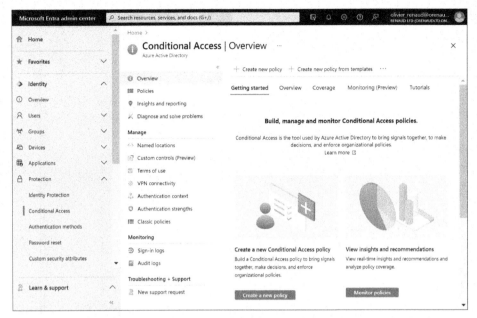

FIGURE 3-17 The Conditional Access screen in Microsoft Entra admin center

When creating a new conditional access policy using the interface shown in Figure 3-18, administrators can configure the following elements:

- **Users** Specifies the users and groups to which the policy will apply
- **Target Resources** Identifies the cloud apps or other protected resources to which the policy applies
- **Conditions** Specifies the conditions the user must meet to be granted access, such as the following:
  - **Device Platforms** Specifies the allowed platforms for the user's device, such as Windows, macOS, Android, and iOS
  - **Location** Specifies the allowed physical locations for the user
  - **Client Apps** Specifies the client applications in which the user will be allowed to work
  - **Filter For Devices** Includes or excludes devices from the policy based on the values of specific device properties
- **Grant** Specifies whether user access to the target resources should be blocked completely or granted with one or more conditions, such as the need for a password change, multifactor authentication, or a hybrid Entra ID-joined device
- **Session** Specifies session limitations for specific apps, such as how long a user's access persists before reauthentication is necessary and whether browser sessions are persistent

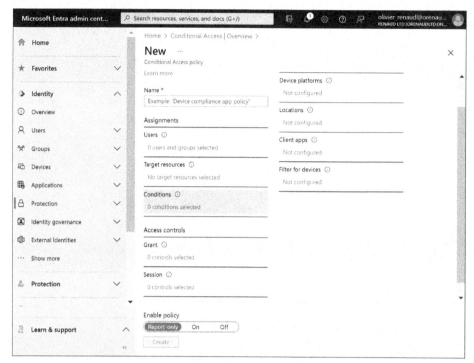

FIGURE 3-18 The Conditional Access screen in Microsoft Entra admin center

Selecting the **On** option in the **Enable Policy** selector activates the policy and applies it as configured.

Quick check

- Which of the following elements creates hybrid identities by replicating on-premises identities to the cloud?
    - Entra ID
    - Azure AD Connect
    - Password hash synchronization
    - AD DS

Quick check answer

- Azure AD Connect is a software tool that runs on the on-premises network and replicates Active Directory domain Services identities to Azure Active Directory in the cloud, creating hybrid identities.

Skill 3.2: Describe threat protection solutions of Microsoft 365

Originally, Windows Defender was the name of Microsoft's antivirus feature for Windows XP. Now called Microsoft Defender Anti-Virus, that feature still exists in Windows 10 and 11. However, the brand has grown, and Microsoft 365 Defender is now the name of a unified protection suite that detects, isolates, and remediates threats wherever they occur in the Microsoft 365 infrastructure.

Describe Microsoft 365 Defender, Defender for Endpoint, Defender for Office 365, Defender for Identity, Defender for Cloud Apps, and the Microsoft 365 Defender Portal

As shown in Figure 3-19, Microsoft 365 Defender treats security as though it's divided into four domains: Identity, Endpoints, Apps, and Email/Collaboration Data. On many enterprise networks, the security operations for the four domains are separate, as each of them requires intense scrutiny. So, the people responsible for Identity security might not know about everything happening on the Apps security team.

Integrated Microsoft 365 Defender experience

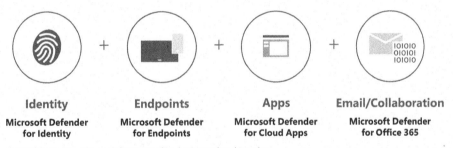

Identity	Endpoints	Apps	Email/Collaboration
Microsoft Defender for Identity	**Microsoft Defender for Endpoints**	**Microsoft Defender for Cloud Apps**	**Microsoft Defender for Office 365**

FIGURE 3-19 The Microsoft 365 Defender security domains

Many enterprises have separate security operations that each function within just one domain, or perhaps two, but none see the whole enterprise security picture. Attacks always begin in one of the four domains, but after gaining initial access to the network, attackers often move laterally between domains, rendering them partially invisible to single-domain detection procedures.

For example, an attacker might trick a user into revealing their password in an enterprise with domain-based security. This compromises the user's identity and allows the attacker to access the network. The team responsible for identity security might recognize the attacker's efforts, note the unauthorized access to the network, change the user's password, and prevent such attacks from happening again, but that is the limit of their brief.

This is because once inside the network, the attacker might have used the stolen identity to take control of an application, thus moving laterally from the Identity domain to the Apps domain, as shown in Figure 3-20. The Apps security people might detect unauthorized access to the application, but they, too, are not fully aware of events outside their domain. This is not neglectful because the amount of incoming signal information to monitor in each domain is huge.

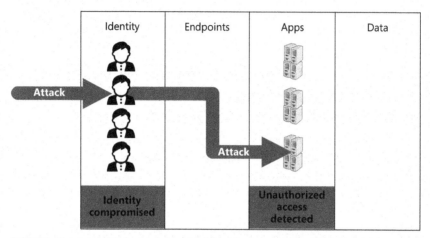

FIGURE 3-20 Lateral attack across security domains

The domain divisions mean nothing to an attacker, of course, but there will never be a complete picture of the current attack or future attacks unless the information gathered by the two separate teams—Identity and Apps—is collated and analyzed together, along with information from the Endpoints and Data teams.

This collation and analysis of information from all four domains is what the Microsoft 365 Defender suite is designed to do. Microsoft 365 Defender consists of a separate application for each of the four security domains, as follows:

- Microsoft Defender for Endpoint
- Microsoft Defender for Office 365
- Microsoft Defender for Identity
- Microsoft Defender for Cloud Apps

These separate applications all report to a central Microsoft 365 Defender engine that analyzes the input from the four domains and compiles a composite security picture that covers the entire enterprise infrastructure. Administrators can use the Microsoft 365 Defender portal to monitor and manage the ongoing security processes.

The following sections describe the capabilities of the Microsoft 365 Defender applications.

Microsoft Defender for Endpoint

Endpoints are the devices connected to a network: computers, smartphones, tablets, wireless access points, routers, and firewalls. All endpoints are potential points of vulnerability, and

Microsoft Defender for Endpoint is designed to discover, configure, and monitor these endpoints. Defender for Endpoint can also remediate the issue when it detects suspicious behavior.

As with all of the Microsoft 365 Defender products, management of Defender for Endpoint is integrated into the Microsoft 365 Defender portal. Microsoft Defender for Endpoint is available in two plans, plus an add-on for Plan 2, as shown in Table 3-2.

TABLE 3-2 Microsoft Defender for Endpoint products

Defender for Endpoint Plan 1	Defender for Endpoint Plan 2	Defender Vulnerability Management add-on for Plan 2
Next-generation antivirus and antimalware protection	All Defender for Endpoint Plan 1 features	All Defender for Endpoint Plan 2 features
Attack surface reduction	Device discovery and inventory	Security baselines assessment
Manual response actions	Vulnerability management	Blocking of vulnerable applications
Centralized management	Threat analytics	Hardware and firmware assessment
Security reports	Automated investigation and response	Network share analysis
Support for Windows 10, Windows 11, iOS, Android OS, and macOS devices	Endpoint detection and response	Authenticated scan for Windows

Microsoft 365 Enterprise E3 includes Plan 1, and Enterprise E5 includes Plan 2. Mixed licensing scenarios are available, in which a tenancy includes both Plan 1 and Plan 2 clients. There is also a standalone Microsoft Defender for Business product, designed for networks of up to 300 users, which includes many of the Defender for Endpoint features found in Plans 1 and 2.

Defender for Endpoint provides tools for investigating endpoint security threats, including the following:

- **Vulnerability management**   Defender for Endpoint continuously monitors the network (as shown in Figure 3-21), inventories hardware and software components such as certificates and browser extensions, discovers potential vulnerabilities, assesses their associated risks, and remediates them.

- **Attack surface reduction**   Minimizes the attack risk by restricting users to only the resources they need. Using zero trust principles, attack surface reduction allows administrators to designate applications as trusted and specify folders that only trusted applications can access. In the same way, network protection prevents endpoints from communicating with websites suspected of hosting malware, phishing attempts, and other suspicious behaviors.

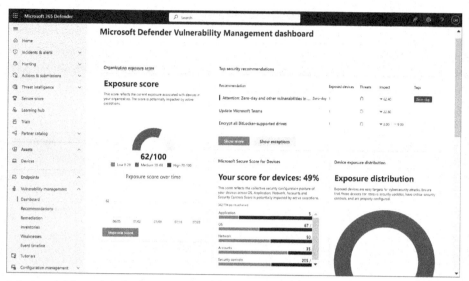

FIGURE 3-21 Microsoft Defender Vulnerability Management dashboard

- **Endpoint detection and response** Provides near real-time detection of attacks, generating alerts that it incorporates into incidents describing similar threats. This enables administrators to analyze security events based on evidence gathered over time.

- **Automated investigation and remediation** After generating alerts, Defender for Endpoint initiates an investigation by scanning its records for similar occurrences on other systems and using artificial intelligence. Defender executes remediations based on automation levels configured for machine groups, as follows:

    - **Not protected** Turns off all remediation.

    - **Semi** Requires administrator approval for particular types of remediation.

    - **Full** Performs remediations automatically.

- **Endpoint attack notifications** Formerly known as Microsoft Threat Experts, Defender proactively hunts for common threats and generates alerts when it finds them.

Microsoft Defender for Office 365

Microsoft Defender for Office 365 is designed to provide protection from attacks arriving through email messages, web links, and Microsoft 365 collaboration tools, including Microsoft Teams, SharePoint, and OneDrive. While all accounts using Microsoft Exchange Online for email are protected by Exchange Online Protection (EOP) against spam, phishing, and malware attempts, Microsoft Defender for Office 365 includes more extensive protection, including the ability to interact with the main Microsoft 365 Defender engine.

Microsoft Defender for Office 365 is available in two plans, as shown in Table 3-3. Plan 1 includes more extensive malware, phishing, email attack detection capabilities; Plan 2 goes beyond the real-time detection of email and collaborative documents and adds automated attack investigation, threat hunting, and attack simulators that administrators can use for training purposes.

Microsoft 365 Enterprise E5 includes Plan 2, but for other Microsoft 365 subscriptions, Defender for Office 365 must be purchased as a standalone subscription.

TABLE 3-3 Microsoft Defender for Endpoint products

Defender for Office 365 Plan 1	Defender for Office 365 Plan 2
Safe attachments	All Plan 1 features
Safe links	Threat trackers
Safe attachments for SharePoint, OneDrive, and Microsoft Teams	Threat Explorer
Anti-phishing protection	Automated investigation and response (AIR)
Real-time detections	Attack Simulator
	Advanced hunting
	Microsoft 365 Defender integration

Microsoft Defender for Identity

Microsoft Defender for Identity, formerly known as Azure Advanced Threat Protection (Azure ATP), is a product that protects the identities stored in Active Directory. There was at one time a separate Defender for Identity management portal, but the interface has now been integrated into the Microsoft 365 Defender portal.

Defender for Identity monitors the Active Directory communications involved in identity creation, management, authentication, and authorization and creates a profile of each user's identity-related activities. The signal is then sent to Microsoft 365 Defender, which collates it with the signals from the other Defender products, as shown in Figure 3-22, to create a comprehensive picture of any attacks that occur. The identity information gathered by Defender for Identity is a crucial contributor to the overall security context developed by Microsoft 365 Defender.

Defender for Identity also helps administrators reduce the existing identities' attack surface by generating reports that suggest configuration best practices and identify potential weaknesses.

Defender is also aware of the tendency of attackers to attempt to compromise low-privilege identities and then move laterally within the network to gain access to more sensitive information. By detecting identities that have been compromised and analyzing the signals generated by Active Directory, Defender for Identity can track these lateral movements and identify other accounts that might have been compromised.

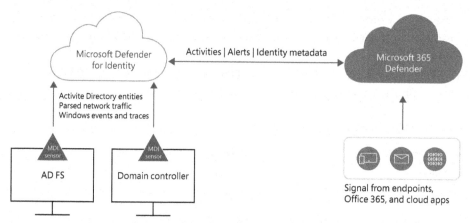

FIGURE 3-22 Microsoft Defender for Identity architecture

One of the biggest problems for IT security personnel in the enterprise is the overabundance of alerts, particularly in identity security. For example, every sign-on failure can generate an alert, which might result from an attempted attack or just a misspelled password by a user. Defender for Identity's analytical capabilities helps reduce the number of alerts brought to the attention of administrators by identifying only those relevant to the network's attack posture and creating a detailed attack timeline that omits the irrelevant.

Microsoft Defender for Cloud Apps

Microsoft Defender for Cloud Apps is a *cloud access security broker (CASB)*, essentially an intermediary between Microsoft 365 cloud users and the cloud-based Software as a Service (SaaS) apps they run. Like the other Defender products, the administrative interface for Defender for Cloud Apps has been integrated into the Microsoft 365 Defender portal.

Defender for Cloud Apps monitors the apps the network users are accessing to ensure that the apps are authorized and used safely. The product includes the main features shown in Figure 3-23:

- **Cloud app discovery** Defender for Cloud Apps uses network traffic analysis and other techniques to perform a pattern search in the Microsoft cloud app catalog of 25,000 applications. After identifying all of the cloud apps being used on the network, Defender then assesses each app as a potential threat based on more than 90 risk factors and displays the resulting information in a dashboard like the one shown in Figure 3-24. Administrators can selectively sanction the apps they want users to access while desanctioning those they do not.

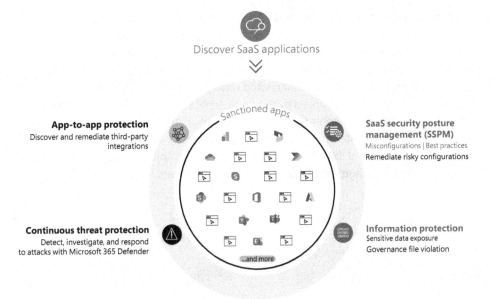

Discover SaaS applications

App-to-app protection
Discover and remediate third-party integrations

Sanctioned apps
...and more

SaaS security posture management (SSPM)
Misconfigurations | Best practices
Remediate risky configurations

Continuous threat protection
Detect, investigate, and respond to attacks with Microsoft 365 Defender

Information protection
Sensitive data exposure
Governance file violation

FIGURE 3-23 Microsoft Defender for Cloud Apps features

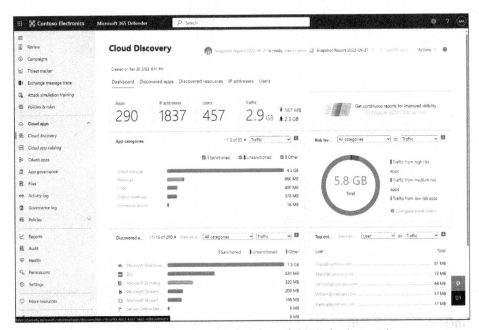

FIGURE 3-24 The Cloud Discovery dashboard in the Microsoft 365 Defender portal

- **SaaS security posture management** Every SaaS app is different, and administrators often cannot practically learn the configuration peculiarities of dozens or hundreds of sanctioned apps. Defender for Cloud Apps, using the information in the cloud app library, compares the best practices for each app with its current configuration settings and generates recommendations for revised settings and actions. Defender for Cloud Apps supports using APIs supplied by the cloud application providers for sanctioned applications. These APIs enable Defender to function as an intermediary between cloud applications and the enterprise's users, as shown in Figure 3-25, by accessing activity logs, user accounts, and data sources. Defender for Cloud Apps can then use this information to monitor usage, enforce policies, and detect threats.

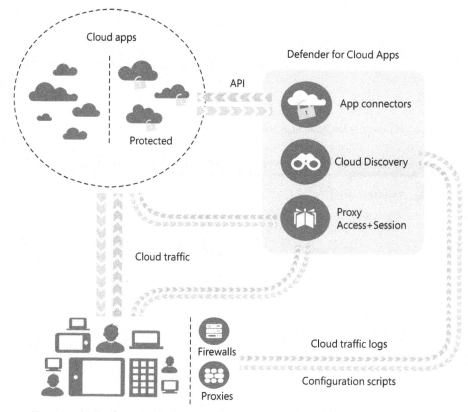

FIGURE 3-25 Interactions of Defender for Cloud Apps with an enterprise network and cloud applications

- **Information protection** Defender for Cloud Apps is integrated into the Microsoft 365 Data Loss Protection (DLP) engine, which enables Defender to scan cloud apps for sensitive data, log its location and who is accessing it, and take actions such as applying a label or even blocking user access.

- **Continuous threat protection**   As noted earlier, Defender for Cloud Apps is integrated into Microsoft 365 Defender, which makes it part of the high-level Microsoft 365 security posture, continuously monitoring cloud app alerts and integrating them into the enterprise attack investigations.

- **App-to-app protection**   Open Authorization (OAuth) is a standard that enables one app to access information on another app on a user's behalf. This is naturally a security concern, and Defender for Cloud Apps can add help by adding protection to the app-to-app communications with application governance. Application governance takes the form of policies that determine how apps communicate with each other, as well as actions and alerts that can remediate problem situations.

Describe Microsoft Secure Score benefits and capabilities

Microsoft Secure Score is a feature found in the Microsoft 365 Defender portal that displays a dashboard of the network's overall security posture, as shown in Figure 3-26. Secure Score is designed to help administrators learn more about the inner security workings of their networks.

The **Secure Score** is a percentage found in the upper-left corner of the dashboard that reflects the number of points administrators achieve by performing security-related tasks and enacting items from the list of recommendations provided by Microsoft 365 Defender.

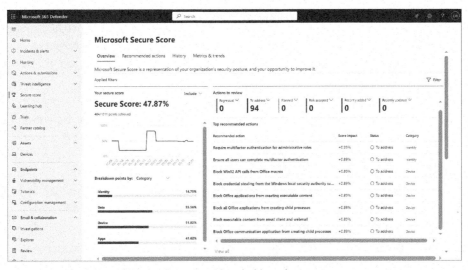

FIGURE 3-26 The Microsoft Secure Score Overview dashboard

Directly beneath the Secure Score is a series of graphs that break down the score by specifying how many points were achieved in each of the four standard security categories: identity, data, device, and apps. Next to the graphs is the list of recommendations provided by Microsoft 365 Defender for each of the four categories and each licensed application.

For example, the first recommendation in the list calls for requiring multifactor authentication during administrative sign-ins. Double-clicking the recommendation switches the Microsoft Secure Score display to the **Recommended Actions** tab and opens a sidebar with more information, as shown in Figure 3-27.

FIGURE 3-27 A recommended action in the Microsoft Secure Score dashboard

This particular recommendation states that it is worth a possible nine points or 0.89 percent of the Secure Score value. As administrators complete the recommended task according to the instructions on the **Implementation** tab, Defender adds the points to the score and recalculates the Secure Score value.

Some tasks have binary solutions; an administrator either completes the task or does not and receives all or none of the points. In recommendations like this one, however, Defender awards partial points for partially completed tasks. It is also possible for the network to lose points and for its score to regress, such as when additional users who suffer from a security condition and are already recommended for remediation are added to the network.

Secure Score is not intended to be a set of instructions that administrators must follow by rote. Every enterprise network has its own needs and peculiarities, so there might be some recommendations that are not practical or possible in a specific situation.

For example, Defender might add the Block Win32 API calls from Office macros recommendation to a Secure Score page because it can help to prevent malicious code from being introduced into the network. However, if the network has users that require those API calls to do their jobs, then the administrators can create an exception like the one shown in Figure 3-28, indicating that they are willing to accept the risk or that they have some other means of preventing macro intrusions in place.

FIGURE 3-28 Creating an exception in the Microsoft Secure Score dashboard

Describe how Microsoft 365 addresses the most common types of threats against endpoints, applications, and identities

Risk management is a highly specialized undertaking heavily dependent on the type and sensitivity of the information to be protected and the nature of the threats to which the network is most vulnerable. For example, an organization that consists mostly of IT professionals will not be overly susceptible to phishing attacks because they have more awareness of them and experience with them. On the other hand, an organization of users with little or no IT expertise will be far more vulnerable to this particular threat and will require more effort to prevent this type of attack.

Microsoft 365 includes a wide variety of security tools that make it possible to predict, prevent, and react to many different kinds of threats. Many of these tools are discussed individually in this chapter and elsewhere in this book. The nature of each tool's function is explained in relation to the types of threats it addresses. However, Microsoft recently announced an effort to organize Microsoft 365's security components under the single name *Microsoft 365 Defender*, which places the tools into the following categories:

- **Endpoints** Tools that protect user devices and sensors from the effects of loss, theft, and attack, such as Microsoft Defender for Endpoint, Microsoft Intune, and Configuration Manager

- **Cloud apps** Tools that protect Software as a Service (SaaS) applications, such as Microsoft Defender for Cloud Apps and Exchange Online Protection

- **Identities** Tools that authenticate, authorize, and protect the accounts of standard users and privileged administrators, such as Microsoft Defender for Identity, Windows Hello, Azure Active Directory Identity Protection, and Privileged Identity Management

- **User data** Tools that analyze documents and messages for sensitive or malicious content, such as Microsoft Defender for Office 365, Exchange Online Protection, Azure Information Protection, and Data Loss Prevention

However, Microsoft 365 Defender is meant to be more than just a list of individual tools. Microsoft 365 Defender also gathers information from all these security components and accumulates them in a single Microsoft 365 Defender portal, as shown in Figure 3-29.

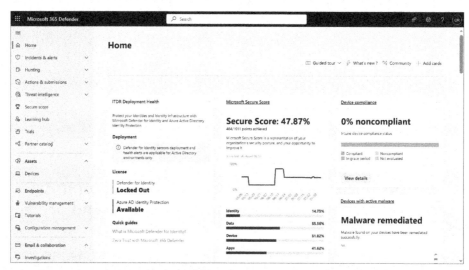

FIGURE 3-29 Microsoft 365 Defender portal

Microsoft 365 Defender goes beyond the reactive approach to security and provides tools that can be proactive by detecting attacks and other security issues before they occur or when they have barely begun. The various Defender tools are all designed to monitor the behavior of users, devices, and other network resources and analyze the information they collect to detect and anticipate suspicious behavior. The intelligence the tools apply to the task is based on the Microsoft Intelligent Security Graph, a web of security relationships that spans the entire network. Microsoft's Cybersecurity Reference Architecture, shown in Figure 3-30, illustrates these relationships.

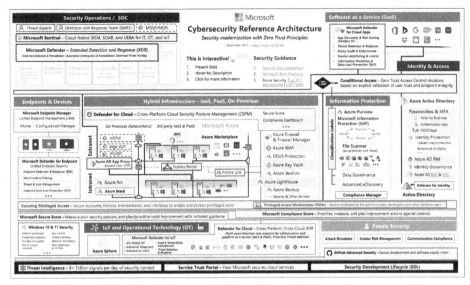

FIGURE 3-30 Microsoft Cybersecurity Reference Architecture

> **NEED MORE REVIEW?** **MICROSOFT CYBERSECURITY REFERENCE ARCHITECTURE**
>
> For an interactive PowerPoint version of the architecture shown in Figure 3-30, see
> *https://aka.ms/MCRA*.

The predominant threats to endpoints, applications, and identities are as follows:

- **Endpoints** Threats to endpoints can include various types of malware, including phishing attempts and ransomware. What often makes endpoints extra vulnerable, however, is when the devices are not compliant with the safety standards imposed by the management. Devices without the latest security patches or not protected by updated antivirus software can provide ingress to the network that attackers can exploit.

- **Applications** Shadow IT—the use of unauthorized applications—can leave a network open to a variety of attacks, including the introduction of malware or spyware to the network, as well as infrastructure attacks, such as Denial of Service (DoS) and Distributed Denial of Service (DDoS).

- **Identities** Credential theft is the chief threat against identities, which can take the form of social engineering, keystroke capture, and even brute force attacks.

A typical enterprise network today faces security threats from many directions and at many levels. Administrators must know that attackers frequently take advantage of vulnerabilities in an enterprise's identities, documents, or endpoints. The following sections examine how the Microsoft 365 security tools address each area.

Protecting identities

All identities are a potential source of risk for the entire network, no matter what level of privileges they possess. Once attackers compromise one identity, it becomes relatively easy to spread laterally within the enterprise and compromise others. Therefore, administrators should try to protect all identities, not just the ones with administrative privileges.

One of the key innovations of Microsoft 365 is the greater emphasis on proactive threat detection and remediation. Microsoft Entra ID (formerly Azure AD) can provide this type of security for user accounts with a feature called Microsoft Entra ID Protection. Identity Protection evaluates the sign-in activities of individual user accounts and assigns risk levels that increment when multiple negative events occur. There are two risk levels associated with each identity, as follows:

- **Sign-in risk**   The probability that an unauthorized individual is attempting to authenticate with another person's identity
- **User risk**   An accumulated probability that a specific identity has been compromised

Microsoft Entra ID Protection recognizes the following risk events and modifies an identity's two risk levels based on the order and frequency in which they occur:

- **Atypical travel**   The user signs in from an atypical location for the user or is geographically impossible based on the user's other recent sign-ins. Microsoft Entra ID takes into account the travel time between the locations and gradually develops its own profile of the user's habits, which helps to prevent the occurrence of false positives (that is, conclusions of risk from sign-in patterns that are common for that user).
- **Anonymous IP address**   The user signs in from a browser that suppresses the user's IP address, such as Tor or a virtual private network (VPN) client. The user signing on might or might not be the identity owner, but Entra ID considers the anonymity to be suspicious.
- **Unfamiliar sign-in properties**   The user signs in from a client with unfamiliar properties, such as a new location, an unusual IP address, or an autonomous system number (ASN), based on the user's previous activities. For new identities, there is a period of information gathering that lasts at least five days, during which Entra ID makes no risk assessments using this criterion.
- **Malware-linked IP address**   An identity is associated with an IP address previously used to contact a known bot server on the Internet. The system is then assumed to be infected with malware and considered to be a risk.
- **Leaked credentials**   An identity is determined to use credentials known to have been compromised. Microsoft gathers information about such credentials from numerous sources, including law enforcement agencies, security consultants, and illicit websites.

When these events occur, Entra ID evaluates them and modifies the behavior of the authentication process according to criteria established by administrators. There are obviously many possible combinations of behaviors that Entra ID might have to take into account when evaluating the risk levels of an identity. For example, if the same risk events occur repeatedly, the risk levels will continue to rise until a drastic reaction, such as blocking all access to the identity, might be required.

The basic Azure AD Identity Protection process is illustrated in Figure 3-31.

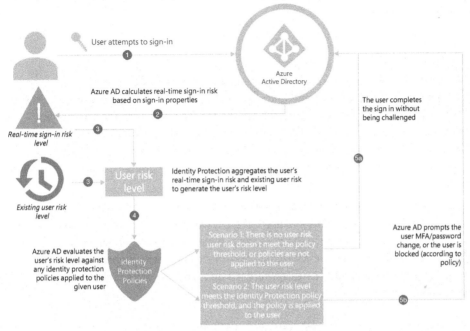

FIGURE 3-31 The Azure AD (Entra ID) Identity Protection risk evaluation process

For example, when a user attempts to sign in with a simple password from an anonymous IP address, Entra ID determines that it is a risk and assigns it a sign-in risk level of medium. This risk level causes Entra ID to implement a Conditional Access policy that imposes a specific action, such as requiring multifactor authentication during the sign-in process. If the user successfully completes the multifactor authentication, the user risk level remains unchanged.

However, if the user fails to complete the multifactor authentication, Entra ID considers this to be a possible indication that the identity has been compromised and raises the user risk level. The next time the user attempts to sign on, the process might proceed completely normally, with no sign-in risk detected; however, the user risk level associated with the identity persists, and Entra ID might be configured to prompt the user to change the password.

Entra ID Protection is included only with the Entra ID P2 (formerly Azure Active Directory Premium P2) plan, supplied with the Microsoft 365 Enterprise E5 edition.

EXAM TIP

The additional security provided by Azure AD Identity Protection applies only to cloud-based identities, not the on-premises identities in Active Directory Domain Services. Microsoft's increased emphasis on cloud-based solutions, such as Microsoft 365, means that the latest innovations in security and other areas are not being ported to the traditional on-premises versions. For this reason, Microsoft recommends that enterprise networks shift more of their applications and services away from on-premises servers and into the cloud. When preparing for the MS-900 examination, candidates should be conscious of this emphasis on the cloud and carefully distinguish Microsoft's cloud-based products from its on-premises products.

Protecting documents

The fundamental purpose of identities is to protect documents and other data. When protecting identities, the threat of lateral penetration forces administrators to apply equal protection to all of them, regardless of their privileges. However, the security can and should be more selective when protecting documents. While an enterprise might have hundreds or thousands of identities to protect, it might easily have hundreds of thousands or millions of documents, which makes applying equal protection to them all impractical. Therefore, administrators need to identify sensitive data documents requiring more protection.

As discussed earlier in this chapter, Azure Information Protection (AIP) and Data Loss Prevention (DLP) enable administrators and users to apply classification labels to documents and specify security measures applied to the documents based on those labels. While these tools can, in some cases, detect sensitive data within documents based on criteria that administrators specify, there are many other cases in which it is up to the users to apply the labels correctly to their documents.

> **NOTE INFORMATION PROTECTION AND DATA LOSS PREVENTION**
>
> For more information on Azure Information Protection and Data Loss Prevention, see the "Data" section earlier in this chapter.

The technological aspects of implementing tools such as AIP and DLP are relatively straightforward; however, the implementation's administrative, cultural, and educational aspects can be more troublesome, especially in a large enterprise. For these tools to function effectively, the classification labels representing the various levels of data sensitivity must be understood by everyone involved and applied consistently throughout the organization.

When the intention is to create a single classification label taxonomy that the entire enterprise will use, it makes sense for representatives from all areas and all levels of the enterprise to have a say in the design of that taxonomy. Unless the terms used for the labels mean the same thing to everyone, there is a chance that documents could be labeled incorrectly or, worse, not labeled at all when they should be.

With the labeling taxonomy agreed on and in place, the next step in the deployment—as with all new programs—should be a pilot deployment. With a small group of representative users applying labels to their documents and with DLP configured to classify a subset of the company's documents automatically, careful monitoring of the labeling process and evaluation of the classified documents will almost certainly disclose some incorrect labeling, requiring modifications to the tools themselves or to the users' procedures. Successive iterations of the taxonomy and the DLP algorithms will likely be needed before the system is completely reliable.

The final phase of the deployment—and arguably the most difficult one—will be educating all the organization's users on the labeling system, how it works, and why it is necessary. This is particularly true for users not involved in the technology behind the system. Document protection is not a problem that administrators can solve only with technology; the human factor is also critical.

Protecting endpoints

At one time, enterprise network security consisted of company-owned computers (deployed and managed internally), and protected using password policies, firewalls, antivirus software, and dial-up and virtual private network connections for a few remote users. Network administrators controlled all the equipment, and a generation of *Client Management Tools (CMTs)* appeared, such as Microsoft's *System Center Configuration Manager (SCCM)*. Now part of the Microsoft Intune family of products and called just Configuration Manager, the tool provides a unified management solution that enables administrators to inventory hardware, deploy operating systems and applications, update software, manage licenses, and remotely control computers all over the enterprise.

Unfortunately, management platforms like SCCM were designed for use with on-premises computers only, and they communicate over local area networks (LANs). As mobile computing devices became increasingly common, a new management platform was needed, one that could function through the cloud. *Mobile Device Management (MDM)* was the first iteration of that new platform. MDM products typically exercise complete control over the mobile devices they manage, and as a result, it became common for organizations using the products to own the devices as well.

However, workers often had problems with the usability constraints imposed by company-owned, company-managed devices. These problems only became more severe as people began to purchase their own smartphones and find them easier to work with than their MDM-managed company devices. This eventually resulted in the BYOD (Bring Your Own Device) concept, which certainly pleased users but made administrators' lives more difficult.

To provide adequate security on devices the company does not own, a new evolutionary step in the development of management products was needed, and *enterprise mobility management (EMM)* tools, such as Microsoft Intune, were the result. Using Intune, administrators can enroll, configure, and manage mobile devices on several different operating system platforms, wherever the devices happen to be. Administrators can even intervene when a threat to security occurs by blocking a device's access to the company network and erasing any sensitive information stored on it.

However, despite the advances in mobile computing and mobile device management, on-premises devices, applications, and services have not gone away and still need to be managed. CMTs and EMMs are different types of management platforms in many fundamental ways. Both require administrators to have significant training and experience, but the two generally do not overlap. A need arose for a management platform that could work with both on-premises and cloud-based devices, as shown in Figure 3-32; this management platform also needs to be extendable to include new technologies as they develop, such as wearables and the Internet of Things (IoT). This new platform has come to be known as *unified endpoint management (UEM)*.

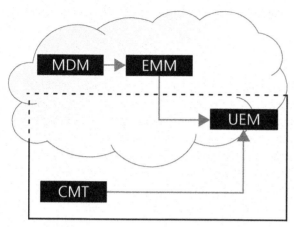

FIGURE 3-32 Development of Unified Endpoint Management

The term *endpoint* has come to be used to refer to any user device, including desktop computers, laptops, printers, tablets, smartphones, and newer technologies, such as wearables and Internet of Things devices. Unified endpoint management aims to eliminate the need for separate management tools for on-premises and mobile devices. An ideal UEM solution is a "single-pane" administration platform that can manage the applications, identities, resources, updates, security, and policy compliance for all the endpoints in the enterprise, regardless of their locations, device types, or operating systems.

> **NOTE INTERNET OF THINGS**
>
> As mobile networking moves beyond the now ubiquitous smartphone, the next evolution appears to be the Internet of Things (IoT), in which mobile computing devices are embedded in various types of tools, appliances, and systems. Home and building automation is a growing market for IoT devices, including thermostats, light switches, refrigerators, and large-scale industrial and utility systems.
>
> In the healthcare industry, IoT devices—including heart rate, blood pressure, and blood glucose monitors—can monitor patients' conditions both inside and outside hospitals; also, they can control implanted devices, such as pacemakers and defibrillators. Automobiles and other vehicles are also common applications for IoT, which can provide location monitoring, toll collection, and traffic control services.
>
> All these device types require management by network administrators and could conceivably be as much of a security threat as any of the other mobile computing devices in use today. For example, one can only imagine the chaos if an attacker managed to penetrate a hospital network or a city's power grid.

In Microsoft 365, UEM capability is implemented in the Microsoft 365 Enterprise and Business Premium products and in the Enterprise Mobility + Security (EMS) product. Microsoft Intune is also available as a separate product in two plans and a suite that provides a range of capabilities. The Microsoft tools relevant to the UEM effort in an enterprise are as follows:

- **Microsoft Entra ID (Azure Active Directory Premium)** The cloud-based directory service that manages identities and provides authentication and authorization for all the Microsoft 365 applications and services, including all the endpoint management tools.

- **Azure AD Connect** An on-premises tool replicating user identities on AD DS domain controllers to Entra ID identities stored in the cloud so that users can sign in through the cloud and administrators can take advantage of the Entra ID identity security features. For more information, see "Microsoft 365 deployment" in Chapter 2, "Describe Microsoft 365 apps and services."

- **Microsoft Intune** A cloud-based enterprise mobility management (EMM) service that enables administrators to enroll mobile devices, deploy apps, and enforce security policies.

- **Configuration Manager** An on-premises CMT that administrators can use to inventory computer hardware, deploy operating system images on internal workstations, manage applications, apply software updates, and enforce device compliance policies.

- **Azure Information Protection (AIP)** A cloud-based tool that enables users and administrators to apply classification labels to documents and implement various types of protection based on the labels, such as access restrictions and data encryption.

- **Microsoft Advanced Threat Analytics (ATA)** An on-premises platform that captures network traffic and log information and analyzes it to identify suspicious behaviors related to multiple phases of the attack process.

- **Microsoft Defender for Endpoint** A cloud-based service that discovers, configures, and monitors endpoints, providing capabilities such as vulnerability management and attack surface reduction.

- **Microsoft Defender for Cloud Apps** A cloud-based service that analyzes traffic logs and proxy scripts to identify the apps that users are accessing—including unauthorized apps—and enables administrators to sanction or unsanction individual apps and connect to APIs supplied by cloud app providers to perform cloud app security analyses.

- **Microsoft Defender for Identity** A cloud-based threat prevention, detection, and remediation engine that uses machine intelligence to look for security threats unique to the Azure environment by analyzing user behavior and comparing it to known attack patterns.

NOTE **MICROSOFT ATA**

For more information on Microsoft Advanced Threat Analytics, see the "Describe analytics capabilities in Microsoft 365" section in Chapter 2, "Describe Microsoft 365 apps and services"

Management of the various types of endpoints presents administrators with a variety of issues that they must address, including the following:

- **User-owned devices**   When workers use their own devices, administrators must define a policy specifying what degree of control the organization will have over them and what company resources the devices will be permitted to access. This can be a difficult task because, while the organization must protect its resources, users are often unwilling to turn over full control of their property to the company. Windows Intune provides administrators with both Mobile Device Management (MDM) and Mobile Administration Management (MAM) capabilities, which provide different levels of management control to suit the needs of the organization and the users.

- **Mobile device networking**   Mobile users often connect to outside wireless networks, such as those in coffee shops and other businesses, which are unsecured by the enterprise. This leaves the devices open to intrusion by outside persons, exposing them to threats that can jeopardize the device, the data stored on it, and the enterprise network. Administrators can use Microsoft Intune or other tools to create and enforce mobile device policies requiring devices to have malware prevention tools, software updates, and other forms of protection to repel threats.

- **Device loss or theft**   Any mobile device is liable to be lost or stolen, with the accompanying danger that any sensitive data stored on the device might be compromised. Users might also leave the company under less-than-friendly circumstances, taking their personal devices with them. In some cases, the cost of replacing the device hardware can be less than that of identifying the data that has been lost and re-creating it. Administrators must prepare for these situations by devising a Microsoft Intune policy that remotely protects the organization's resources, even when the mobile device is in hostile hands.

- **Infected devices**   Mobile devices that become infected with malware while connected to outside networks can bring that infection into the enterprise, damage documents, and pass the infection along to other systems. Administrators must classify and protect all mobile devices connecting to the enterprise network as potential threats.

- **Device data synchronization**   While data stored in the Microsoft cloud is replicated to multiple datacenters for protection, mobile devices working outside the company premises might not always be connected to the cloud. Therefore, when users work with company documents while offline, any revisions they make to the documents are not saved to the cloud or backed up until they next connect to a network. Therefore, this revised data can be lost if the device is damaged, lost, or stolen before it next connects to the cloud.

- **Password changes**   One of the more common tasks for help desk personnel and administrators is changing users' passwords. This task is even more common when Microsoft Entra ID Protection is configured to require a password change when their authentication-based risk levels reach a certain value. Self Service Password Reset (SSPR) enables users who have been successfully authenticated to change their passwords rather than require the intervention of an administrator.

Describe the capabilities and benefits of Microsoft Sentinel and Microsoft 365 Lighthouse

Security Information and Event Management (SIEM) is a type of product that combines two technologies: security event management (SEM) and security information management (SIM). Together, the two technologies form a solution that can gather and analyze information about a network's security events. SIEM tools collect information from logs and various other security mechanisms and evaluate it to identify and prioritize potential security hazards, generate alerts, and combine related alerts into incidents.

When SIEM has a drawback, it is often an overabundance of alerts that administrators often cannot practically investigate and handle individually. *Security orchestration, automation, and response (SOAR)* is a newer technology that uses artificial intelligence to prioritize incidents better and perform automated remediations, which reduces the burden on the network's security administrators. Microsoft Sentinel combines both SIEM and SOAR technologies into one comprehensive product. Microsoft 365 Lighthouse is a tool designed to enable service providers to provide security services to their clients using a cloud-based portal.

Microsoft Sentinel

Microsoft Sentinel combines SIEM and SOAR functionality into a tool that provides a high-level view of an enterprise network's security posture. As shown in Figure 3-33, Sentinel divides its functionality into four basic categories.

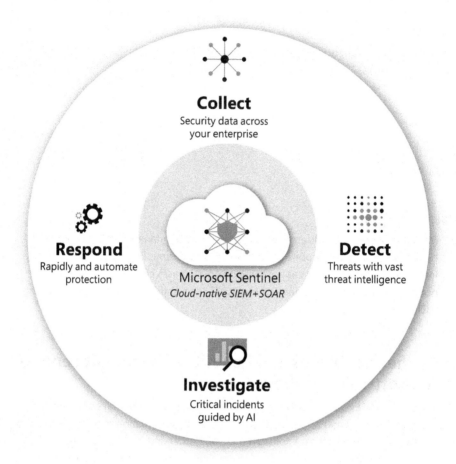

FIGURE 3-33 Functions of Microsoft Sentinel

- **Collect** Microsoft connectors enable Sentinel to exchange information in real time with all of the Microsoft 365 Defender and Microsoft Entra (Azure) services and connectors to other Microsoft 365 services and third-party security products. There is also a thriving Sentinel development community that produces its own connectors, and administrators can create custom connectors as well.

- **Detect** With the data gathered from the connectors, Sentinel identifies potential security-related behavioral anomalies, such as excessive numbers of failed sign-on attempts, and generates alerts.

- **Investigate** Sentinel uses analytics to investigate similarities and patterns in the alerts it has detected and combine them into incidents, as shown in Figure 3-34, which can provide administrators with a better overall picture of an attack effort. Selecting an incident allows administrators to view its severity and all of the alerts involved. Sentinel can also proactively hunt for security threats based on a global database of attack techniques.

- **Respond** Sentinel's SOAR capabilities allow administrators to automate predictable tasks like endpoint onboarding, incident response, and threat remediation. Sentinel is integrated with Azure Logic Apps, making it possible to create automation rules, playbooks, and workflows that contain responses to specific security threats.

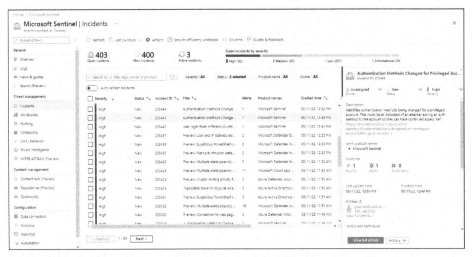

FIGURE 3-34 The Incidents page in the Microsoft Sentinel portal

Microsoft Sentinel pricing is based on the amount of data stored in the Azure Monitor Log Analytics workspace. Users can opt to pay for the storage space as they go or select a commitment tier for a specified number of gigabytes per day, which provides substantial savings.

Microsoft 365 Lighthouse

Small- and medium-sized businesses often lack IT personnel with a sufficient security background to manage and monitor the network using the tools provided in Microsoft 365. This creates a market for managed service providers (MSPs) who can lend their security expertise to their clients to help them protect their networks. *Microsoft 365 Lighthouse* is a cloud-based administration portal intended to provide MSPs with sufficient access to their clients' networks security tools on their clients' networks without giving away the keys to the kingdom.

Microsoft Lighthouse is based on a portal that enables MSPs to view all of their tenants' networks in one place and focus on individual tenants, users, endpoints, and even threats. The tool can onboard new users and devices using security configuration baselines that the MSP can tailor to specific tenants.

Once onboarded, Lighthouse can track user activities and identify users at risk for security problems, as shown in Figure 3-35. The list identifies the users, provides their current status, and allows the MSP to select users to display more details about their risky behavior. The MSP can then take action by emailing the risky users, changing their passwords, requiring them to use multifactor authentication, or even preventing specific users from signing on.

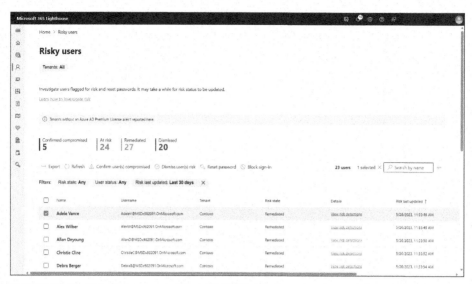

FIGURE 3-35 The Risky Users page in Microsoft 365 Lighthouse

Lighthouse enables MSPs to interact with their tenants from other directions as well. For example, instead of working with the users' identities, an MSP can open the **Threat Management** page, shown in Figure 3-36 and display a list of all the threats detected on the tenants' systems. MSPs can then work with individual threats and remediate all of their instances—on multiple users or even multiple tenants—at once.

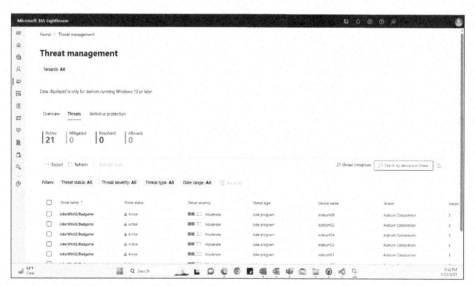

FIGURE 3-36 The Threats tab on the Threat Management page in Microsoft 365 Lighthouse

MSPs must be enrolled in Microsoft's Cloud Solution Provider (CSP) program to manage their tenants with Microsoft 365 Lighthouse, but no additional costs are involved. There are no requirements for the tenants the MSPs are managing.

Skill 3.3: Describe trust, privacy, risk, and compliance solutions of Microsoft 365

Microsoft 365 includes a large number of security tools that work together in various ways to provide a network with trust, privacy, risk, and compliance solutions. Some of these solutions are discussed in the following sections.

Describe the Zero Trust model

At one time, enterprise security could be considered a perimeter surrounding an organization. Data remained largely within the organization's sites and could be protected from unauthorized access by firewalls, virtual private networks (VPNs), and physical barriers. Even when data began to be accessible beyond the organization using Internet websites and portable devices, the company still owned and managed these potential attack vectors.

The assets an organization needs to protect, sometimes called its *digital estate*, have grown enormously in recent years, and so have the enterprise's means of ingress and egress. This digital estate certainly includes the company's data, but it also includes the users who access the data and the systems and devices by which they access it. All three of these assets are potential weak points in an enterprise security system, and all three need protection (see Figure 3-37).

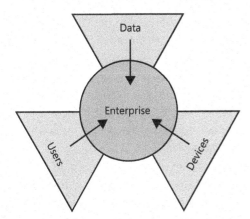

FIGURE 3-37 The enterprise asset types needing protection

The commitment to the cloud required by adopters of Microsoft 365 creates a new attack vector. However, to fully protect the company's data, IT administrators now have to be concerned with the cloud, and they must be concerned with security for devices that are not directly owned by the organization, not located within the organization, and, in some cases, owned by users who are not even employees of the organization.

Therefore, the primary storage for an organization's data can be located in the cloud or on servers kept on-premises. In many cases, the data is split between the two. That means administrators must be responsible for the security of both. However, in addition to the primary storage locations, the devices workers use to access the data are also potential attack vectors. The increasing adoption of the BYOD paradigm complicates the process of securing data that might be stored in someone's pocket on a device that might not be fully manageable by enterprise administrators.

The security problem also extends beyond the logical extremities of the enterprise to the partners, clients, and consultants with which employees share data. These people use their own systems and devices that are even farther out of reach of the enterprise administrators. All these attack vectors can provide intruders with a way into the enterprise network, and once sophisticated intruders are inside, they often manage to stay there and extend their influence.

While there are always a certain number of casual cybercriminals who are relatively easy to repulse, the serious, professional penetration attempts that often afflict large enterprises can be incredibly sophisticated and take place over long periods of time. Microsoft 365 includes a powerful array of security tools that allow administrators to implement various types of protection over the company's data and the devices that access it, but these tools are not simple turnkey solutions. Enterprise administrators must design a security plan that prioritizes the sensitivity of the company's data, assesses the vulnerability of the systems and devices on which the data is stored, identifies the users and their data needs, and specifies how the Microsoft 365 tools will be used.

These complicating elements in today's enterprise networks—such as remote users and BYOD policies—call for a rethink of the perimeter security model. The original principle was to keep all potentially dangerous elements outside the network perimeter—or near the perimeter—in a secure subnet. These days, the potential dangers are everywhere, both inside and outside the network perimeter, and a more comprehensive approach is needed.

For example, in the traditional network security architecture, the assumption is that anyone authenticated and allowed inside the perimeter (physically or virtually) is considered a trusted user and needs no further validation. In the modern business world, this is certainly not the case. Threats can be present inside the perimeter and can even originate from validated users within the organization itself, whether those users are malicious or merely gullible. This is why the new security model currently gaining acceptance is called Zero Trust.

Zero Trust is a security architecture based on the principle of "never trust, always verify." Simply put, all requests, devices, and users must be authenticated and authorized every time they attempt to access a protected resource. Even on-premises employees who have already been authenticated while logging on to the network will continue to be verified whenever they access protected network resources.

The fundamental principles of a Zero Trust environment are as follows:

- **Verify explicitly** Identity verification is a continual process for every attempt to access a protected resource at every level, including identity, location, device condition, and data sensitivity.

- **Use least privileges**   The least privileges concept calls for users to start with no access to the network at all and then receive privileges for the resources they require to perform their jobs. Users are granted access only to the resources they need (called Just-Enough-Access, or JEA), and for only the length of time they need it (called Just-In-Time or JIT access).

- **Assume breach**   Every access request is assumed to be that of an attacker who has already penetrated the network and is attempting to move laterally within it to access other protected resources. By comparing current user activity with known attack behaviors, Microsoft 365 can contain genuine attacks by restricting them to a limited part of the network.

Due to outside events, the evolution of the modern enterprise network has been forced to accelerate in recent years. Because many more people work remotely and use personal devices to access company data, location-based security architectures like the traditional network perimeter are no longer practical. The Zero Trust architecture no longer relies solely on users' locations to determine their trustworthiness.

Compared to the perimeter model, which authenticates users only once and then trusts them until they log off, the Zero Trust model calls for users to be authenticated and authorized constantly as they move about within the network and access different resources.

Zero Trust is not an application, service, or Microsoft 365 feature. Rather, it is a philosophy administrators can apply to their network's security posture design. All organizations have to assess their security needs and the threats they face. Zero Trust focuses on six critical security areas, as shown in Figure 3-38, each of which administrators should consider in their planning.

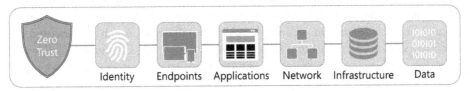

FIGURE 3-38 Six security criteria of the Zero Trust architecture

The six security criteria central to the Zero Trust security architecture are discussed in the following sections.

Identity

It's easy to build a perfectly secure house; just leave out all the windows and doors. Your possessions will be safe, but you won't be able to get at them. In the same way, it would be easy to build a perfectly secure network by establishing a formidable perimeter around the sensitive resources and not letting anyone at all through it. This would be pointless, of course. Workers need access to those sensitive resources, and identities are the basis of that access. In enterprise networking, an *identity* is a collection of attributes uniquely describing a *security principal*—a specific individual and the resources they can access.

For data to be secure, the most fundamental types of protection are as follows:

- **Authentication** Confirming that the individuals accessing the data really are who they claim to be
- **Authorization** Confirming that the individuals have been granted appropriate levels of access to the data they need

Securing network users' identities is the process of making these procedures as safe and impenetrable as they can be.

The identities of an organization's users are a prime target for cybercriminals because stealing a user's name and credentials enables the attacker to access everything the user knows about the company. News stories regularly report thefts of large blocks of identities from major companies, which endanger the companies' sensitive data and their employees' personal lives. For example,

- **For employees** The theft of the names, addresses, and Social Security numbers that are part of any organization's human resources records leaves users open to credit fraud and numerous other criminal intrusions.
- **For the organization** Identity theft can be catastrophic in many ways, resulting in data theft, damage, or destruction that can prevent the company from doing business and cost it vast amounts of money.

Attacks attempting to steal user identities can be extremely simple or incredibly sophisticated. A major security breach for an organization can begin with a single intruder that calls an unsuspecting employee on the phone, claims to be Jack Somebody from account maintenance in the IT department, and talks the employee into disclosing their login name and password. Once the intruder has one user's credentials, it becomes easier for them to gain others. This sort of lateral movement within the organization's security infrastructure can be a slow and methodical process for the intruder that eventually yields access to an identity with high-level network access, leading to a major security event. This is why administrators should take pains to protect all the organization's identities, not just the ones with elevated privileges.

In Microsoft 365, Microsoft Entra ID (formerly known as *Azure Active Directory*) allows administrators to create user identities, as shown in Figure 3-39, and performs the authentication and authorization processes. Entra ID is a cloud-based directory service alternative to *Active Directory Domain Services (AD DS)*, the on-premises directory service for Windows networks since 1999. The primary objective of creating Entra ID is to service identities and authenticate and authorize cloud-based resources. This is an essential element of administering Microsoft 365.

An Entra-based Active Directory implementation is necessary for Microsoft 365, even when an AD DS installation is already in place, because AD DS is limited to providing on-premises security functions. Users must access the on-premises network to sign in to their organization's AD DS domain controllers. The only way a remote user can authenticate to the company network using AD DS is to establish a connection to an on-premises server, such as a virtual private network (VPN) connection.

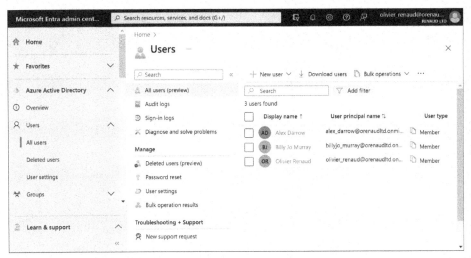

FIGURE 3-39 Azure Active Directory in Microsoft Entra admin center

Entra ID is strictly cloud-based and enables users working anywhere and with any device to sign in to the organization's Microsoft 365 network and gain access to its services. Another advantage of a cloud-based directory service is that administrators can create identities for people outside the organization, such as partners, clients, vendors, or consultants, who need occasional or restricted access to company resources.

> **NOTE USING ENTRA ID WITH AD DS**
>
> Entra ID and Active Directory Domain Services are not mutually exclusive. For an organization with an AD DS infrastructure in place, it is possible to deploy Entra ID and create hybrid identities by synchronizing the two directory services using a tool called Azure AD Connect. For more information, see "Describe identity and access management solutions of Microsoft 365" later in this chapter.

Creating an identity in Microsoft 365 is a simple matter of supplying name values in a form like the one from the Azure Active Directory section of the Microsoft Entra admin center shown in Figure 3-40. The Microsoft 365 admin center contains a similar form that also enables the identity creator to assign product licenses, such as a Microsoft 365 license, to the user. While creating identities is a quick and easy process, securing them can be considerably more complicated.

Identities apply to users and devices, services, applications, or any other network entities that access protected resources. In a Microsoft 365 environment based on Zero Trust, all identities are authenticated and authorized by Azure Active Directory each time they request access to a new protected resource. Depending on the sensitivity of the requested resource, this process can also include multifactor authentication and/or the application of conditional access and least privileges policies.

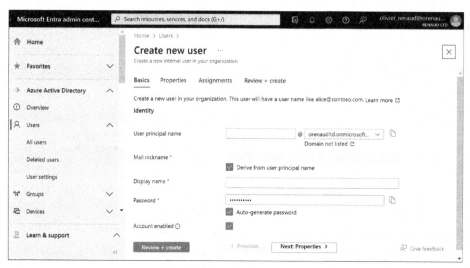

FIGURE 3-40 Creating an Entra ID user account

Endpoints

An *endpoint* is any device that connects to the network from any location, whether the device belongs to the company, an employee, or a guest user. Zero Trust calls for security policies to be applied and enforced uniformly on endpoints of all types by tools such as Microsoft Intune, regardless of the users' identities or the devices' locations. Devices have identities as well, which must be validated during every transaction.

If one of the two main innovations of Microsoft 365 is the use of cloud-based services, the other is the ability of users to access those services using many different types of devices that run on various computing platforms and work at any location with Internet access. As noted earlier, VPN connections have long enabled remote users to access the company network from home or while traveling, using a laptop or desktop. In subsequent years, there were a few mobile devices—nearly always supplied to users by the company—that were able to access a remote network but with limited utility, such as email only. Today, Microsoft 365 enables remote users working with desktops, laptops, tablets, and smartphones to access virtually any enterprise service or resource they could access using an on-premises workstation. However, the trick is to make this access possible while also making it secure.

Therefore, device security in Microsoft 365 must address two relatively new issues:

- Mobile devices that frequently operate outside of the organization's protective perimeter
- The increasing use of BYOD mobile devices that are not selected and owned by the company

Because mobile devices can access any and all sensitive information maintained by the enterprise, there must be some means to protect that information from the threats to which all mobile devices are subject, including loss, theft, and misuse.

ENDPOINT SECURITY

While administrators can still use traditional access-control measures, such as file system permissions, to regulate who can work with the organization's sensitive data, the Azure Active Directory and Microsoft Intune services are primarily responsible for ensuring that the devices used to access that data are safe. Microsoft 365 supports a large number of mobile computing platforms, including the following:

- Windows 10/11
- Android
- Android enterprise
- iOS
- macOS

The interaction between mobile devices and the Microsoft 365 cloud services is complex, as shown in Figure 3-41. However, as you can see in the diagram, Microsoft Intune functions as a clearing house for many of these services and uses Entra ID for authentication and authorization.

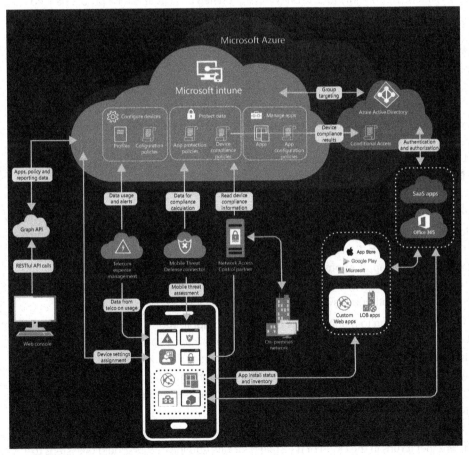

FIGURE 3-41 Microsoft Intune service architecture

Even when organizations have a BYOD (Bring Your Own Device) policy for their users' endpoints, those devices must be subject to some form of enterprise endpoint security. This is the primary function of Microsoft Intune, which is Microsoft 365's endpoint management tool; administrators use Intune to enroll users' devices and exercise some degree of management on them. By creating health compliance policies using Intune, enrolled devices can be checked for adherence to those policies before Entra ID authorizes them to access enterprise services and information. This is known as *conditional access*. Because Entra ID and Intune operate in the cloud, they can control access to the other Microsoft 365 services from any location.

MDM AND MAM

Securing devices begins with their enrollment using Microsoft Intune when administrators must decide what type of management they will impose on the device. *Mobile Device Management (MDM)* grants the organization nearly complete control over the device, requiring the user to comply with all the enterprise policies. MDM even allows an administrator to remotely wipe the entire device if lost or stolen, ensuring that any sensitive data is not compromised further.

MDM is intended primarily for use on company-owned devices; it can be problematic to some users who might not like the idea of granting the organization such comprehensive control over their personal property. For example, MDM policies might require smartphone users to sign on with a password or use another authentication mechanism every time they use their phones—which users might find inconvenient.

The alternative is *Mobile Application Management (MAM)*, which gives administrators control over specific applications running on a device but not the entire device itself. For example, a policy in MAM might require the users to sign in when using Microsoft Exchange to access their email, but MAM cannot require them to sign in every time they turn on their phones. MAM also enables administrators to wipe company data from the phone but only the data associated with the managed applications.

Applications

Applications are the doorways through which users access the data they need, some of which might be highly sensitive. Part of the Zero Trust initiative includes ensuring that the security capabilities built into applications are deployed, such as in-app permissions and other security-related configuration settings. Administrators should also monitor applications for unusual patterns of usage or other behavior.

However, in addition to managing the organization's applications, IT personnel have another concern. One of the biggest issues regarding application security is company employees' use of unauthorized applications—sometimes known as *shadow IT*. At one time, shadow IT mostly took the form of software on personal disks brought into the office and shared among users. Today, however, unauthorized applications are more likely to be installed from the cloud or run as a cloud service.

Any application running on a device that accesses sensitive network data is a potential threat, whether it runs in the cloud or is installed locally. Administrators should take steps to detect the presence of applications that might be dangerous to the network. The process of locating shadow IT applications is called cloud app discovery. Microsoft Defender for Cloud Apps (formerly known as Cloud App Security) is the Microsoft 365 tool that does this.

Microsoft Defender for Cloud Apps is a cloud-access security broker application that scans network resources to detect the cloud applications that users are running. It also can detect unauthorized Infrastructure as a Service (IaaS) and Platform as a Service (PaaS) products that might be in use. The objective here is to detect cloud applications that have not been approved by the IT department and could threaten enterprise network security.

Network

Networks provide users with access to the data they need, but they are also a major point of vulnerability. Dividing a network into segments with access controls at each hop can prevent attackers from moving laterally through the network once they gain access. Networks in a Zero Trust environment should also use end-to-end encryption to protect data while in transit.

The traditional network security model calls for constructing a perimeter surrounding the enterprise premises; this model has servers, workstations, and users inside the perimeter and firewalls protecting them by filtering out unwanted traffic. Remote users could connect to enterprise resources only by establishing a secured connection to a remote access server located in a screened subnet on the perimeter network. A Microsoft 365 installation places substantial and potentially vulnerable resources in the cloud outside the network perimeter, requiring a revised network security model.

Remote users might still connect to on-premises servers for some functions, but others will connect directly to cloud services. Also, the new emphasis on mobile devices means that users will be accessing enterprise resources from a wider variety of locations, including public locations, such as hotels and coffee shops, over which the company has no control.

The Microsoft 365 deployment process begins with an assessment and possibly redesigning the network to ensure that Internet bandwidth and proximity to the nearest Microsoft cloud endpoint are optimized. Also, adapting the security model to a network infrastructure that includes cloud services requires a shift in emphasis from perimeter security to endpoint security, in which the focus is placed more on securing the locations of the data and the locations of the users accessing the data than on the network medium connecting them.

> **NOTE MICROSOFT 365 DEPLOYMENT**
>
> For a more detailed examination of the Microsoft 365 deployment process, see "Describe endpoint modernization, management concepts, and deployment options in Microsoft 365" in Chapter 2, "Describe Microsoft 365 apps and services."

Endpoint network security means that the protective features built into the Microsoft 365 cloud services take on a more prominent role in the enterprise security strategy. Microsoft 365 administrators do not have control over the network traffic reaching the cloud services, nor can they erect a perimeter around every remote or mobile device that accesses the enterprise services. Therefore, instead of trying to block malicious traffic with firewalls, security comes from mechanisms such as multifactor authentication, Data Loss Prevention, and Cloud App Security.

This does not mean the networks cease to be vulnerable or can be left unprotected. Administrators must be wary of the threats that have always afflicted networks, including unauthorized packet captures, unprotected Wi-Fi networks, and rogue access points. For example, if an enterprise allows both managed and unmanaged devices to access company resources—regardless of the policies they use to control that access—it is still a good idea to keep the managed devices on a separate wireless network from the unmanaged ones. Also, appropriate security and encryption protocols must still protect internal Wi-Fi networks, and their administrative passwords and preshared keys must be modified regularly.

Infrastructure

Infrastructure is an inclusive term encompassing all of a network's hardware and software, both physical and virtual, on premises and in the cloud, as well as the facilities and services that house and protect them. The infrastructure of a typical enterprise network presents many potential attack vectors, and administrators should make every attempt to block them. IT personnel can keep software products updated and use infrastructure monitoring technologies that detect unusual and problematic behavior, such as Security Information Event Management (SEIM) and Security Orchestration, Automation, and Response (SOAR).

Data

All the security functions applying to the other five Zero Trust criteria essentially protect the organization's data—its most valuable resource. Administrators must consider the data's security in all possible states: in-motion, at-rest, and in-use. Depending on the nature and sensitivity of the data, each state might require different security measures. Microsoft 365 supports tools that can label, classify, and encrypt data to protect it in all states, such as Data Loss Prevention (DLP) and Azure Information Protection (AIP).

The traditional method for securing documents is to apply access control permissions to them. Permissions take the form of access control lists that are stored as attributes of individual files and folders. An *access control list (ACL)* consists of multiple *access control entries (ACEs)*, each of which specifies a security principal, such as a user or group, and the permissions that grant the principal a degree of access to the file or folder.

Permissions have been around for decades, enabling users and administrators to restrict access to particular documents, but they must be applied manually and are difficult to manage for a large document collection. Someone also must keep track of which documents contain sensitive information that requires additional protection.

Therefore, Microsoft 365 includes security mechanisms, such as Azure Information Protection (AIP) and Data Loss Prevention (DLP), which can protect documents in other ways. The process of identifying documents containing sensitive data and securing them consists of the following four steps:

- **Discovery** The process of locating documents that contain sensitive information, either by automatic detection based on established data patterns or by prompting users to apply classification labels

- **Classification** The application of labels to documents containing sensitive information, indicating what types of protection should be applied to them

- **Protection** The application of specific security mechanisms to documents based on the classification labels that have been applied to them

- **Monitoring** The process of tracking document access trends, activities, and events and taking action when necessary

The process of discovering documents containing sensitive information is highly dependent on three factors:

- The nature of the organization

- The type of business in which the organization is engaged

- The policies or regulations with which the organization must comply

Tools like Data Loss Prevention have preconfigured sensitive information types that enable the automated discovery of documents that contain common data patterns, such as credit card and Social Security numbers. Also, administrators can create customized sensitive information types that can discover documents containing specific industry-based keywords and data patterns.

Like a physical label, the sensitivity labels applied by tools like AIP and DLP can warn users that a document contains sensitive information and recommend that users take certain actions. The labels persist with the documents as they travel to different systems and are opened in other applications—even on other computing platforms. However, AIP and DLP labels can also be configured to apply various types of protection, like those shown in Figure 3-42. The labels can

- Cause documents to be encrypted—at rest and in transit

- Be limited to use with specific applications

- Be restricted to specific users or devices

- Be configured to expire

- Be deleted after a specified lifespan

Once the document classification and protection phases are complete, administrators are still responsible for monitoring the reports and alerts generated by the security tools. For example, repeated attempts to access or share protected documents by the same user or device can indicate the presence of a security breach, even if the attempts fail. The monitoring process should also include remediation so that an administrator who notices anomalous behavior can intervene by revoking document access privileges or quarantining files.

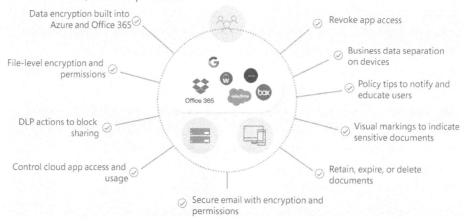

Protect sensitive information across devices, cloud services, and on-premises

Data encryption built into Azure and Office 365

File-level encryption and permissions

DLP actions to block sharing

Control cloud app access and usage

Secure email with encryption and permissions

Revoke app access

Business data separation on devices

Policy tips to notify and educate users

Visual markings to indicate sensitive documents

Retain, expire, or delete documents

FIGURE 3-42 Microsoft 365 document protection mechanisms

Describe Microsoft Granular Delegated Admin Privileges (GDAP) principles

One of the recurrent problems for partners and other service providers supporting Microsoft 365 customers is the allocation of access permissions that enable the partner to work on the customer's systems and services on their behalf. A feature called *delegated administration privileges (DAP)* has long made that possible, but DAP grants the partner full Global Admin privileges over the customer's tenancy.

Many customers might be hesitant to grant those privileges, and rightly so; if the partner's systems become compromised, then the customer could also be compromised—as could all the partner's other customers. Also, when the partner has multiple people working on a customer's network, all using the same Administrator account, it can become difficult to maintain accountability for the changes made. These are vulnerabilities that can be a dealbreaker for a partner/customer relationship.

Granular delegated admin permissions (GDAP) is a revision of DAP that enables partners to assign more specific Entra ID permissions to their users, fulfilling the least-privilege requirement of the Zero Trust initiative. Partner personnel managing the customer's Azure subscriptions—such as creating and configuring users—are made members of an Admin Agent security group that grants them the privileges they need, as shown in Figure 3-43.

Follow these steps to assign GDAP privileges:

1. The partner first requests a relationship with the customer in the Microsoft Partner Center, which specifies a time limit for the privileges to be granted (with a two-year maximum) and the Entra ID roles the partner should be assigned.

2. The Partner Center generates an email containing the request and sends it to the customer.

3. Once the customer approves the request, the partner can use the **Admin Relation-ships** page in the Partner Center to create security groups and assign Entra ID roles to them.

In addition to entering into a different type of partner/customer relationship, GDAP also makes it easier for either party to terminate that relationship without manually denying privileges.

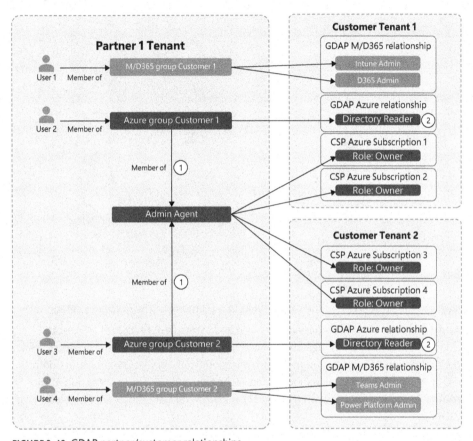

FIGURE 3-43 GDAP partner/customer relationships

Describe Microsoft Purview and compliance solutions such as insider risk, auditing, and eDiscovery

For many IT professionals, the prospect of implementing vital services and storing important company information in the cloud is met with significant trepidation. They might have an instinctive reluctance to trust an IT infrastructure not implemented on computers the company owns and housed in their own datacenters. They might also hesitate to give up their control over those computers and their resources. Also, there might be statutes and standards to which the IT infrastructure must comply, whether because of contracted terms, company policies, or governmental requirements.

Service Trust Portal

Microsoft is aware of these trust issues and has created a central storehouse called the Service Trust Portal (STP) for information about them. STP is a website, shown in Figure 3-43, available to everyone at *http://aka.ms/stp*, although some parts of the site are restricted to registered users of Microsoft 365 and other products. See Figure 3-44.

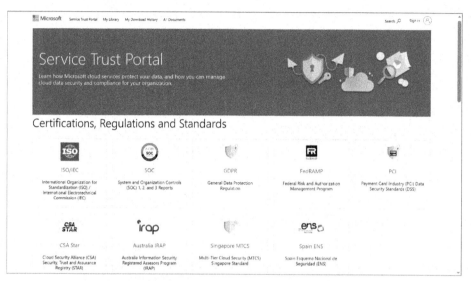

FIGURE 3-44 The Microsoft Service Trust Portal website

Among the many resources on the site are links to documents in the following categories:

- **Audit Reports**   Provide independent audit and assessment reports of Microsoft's cloud services, evaluating their compliance with standards such as those published by the International Organization for Standardization (ISO), Service Organization Controls (SOC), National Institute of Standards and Technology (NIST), Federal Risk and Authorization Management Program (FedRAMP), and General Data Protection Regulation (GDPR)

- **Documents & Resources**   Consist of a large library of documents, including white papers, FAQs, compliance guides, penetration test reports, Azure security and compliance blueprints, and other data protection resources

- **Compliance Manager**   Assesses and scores an organization's regulatory compliance based on multiple published standards

- **Industries & Regions**   Provide documents containing compliance information for specific industries—such as education, financial services, government, health care, manufacturing, and retail—and specific countries, including Australia, Czech Republic, Germany, Poland, Romania, Spain, and the United Kingdom

- **Trust Center** Links to the Trust Center site, which provides documentation on how Microsoft supports security, privacy, compliance, and transparency in its cloud services

- **Resources** Provide information about Microsoft's global datacenters, security and compliance information for Microsoft 365, and a FAQ list for the Service Trust Portal

- **My Library** Enables users to pin documents from the site onto a separate user page for quick reference later

Microsoft Purview

Microsoft Purview is an umbrella brand that includes Microsoft's data risk, compliance, and governance tools, some of which were, at one time, separate products. For example, Azure Purview and the Microsoft 365 Compliance Manager are now available through the Microsoft Purview portal, shown in Figure 3-45.

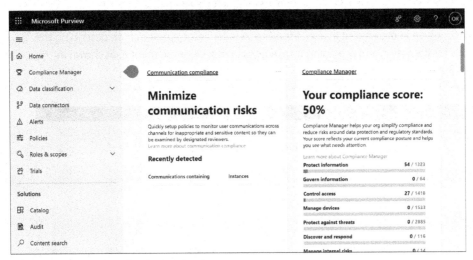

FIGURE 3-45 The Microsoft Purview portal

Compliance Manager

Compliance Manager—now incorporated into the Microsoft Purview portal—is a risk assessment tool that enables an organization to track and record its activities to achieve compliance with specific certification standards. An assessment of an organization's compliance posture is based on the capabilities of the Microsoft 365 cloud services and how the organization uses them, compared to an existing standard, regulation, or law.

The home page for the **Compliance Manager** tool in the **Purview** portal contains an **Overview** tab that displays the general compliance score for the network and a list of key improvement actions, along with their status, Impact values, and completion states, as shown in Figure 3-46.

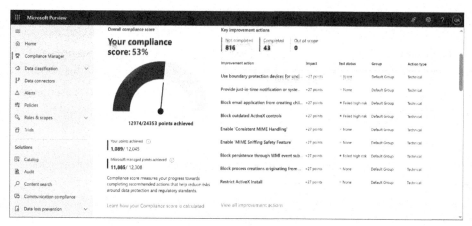

FIGURE 3-46 The Compliance Manager page in the Microsoft Purview portal

Selecting an improvement action displays a detailed information screen describing the reasons for the action and providing instructions on how to implement it, as shown in Figure 3-47.

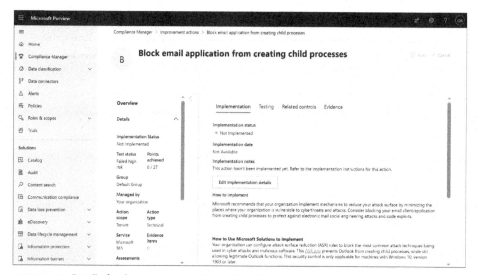

FIGURE 3-47 Detail of an improvement action in Compliance Manager in the Microsoft Purview portal

Enterprise networks can be subject to a wide variety of compliance standards, and Compliance Manager includes a long list of regulations, shown in Figure 3-48. Administrators can select a particular standard and configure Compliance Manager to assess the network and determine to what degree it is compliant with the selected standard.

FIGURE 3-48 The Regulations tab in Compliance Manager in the Microsoft Purview portal

Auditing

Microsoft Purview includes auditing capabilities that log operations for many Microsoft 365 applications and services. Administrators can search the audit log directly from the Microsoft Purview portal, providing detailed information that can be useful during security, compliance, and legal investigations.

Microsoft Purview can provide two levels of audit logging, as follows:

- **Audit (Standard)**   Standard auditing is enabled by default in Microsoft Purview, with logs that retain event entries for 90 days before deletion. Administrators can search the log from the **Audit** page in the Microsoft Purview portal, as shown in Figure 3-49, or by using the Search-UnifiedAuditLog cmdlet in Windows PowerShell.

- **Audit (Premium)**   Premium auditing stores Active Directory, SharePoint, Exchange, and OneDrive events for a full year, while retaining all other log entries for the standard 90 days. Administrators can also create their own log retention policies that extend the storage of logged events based on specific criteria, such as the service that generated the log entry. Audit (Premium) also provides intelligent insights into the logged information, making it more useful for investigations of security incidents.

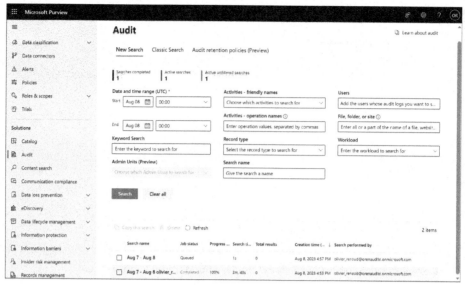

FIGURE 3-49 The Audit page in the Microsoft Purview portal

eDiscovery

In addition to its auditing capabilities, Microsoft Purview includes a feature called eDiscovery, which is a tool for locating and packaging digital information for use as evidence in internal investigations, compliance efforts, and legal cases. eDiscovery can perform comprehensive searches across a wide range of Microsoft 365 data sources, as shown in Figure 3-50, including Exchange Online, SharePoint, Microsoft Teams, OneDrive, Microsoft 365 Groups, and Viva Engage. The tool can then export the search information and place a legal hold on the sources as needed.

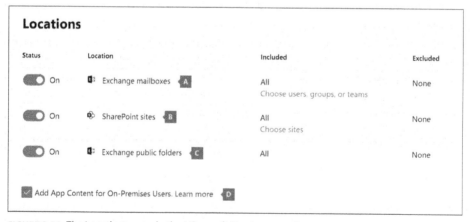

FIGURE 3-50 The Locations page in the Microsoft Purview portal

eDiscovery is available in three versions, depending on the Microsoft 365 subscription level, as follows:

- **Content Search**   Provides keyword search and export capabilities for Microsoft 365 data sources
- **eDiscovery (Standard)**   Provides the same search and export capabilities as the Content Search option, plus the ability to create individual cases and assign custodians to them with exclusive access
- **eDiscovery (Premium)**   Provides all the capabilities of eDiscovery (Standard), plus a complete end-to-end workflow and intelligent analytics that enable investigators to focus on the most relevant content

Describe how Microsoft supports data residency to ensure regulatory compliance

When people speak of storing data in the cloud, the implication is that the cloud is a single, unified resource on the Internet, which can store virtually unlimited amounts of data. This is not the case, however. Physically, the cloud is a series of datacenters in diverse locations. Different service providers have varying amounts of resources in various locations, but for Microsoft and the other large service providers, the cloud takes the form of hundreds of datacenters scattered around the planet.

Where a tenant's data is located in the Microsoft cloud can be a critical factor, not only in the network's performance of the network but also in the tenant's compliance with any regulatory standards to which it is subject. From a performance standpoint, it is preferable for a tenant's cloud data to be stored in a facility that provides the best possible performance. In some cases, the best location for a tenant's data might simply be the nearest datacenter, but this is not always the case. Not all datacenters provide the same level of performance, so it might be possible for the best performance to be realized from a more distant facility.

Some tenants must comply with regulations regarding where and how they store their data, which can easily be a more critical factor in their data residency. Government contracts, educational institutions, and even some commercial client agreements might stipulate that data be stored in a certain place and way.

For example, U.S. government contracts might specify that data must be stored in a United States facility—or at least in a facility not located in a nation considered to be hostile. Some contracts might even forbid the use of cloud storage entirely and require a company to maintain its data in an on-premises datacenter.

For these reasons, it can be important for IT administrators to understand exactly where their data is going; "the cloud," in these cases, is not a sufficiently detailed location.

When an organization creates a new tenant in the Microsoft Entra portal, it must select a location, as shown in Figure 3-51. Entra will create the tenancy in a datacenter located in the selected country. This location cannot be changed once the tenancy is created.

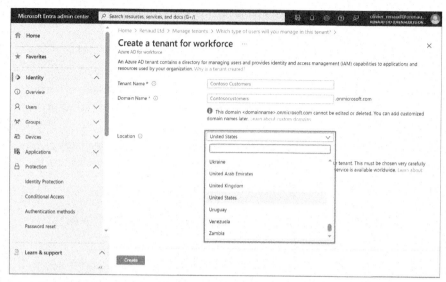

FIGURE 3-51 Selecting a location for a new tenancy in the Microsoft Entra admin center

For Microsoft tenants in the United States and other major countries, many datacenters support all of the Microsoft cloud services. However, not every country has datacenters that support all Microsoft 365 services. Exchange Online, SharePoint, and Microsoft Teams are available virtually everywhere. However, when a particular service is unavailable in a selected location, Microsoft will choose the nearest geographical location that supports it.

To see exactly where a tenant's data is located for each Microsoft service, they can look at the Microsoft 365 admin center on the **Org Settings** page, under **Organization Profile > Data Location**, as shown in Figure 3-52.

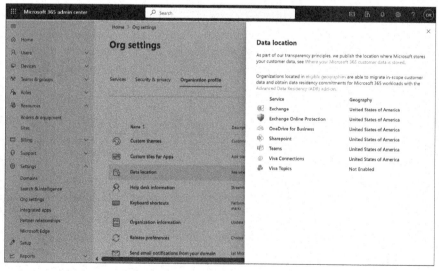

FIGURE 3-52 The Data location screen in the Microsoft 365 admin center

Describe information protection features such as sensitivity labels and data loss prevention

Microsoft 365 has various features that contribute to protecting the organization's data, many of which have already been mentioned in this and the previous chapters. These features are discussed in the following sections.

Microsoft Entra ID (Azure Active Directory Premium)

Active Directory (AD) is a directory service that has been a part of the Windows Server product since the Windows 2000 Server release. A directory service is a database of objects, including users and computers, that provides authentication and authorization services for network resources. Authentication and authorization are essentially the front gates of information protection, providing basic, password-based security.

Microsoft Entra ID (formerly known as *Azure Active Directory or Azure AD)* is a cloud-based AD equivalent that can provide Microsoft 365 users with single-sign-on capability that enables them to access all their SaaS applications and services, including Microsoft 365 and any third-party products that administrators have integrated into their environment, from any device, at any location.

Entra ID provides a Microsoft 365 deployment with identity and access management services that extend beyond the on-premises network into the cloud. Entra ID enhances the security of the Microsoft 365 environment by supporting multifactor authentication, which requires users to verify their identities in two or more ways, such as with a password and a fingerprint or some other biometric factor.

Entra ID can also provide authentication and authorization services for internal resources, such as on-premises applications and services. For organizations with an existing Windows Server–based AD infrastructure, Entra ID can connect to internal domain controllers to create a hybrid directory service solution that shares the advantages of both implementations.

Microsoft Intune

As noted elsewhere, *Microsoft Intune* is a cloud-based device and application management tool that is integrated with the authentication and authorization functions provided by Entra ID. While administrators can use Intune to manage their in-house computers and applications, the primary innovation of the product is its ability to manage BYOD, or user-owned, devices, such as smartphones, tablets, and laptops, and enable them to access the organization's protected services, applications, and data securely.

Intune can manage devices running any major mobile operating system, including Android, iOS, MacOS, and Windows. Using Intune, even operating systems that cannot join an Active Directory domain can access protected resources. Intune uses the mobile operating system's protocols and APIs to communicate, building an inventory of devices that can access company applications and data.

Administrators can use Intune to create standards for configuring security settings that a device must meet before accessing protected resources. For example, an administrator can require that a device use a particular authentication type or specify that only certain applications can access company data. Intune can even ensure that sensitive data is removed from a device when an app shuts down. This type of control enables Microsoft 365 to maintain its resources' security without administrators taking complete control over user-owned devices.

Azure Information Protection

Azure Information Protection (AIP) is a system that enables users and administrators to apply labels to documents and emails that classify the information they contain. The labels can be configured to specify how applications treat the information and, optionally, take steps to protect it.

AIP can apply labels to specific documents or follow rules created by administrators to identify sensitive data in any document. For example, an administrator can create a rule that identifies data patterns associated with credit card or Social Security numbers in a Word document as a user creates it. When the user attempts to save the document, AIP warns the user to apply the label, as shown in Figure 3-53.

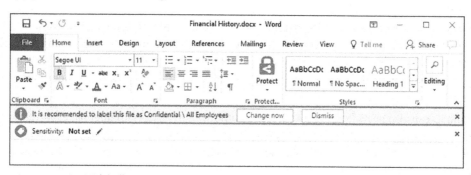

FIGURE 3-53 An AIP labeling recommendation in a Word document

Administrators can also configure AIP labels to be visible in the documents they are applied to. When a user agrees to classify a document as sensitive, the application can apply a watermark or other visual indicator, which will persist in the document wherever it is stored.

AIP can also use *Azure Rights Management (Azure RMS)* to protect documents or emails labeled as sensitive. Based on the rules created by administrators, documents labeled by AIP can be protected using encryption, identity restrictions, authorization policies, and other methods. For example, when an email message contains sensitive data, AIP can control the email client application, preventing users from clicking the **Reply All** or **Forward** button. Similarly, AIP can restrict Microsoft 365 documents to nonprinting or read-only status.

Microsoft Advanced Threat Analytics

Advanced Threat Analytics (ATA) is an on-premises solution that uses information gathered from a wide variety of enterprise sources to anticipate, detect, and react to security threats and attacks. ATA receives log and event information from Windows systems and also captures network traffic generated by security-related protocols, such as Kerberos and NTLM. This traffic provides ATA with information about user authentication and authorization patterns.

Using this gathered information, ATA builds up profiles of applications, services, and users. By examining the normal behavior of these entities, ATA can detect anomalous behavior when it occurs and ascertain whether that behavior is suspicious based on known attack patterns. When it suspects or detects a security breach, ATA displays an alert in the ATA dashboard, such as the one shown in Figure 3-54.

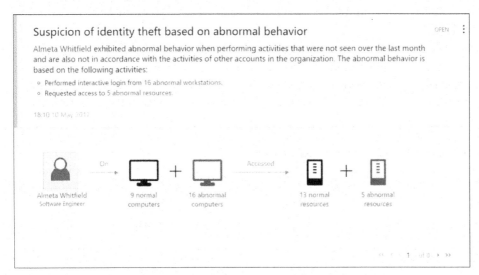

FIGURE 3-54 A Microsoft Advanced Threat Analytics alert to abnormal behavior

ATA is one of several Microsoft 365 technologies that uses advanced intelligence to anticipate user needs before they occur. In this case, the need is for intervention, whether automated or human, in a potentially dangerous security situation.

Microsoft Defender for Cloud Apps

Microsoft's research has determined that many of the hundreds of cloud applications that large enterprises use today are unknown to the IT department and therefore are unmanaged by them. Microsoft has started calling these clandestine cloud apps shadow IT, and they obviously present a security hazard.

Microsoft Defender for Cloud Apps (formerly called Cloud App Security) is a cloud access security broker (CASB) product that enables Microsoft 365 administrators to scan their networks for the cloud apps that users are accessing, assess their security vulnerability, and continuously manage them.

Defender for Cloud Apps examines traffic logs and firewall and proxy information to discover the cloud apps in use. After determining whether the apps are dangerous to data, identities, or other resources, administrators can sanction or unsanction specific apps to allow or prevent user access to them. For apps administrators have sanctioned, Defender uses their own APIs to connect to them and monitor user activity.

Microsoft Defender for Identity

As with the Microsoft Defender Advanced Threat Protection feature included in Windows 10, Microsoft Azure has its own ATP, as do Office 365, Exchange Online, SharePoint, Microsoft Teams, and OneDrive. However, Azure Advanced Threat Protection is now known as Microsoft Defender for Identity. Each ATP engine is designed to use machine intelligence to prevent, detect, and respond to the security threats unique to its environment. In Azure, the primary vulnerability is the identities stored in Entra ID (Azure Active Directory), so the Azure ATP engine looks for anomalous user behavior and compares it to standardized patterns used by attackers.

Azure Information Protection is included in all the Microsoft 365 plans, but it is also available with other Microsoft products in a free version with limited functionality and as a separate subscription in two plans of its own, called Premium P1 and Premium P2. Each subscription level adds features, as shown in Table 3-4, and includes all the features of the lower subscription levels.

TABLE 3-4 Azure Information Protection subscriptions

Plan	Included with	Description
Free	No purchase necessary	Allows consumption of AIP-protected content by users with accounts that are not associated with Azure identities
Azure Information Protection for Office 365	Office 365 Enterprise E3 and above	Provides protection for Office 365 services using custom templates and supporting Office 365 Message Encryption
Azure Information Protection Premium P1	Microsoft 365 Business Microsoft 365 Enterprise E3 Microsoft Enterprise Mobility + Security E3	Provides the ability to use on-premises connectors, track and revoke documents, and manually classify and label documents
Azure Information Protection Premium P2	Microsoft 365 Enterprise E5 Microsoft Enterprise Mobility + Security E5	Provides support for policy-based rules and automated classification, labeling, and protection of documents

Describe the capabilities and benefits of Microsoft Priva

As mentioned frequently in this book, an organization's data is its most valuable commodity, and keeping that data secure is one of the primary functions of Microsoft 365. That company data frequently includes confidential information, however, and it is the responsibility of the IT department not only to keep the data secure but also to maintain its privacy.

Microsoft Priva is a tool that helps administrators establish and maintain the privacy of the company's data in light of the many regulatory laws about data privacy now in place in the U.S. and other countries. Priva is not concerned with protecting data against outside attacks; other Microsoft 365 tools handle that. Regarding data privacy, Priva is concerned mainly with how the organization handles its sensitive data internally.

Microsoft Priva consists of two privacy solutions, as follows:

■ **Priva Privacy Risk Management** Uses built-in or custom policy templates to identify data that is subject to privacy risks, generates alerts when data conforming to a policy is detected, and provides administrators with the ability to investigate and remediate the alerts

■ **Priva Subject Rights Requests** Simplifies and automates the process of responding to legally submitted data subject requests by prioritizing data, implementing workflows, and generating reports

The first task undertaken by Priva is to identify the personal data stored by the company that is at risk. The Priva administration interface is included in the **Microsoft Purview** portal under the **Privacy Management** menu. The **Overview** dashboard, shown in Figure 3-55, specifies the number of items containing personal data and the number of outstanding rights requests. The **Overview** dashboard also displays key insights into the discovered personal data and a list of the current action policy alerts.

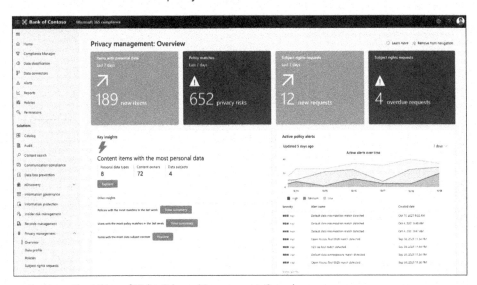

FIGURE 3-55 The Microsoft Priva Privacy Management: Overview page

Priva risk management

Once Priva has identified the data stored by an organization, administrators can select a template to create a policy that will govern the data handling. Priva includes templates to address the following privacy risks:

■ **Data overexposure** Data that is publicly available, shared too widely within the organization, or shared with individuals outside the organization. Prevalence of this type of risk should compel administrators to educate users about data-sharing policies.

■ **Data transfers** Creates policies that detect when data is transferred in an unsafe manner, as determined by the administrator. Depending on the type and sensitivity of the data, administrators can limit unencrypted transfers between departments, geographic locations, or individuals outside of the organization.

- **Data minimization** Potentially sensitive data that has been stored unused for a long period of time can present unnecessary risks. This template can create policies that identify such data and notify its owners to use or delete it.

The **Policies** page in the Microsoft Purview portal allows administrators to create a new data transfers policy, as shown in Figure 3-56, or create a new custom policy from scratch.

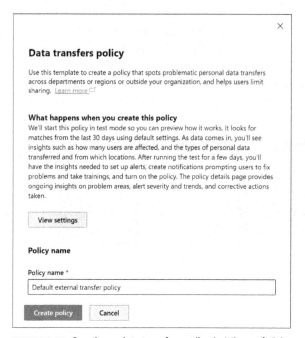

FIGURE 3-56 Creating a data transfers policy in Microsoft Priva

Priva rights requests

In recent years, there has been legislation passed in many countries providing citizens with the right to request that organizations disclose any personal information about them that they possess. These might seem like simple requests to the requestor, but for an organization that maintains a large data store, locating all of the requested information concerning a particular individual can be a difficult and time-consuming task.

Microsoft Priva aids in this process by evaluating the organization's data and prioritizing the content for review as soon as an administrator creates a new rights request. The **Subject Rights Requests** overview page, shown in Figure 3-57, lists the currently in-progress requests and quantifies them by **Top Request Types** and **Status**.

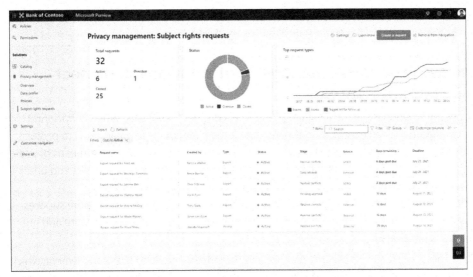

FIGURE 3-57 The Microsoft Priva Privacy Management: Subject Rights Requests page

The process by which data is evaluated and selected for inclusion in the request can be a complicated one that might involve stakeholders throughout the organization. To facilitate this process, Priva creates a Microsoft Teams channel for each request in which the personnel involved can discuss the matter.

For more information about a specific request, administrators can select an entry from the list and open a details page showing the progress of that request, as shown in Figure 3-58.

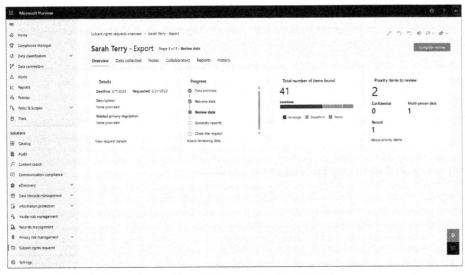

FIGURE 3-58 The detail page for a subject rights request in Microsoft Priva

After evaluating and selecting the data to be included in the request, Priva generates reports for the subject of the request and the company's records.

Describe insider risk management solutions to protect against internal threats

Typically, information is the most valuable resource a business possesses. When considering security measures for an enterprise network, the ultimate end of these measures is to protect the information. Protection against unauthorized users or devices is really just a means of protecting the data that those users can access and store on those devices. Computers and other hardware devices have monetary value, but the physical security measures of a datacenter—for example, the electronic door locks, the security guards, and the fire suppression systems—are there primarily to protect the information stored on the hardware and not so much the hardware itself.

The process of creating a security plan for an enterprise is known as *risk management*, which is the act of identifying the assets that need protection, determining the potential dangers to those assets, assessing the impact of those dangers to the organization, and implementing protective measures appropriate to the assets and the threats. Microsoft 365 includes a large collection of tools that can help with all phases of this process. The security technologies in Microsoft 365 are divided into four areas, as follows:

- Security management
- Identity-based protection
- Information protection
- Threat protection

The technologies in each of these areas are shown in Figure 3-59. An organization seeking to secure its enterprise network is unlikely to need all these technologies. Consider these to be a toolkit from which administrators can select the right tool for each task. Microsoft's Core Services and Engineering Operations (CSEO) group has chosen the technologies protruding from the wheel shown in the figure.

Therefore, the first step of the risk management plan is to identify the types of information the organization possesses and determine the value of each information type to the business.

Identifying and valuing information assets

Companies often generate vast amounts of data with varying levels of sensitivity. It is usually not practical for an organization to implement the ultimate level of security over its data, so it is necessary to classify the information according to its function and value. Therefore, the risk management process should begin with an inventory of the organization's information assets and a determination of each asset's value to the company, considering its need for confidentiality, integrity, and availability. The factors to consider when compiling such an inventory are shown in Table 3-5.

Microsoft 365 technologies and their associated security areas

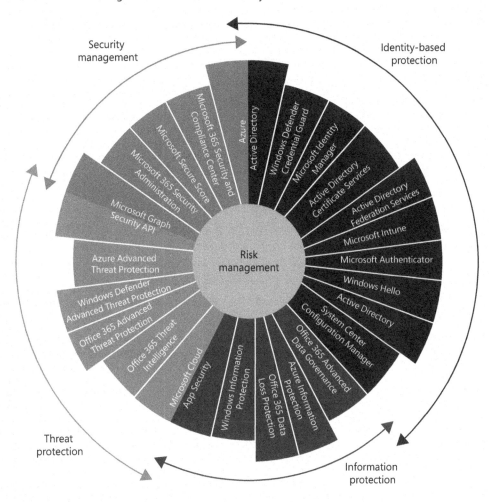

FIGURE 3-59 Microsoft 365 security technologies used by the Microsoft CSEO group

TABLE 3-5 **RISK FACTORS FOR ASSET INVENTORY**

Risk factor	Description	Example
Confidentiality	Access and disclosure of sensitive information by unauthorized persons	What if users' passwords or Social Security numbers were stolen?
Integrity	Modification or damage of sensitive information by unauthorized persons	What if the company's payroll information or product designs were changed?
Availability	Prevention of access to sensitive information by authorized users	What if the company's client list or website was rendered inaccessible?

The definitions used for information types will be specific to the nature of the business and their value to the business. For example, an attack that renders the site unavailable for several days would be inconvenient for a company that uses its website to provide customer support information. For a company that sells its products exclusively on the web, however, the unavailability of its e-commerce website for several days could be economically disastrous.

For a large enterprise, this type of asset inventory is typically not the exclusive province of the IT department. It will likely require the involvement of personnel from various departments and at various levels of the organization, including management, legal, accounting, and even clients and partners outside the company.

The value of an information resource might not necessarily be expressed in monetary terms. A data threat might result in lost productivity, the creation of additional work to restore or re-create the data, fines or penalties to the government or regulating agencies, or even more intangible effects, such as bad public relations or lost customer confidence.

The best practice to quantify the inventoried assets is to create a graduated scale considering all the risk factors particular to the business. A general numerical scale from 1 to 3 or a risk gradation of low, medium, or high would work, with a larger number of grades if the security measures the administrators choose to implement warrant it.

The value or sensitivity of a data asset will determine the nature of the security mechanisms administrators use to protect it. Some data types might be subject to legal or contractual compliance specifications, which impose strict limits on where and how they are stored and who can access them. The security requirements for this most sensitive data might define the highest value on the risk scale, which can call for extreme security measures such as on-premises storage in a secured datacenter, data encryption and redundancy, and highly restrictive access permissions.

Other types of sensitive data might not even be subject to broadly categorical security mechanisms, such as those applied to file folders or specific file types. Microsoft 365 includes the Azure Information Protection (AIP) tool that can apply labels to documents containing sensitive information. Administrators can configure the labels to trigger various types of security, such as watermarks, encryption, and limited access. While users and administrators can manually apply the labels to documents, AIP can also detect sensitive information in documents and automatically apply labels to them. For example, when a user creates a Word document, administrators can configure AIP to detect values that appear to be credit card numbers, as shown in Figure 3-60, and apply a label to the file that calls for a specified degree of protection.

Data that does not greatly threaten confidentiality, integrity, and availability is at the low end of the risk scale. This data will require some protection, but the security at the low end of the scale might be limited just to file system access permissions.

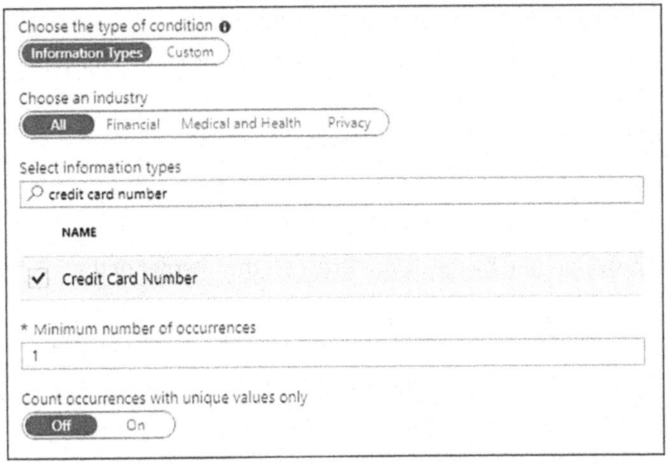

FIGURE 3-60 AIP configuration

Inventorying hardware

Once the data sensitivity and value have been assessed, the next step of the risk-management plan design process is to consider the technology used to store, access, transmit, and process that data. This includes the servers or cloud services where the data is stored when at rest, the client systems and devices used to access the data, the network components that carry the data between the various systems, and the applications that process the data.

In the same way that the data itself is inventoried in the previous phase, there should be an inventory of all the hardware involved in storing the data. This information can be used to locate the precise source of a security breach and to help prevent unauthorized devices from accessing secured company resources.

The primary storage locations for all sensitive company information should be servers in a secured environment, such as a datacenter or server closet, or a cloud service, which should have security policies detailed in the service contract. However, compiling an inventory of client systems and devices can be significantly more complicated. Workstations located at the enterprise sites are presumably already inventoried, but home computers and employees' mobile devices, such as smartphones and tablets, need to be considered. Also, computers and devices belonging to people outside the organization, such as partners, consultants, temporary workers, and customers, need to be considered.

Administrators should document every device that comes into contact with company data. The inventory should include information such as the following:

- **Make** The manufacturer of the device
- **Model** The manufacturer's model name and number for the device
- **Serial number** The manufacturer's serial number for the device
- **Owner** The person or organization that is the owner of the device

- **User**   The person or persons who use the device to access company data
- **Location**   The place where the device is installed or, if mobile, the location of the person responsible for it
- **Service ID**   The owner organization's assigned ID number, if applicable
- **Operating system**   The operating system installed on the device
- **OS version**   The version and build of the operating system running on the device
- **Network provider**   The provider used by the device to access the Internet or the company network
- **Applications**   The applications on the device that are used to access company data
- **Information used**   The specific types of company data that the device can access

For workstations owned by the organization, this information is typically compiled during the system's deployment process and can probably be imported into the inventory. The information-gathering process should be required for systems and devices owned by employees before any access to sensitive company data is permitted.

Verifying inventory information can be difficult for frequent travelers or home computer users, but in the modern management model implemented by Microsoft 365, tight control of hardware devices is an essential element of enterprise security. For devices owned by people who are not employees of the organization, such as customers, the diplomatic aspects of enforcing these policies can be even more difficult. Still, administrators might be able to mitigate them by creating a risk level that provides these users with access only to a limited class of information that is not extremely sensitive.

In addition to the systems and devices that access company data, networking technology can also present an element of risk. The most obvious potential attack vector is wireless network devices, which are vulnerable to outside attacks in a variety of ways. Microsoft 365 includes Microsoft Intune, which enables administrators to create Wi-Fi network profiles that contain preshared keys and other security measures that prevent unauthorized devices from connecting to a company wireless network. Some extremely sensitive data types require special handling, even for wired networks, such as compliance regulations requiring network cables to be enclosed in sealed conduits to protect against wiretapping. Hardware-based security devices, such as firewalls, should also be included in the inventory.

When hardware that accesses sensitive information is compromised, the data is also presumed to be compromised. Administrators can use the hardware inventory to ensure that the operating systems and applications on the devices are updated with security patches and that antimalware and other security tools are updated. Administrators can also use Microsoft 365 tools to create compliance policies so that devices cannot access network resources unless they meet specific requirements, including up-to-date software.

The hardware security elements of a risk management plan can go beyond the capabilities of the tools in Microsoft 365. Protecting the hardware can include other mechanisms, including the following:

- **Physical security** Software-based security measures cannot fully protect the data stored on a computer if intruders have physical access to the machine. Even if the intruders can't compromise the data, they can always destroy it, which can be just as damaging to the organization. Physical measures, even those as simple as a locked door, are basic elements of any risk management plan. For mobile devices, which are always vulnerable to loss or theft, administrators can use Microsoft Intune mobile device management to implement the ultimate hardware solution: remotely erasing the data from the device.

- **High availability** In addition to malicious or criminal intrusion, hardware devices are also liable to failures from wear and tear or destruction from natural disasters, such as fires, earthquakes, and extreme weather. High-availability measures, such as RAID arrays, redundant servers, and duplicate datacenters, can preserve data against loss and ensure that the data remains available to users. For Microsoft 365 data stored in the cloud, the Microsoft Global Network maintains datacenters worldwide, as shown in Figure 3-61, providing subscribers with a 99.9 percent availability rate.

- **Disaster recovery** Data backups and cloud synchronization can enable sensitive data to be restored, even after an attack or a disaster renders the original data or the hardware on which it is stored unusable.

FIGURE 3-61 Microsoft Global Network datacenter locations

Classifying users

The third element of the digital estate that must be considered when creating a risk management plan is the people who actually access the data. Whether deliberately or inadvertently, users are a constant vulnerability—if not an actual threat—to the organization's data. After quantifying the organization's information assets and their value and inventorying the hardware used to store, access, transmit, and process the information, the next step is to list the people with access to the information.

The people with access to the organization's information certainly include employees authorized to create, view, and modify the data. However, a risk management team must also consider the possibility of other individuals accessing the data. Anyone with physical access to computers on which data is stored or from which it is accessible is a potential threat. This includes cleaning and maintenance staff, repair people, and even security guards. Even if an individual doesn't have the credentials needed to sign on to a computer, it is still possible for a person to steal or destroy the computer or remove a hard drive from it.

A risk management plan should include a list of everyone with access to sensitive information and what exact information they can access. Following the Zero Trust philosophy, access control policies should be designed to provide users with permissions only for the data they need and no more. Administrators often do this within the organization by defining roles, granting the roles access to the required data, and then assigning individuals to those roles. This simplifies the process of authorizing new users, moving users to other jobs, and deauthorizing departing users. Then, administrators can create an orderly lifecycle for each user's identity, as shown in Figure 3-62.

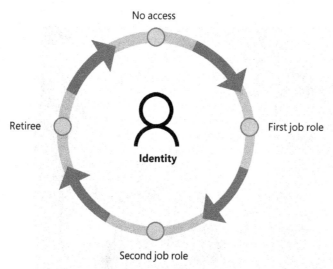

FIGURE 3-62 Identity lifecycle for an individual user

Every person who is granted access to company data should have an individual user account, including people who are working on-site temporarily. Any convenience that might be realized by creating generic guest accounts and assigning them to temporary users as needed will be nullified by the difficulty these accounts can cause when investigating an incident involving data loss or unauthorized access.

The plan must also include the means of ensuring that the individuals signing on to computers are actually the people they purport to be. Password policies can ensure that users create sufficiently long and complex passwords and change them regularly. Microsoft 365 also includes several enhanced authentication mechanisms, including multifactor authentication options calling for a fingerprint scan or a code sent to a mobile phone in addition to a password.

Users with administrative privileges present a greater potential threat to company data. The risk management plan should include policies requiring administrators to use standard user accounts for all typical work functions and administrator accounts only for tasks requiring additional privileges. This helps protect the company data from accidental damage or deletion and reduces the possibility of unauthorized software installation, whether intentional or not. Privileged access user accounts should have their own lifecycle policies with more stringent monitoring and control, as shown in Figure 3-63.

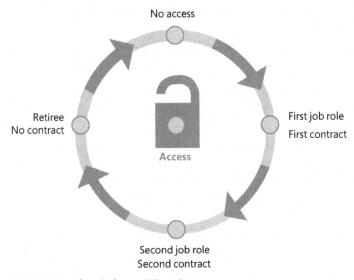

FIGURE 3-63 Lifecycle for a privileged access user account

Of course, even authorized users can be a threat, and the risk management plan should define the specific means by which new employees are vetted, including national (or international) background checks, credit histories, and confirmation of degrees and other credentials. For organizations working with extremely sensitive data, more extensive investigation of new hires might be in order.

Internal users are a major source of security incidents, although the incidents can be unintentional or deliberate. Disgruntled workers and industrial espionage are certainly legitimate causes of data theft or loss. However, simple slips, such as leaving a signed-on computer unattended, can be equally dangerous. In addition to addressing malicious threats, a risk management plan should devote sufficient attention to accidental threats.

Anticipating threats

Arguably, the most difficult part of the risk management planning process is trying to anticipate all the possible threats that could afflict the company's data in the future. The three basic risk factors for the data—confidentiality, integrity, and availability—can be exploited in any number of specific ways, but the general threat categories are listed in Table 3-6.

TABLE 3-6 Risk management threat possibilities

Confidentiality	Integrity	Availability
Theft of data by an internal employee	Accidental alteration of data by an internal user	Accidental damage or destruction of data by an internal user
Theft of data by an external intruder	Intentional alteration of data by an internal employee	Intentional damage or destruction of data by an internal user
Inadvertent disclosure of data	Intentional alteration of data by an external intruder	Intentional damage or destruction of data by an external intruder
		Damage or destruction of data by a natural disaster

The core of the risk management process is to anticipate potential threats in detail and use the information gathered earlier in the data, hardware, and user inventories to estimate the severity and likelihood of each threat. For example, the threat of the company's client sales figures being disclosed when a traveling user misplaces their smartphone is far more likely than a competitor breaking into the company headquarters at night and hacking into a workstation to steal the same information. The severity of the threat in the two scenarios is the same, but the loss of a smartphone is the more likely occurrence, so administrators should expend a greater effort at mitigating that possibility.

In another example, a competitor's burglary attempt might result in the theft of those same client sales figures; in another scenario, this same burglary attempt might cause deliberate damage to the company's web servers, taking the company's e-commerce site down for several days. The likelihood of these scenarios is roughly the same, but the web server damage is the far more severe threat because it interrupts the company's income stream. Therefore, the more severe threat warrants a greater prevention attempt.

Microsoft 365 provides tools administrators can use to predict, detect, and respond to security threats. However, a comprehensive risk management plan goes beyond these types of tools and incorporates purchasing, hiring, building, and administration policies.

Updating the plan

Risk management is not a one-time event; it must be a continual process to be effective. Security threats continue to evolve rapidly, so the protection against them must also evolve. At least once a year, the risk management team should repeat the entire assessment process, updating the inventories of all the organization's information, hardware, and human assets to ensure that no changes have occurred without the company's knowledge. The team must update the threat severity and likelihood matrix as well. New or updated threats will require new security tools, procedures, and policies to protect against them.

In addition to the internal updates of the risk management plan, an organization might want to engage outside contractors to perform a vulnerability assessment, which evaluates the threats in an organization's security infrastructure. Depending on the size of the organization and the current nature of its possible threats, a vulnerability assessment can be a minor and relatively inexpensive procedure or an elaborate and costly undertaking.

Some of the specific types of vulnerability assessments are as follows:

- **Network scan**   Identifies avenues of possible threats through an internal network and Internet connections, including router, firewall, and virtual private network (VPN) configurations

- **Wireless network scan**   Evaluates the organization's Wi-Fi networks for vulnerabilities, including improper configuration, antenna placement, and rogue access points

- **Host scan**   Identifies vulnerabilities in servers, workstations, and other network hosts, including port and service scans, configuration settings, and update histories

- **Application scan**   Examines web servers and other Internet-accessible servers for software vulnerabilities and configuration issues

- **Database scan**   Identifies database-specific threats in database servers and the databases themselves

Another possible method of assessing security vulnerabilities in an organization's risk management system is performing a penetration test. A penetration test is a procedure in which an outside contractor is engaged to attempt an attack on the company's systems to ascertain whether the potential vulnerabilities identified in the risk management process are actual vulnerabilities and to assess the organization's response procedures.

Summary

- The fundamental principles of a Zero Trust environment are verify explicitly, use least-privilege access, and assume breach.

- Microsoft 365 includes security technologies divided into four areas: Security Management, Identity-Based Protection, Information Protection, and Threat Protection.

- An identity is a logical representation of a user in a network environment. To users, an identity is a name they type to sign in to the network. To administrators, an identity is a collection of attributes associated with a particular individual.

- A hybrid identity is an account that exists in a cloud-based directory service such as Entra ID and an on-premises directory service such as Active Directory.

- There are three basic means of authenticating an individual's identity. The individual must supply one or more of the following: something you know, something you are, or something you have. Multifactor authentication requires two or more of these.

- The process of creating a security plan for an enterprise is known as *risk management*.

- Unified endpoint management (UEM) is a management platform that can work with both on-premises and cloud-based devices and be extendable to include new technologies as they develop, such as the Internet of Things (IoT).

- To achieve a true Unified Endpoint Management solution with Microsoft products, a combination of Microsoft Intune and Configuration Manager is needed in an arrangement called *co-management*.

- The Microsoft Defender applications (Defender for Endpoint, Defender for Office 365, Defender for Identity, and Defender for Cloud Apps) all exchange information with the central Microsoft 365 Defender engine.

- Microsoft Sentinel is a combined SIEM and SOAR product that provides an overall view of an enterprise network's security posture and can automatically remediate common security problems when detected.

- The Service Trust Portal (STP) is a central storehouse for information about cloud trust and standards compliance issues.

- Microsoft Purview is a combined data risk, compliance, and governance tool and the interface to features such as security auditing and eDiscovery.

Thought experiment

In this thought experiment, demonstrate your skills and knowledge of the topics covered in this chapter. You can find the answers to this thought experiment in the next section.

Ralph is the Director of the Brooklyn datacenter at Contoso Corp. The company currently has three office buildings in the New York area with 600 users. There are datacenters in all three buildings, all based on Microsoft server products and managed using Microsoft Configuration Manager. The three datacenters are jammed with equipment and have no room for further expansion. Ralph is convinced that it would be better for the company to expand into the cloud and purchase Microsoft 365 subscriptions for the 600 users rather than purchase an additional property and build a fourth datacenter from scratch.

With the cost of real estate and construction in New York being what it is, the financial aspect of a cloud expansion is amenable to the company. However, there is still significant opposition to Ralph's proposal from the other two datacenter directors and the chief technology officer:

1. None of the IT management staff—including Ralph—has much experience with cloud technologies.

2. Some fear that storing company data in the cloud will not be secure.

3. There are concerns that the performance of the company's customer portal—a catalog database that took a great deal of effort to develop—will suffer because of cloud service downtime and Internet latency issues.

Ralph must prepare a presentation that promotes his cloud project and addresses these three concerns. Using what you have learned about cloud service trust and deployment issues, propose a solution for each of the three concerns Ralph must address in his presentation.

Thought experiment answer

Ralph can address the concerns of the other directors and the CTO in the following ways:

1. Microsoft's FastTrack program is designed to provide free support for new cloud sub-scribers during their infrastructure design and implementation processes and ongoing support for the management staff.

2. Microsoft 365 includes tools such as Entra ID Protection, Azure Information Protec-tion, and Microsoft Defender for Office 365 that enable administrators to protect user identities and elevate the security of the company data stored in the cloud based on its sensitivity.

3. Microsoft contracts include a service level agreement guaranteeing 99.9 percent uptime. The Microsoft 365 deployment process also includes a networking phase in which the company evaluates its Internet access infrastructure to ensure that all Micro-soft 365 clients and administrators have sufficient Internet connectivity to regularly access the cloud resources they require.

CHAPTER 4

Understand Microsoft 365 pricing and support

Microsoft 365 is designed to be a complete solution for organizations of various sizes that provides the operating system, productivity applications, and cloud-based services that most users need. For many businesses, Microsoft 365 can be a complete solution; others might have to install additional applications as well.

As discussed in the preceding chapters, candidates preparing for the MS-900 examination must understand the components of the Microsoft 365 packages and the features and benefits they provide. However, they must also be aware of the various licensing options available for Microsoft 365 subscribers, how they are priced, what support options are available, and what the lifecycle of the Microsoft 365 product is expected to be. This information is necessary for IT professionals to make an informed purchasing decision for their organizations.

Skills in this chapter:

- Skill 4.1: Identify Microsoft 365 pricing and billing management options
- Skill 4.2: Identify licensing options available in Microsoft 365
- Skill 4.3: Identify support options for Microsoft 365 services

Skill 4.1: Identify Microsoft 365 pricing and billing management options

Microsoft 365 is not a "one-size-fits-all" product. It is intended to support a range of organization sizes and also organizations with different security and feature requirements. Various product editions have different feature sets and, of course, different prices. As with Office 365, Microsoft 365 is available only by subscription, but unlike Office 365, some Microsoft 365 editions eliminate the need for subscribers to purchase an operating system.

Microsoft 365 subscriptions

Most organizations interested in Microsoft 365 as an introduction to cloud-based networking, either as a new deployment or an addition to a traditional on-premises network, will opt for one of the Microsoft 365 Business options or one of the Microsoft 365 Enterprise subscriptions described in the following sections. In addition, there are specialized versions of Microsoft 365 designed for educational and governmental environments.

Microsoft 365 Business

Intended for small- and medium-sized businesses with up to 300 users, the Microsoft 365 Business product comes in three subscription levels: Basic, Standard, and Premium. All three include the standard Office productivity applications: Word, Excel, PowerPoint, and Outlook, and the Microsoft 365 cloud services: Exchange, SharePoint, Microsoft Teams, and OneDrive. The differences between the levels, other than the prices, are as follows:

- **Microsoft 365 Business Basic**   Includes only the web and mobile versions of the productivity applications

- **Microsoft 365 Business Standard**   Includes all Business Basic features plus downloadable desktop versions of the productivity applications, plus desktop versions of Access and Publisher

- **Microsoft 365 Business Premium**   Includes all Business Standard features, plus Azure Active Directory Premium Plan 1 and the advanced security capabilities of Microsoft Intune and the suite of Microsoft Defender applications

> **NOTE MICROSOFT 365 BUSINESS FOR NONPROFITS**
> In addition to the commercial Microsoft 365 Business Basic, Standard, and Premium subscriptions, Microsoft offers full-featured versions at all three levels for qualified nonprofit organizations at special prices.

Microsoft 365 Business is a comprehensive package for organizations that do not maintain a full-time IT staff, which is the case with many small businesses. Deploying Microsoft 365 workstations is largely automated, and the package includes the Microsoft 365 admin center, which provides a unified interface for the setup and management of identities and devices.

Microsoft 365 Business Premium includes Windows Autopilot, which streamlines the deployment of new Windows workstations or upgrading existing ones. For computers with an earlier version of Windows installed, Microsoft 365 provides an upgrade to Windows 11. In addition to Autopilot, Microsoft 365 includes device management settings in Azure Active Directory that can automatically apply policies to newly deployed workstations, including those for functions like the following:

- Activation of the Microsoft 365 subscription

- Windows 11 and Microsoft 365 updates

- Automated installation of Microsoft 365 productivity applications on Windows 11

- Control of the device's screen when the system is idle

- Access control to Microsoft Store apps

- Access control to Cortana
- Access control to Windows tips and advertisements from Microsoft

Another priority of Microsoft 365 Business Premium is to provide security in areas where small businesses often fall short, as shown in Figure 4-1. The suite of security functions and services included in the product protects all the primary areas of a business network: identities, with multifactor authentication; devices, with management capabilities for on-premises and mobile devices; applications, with usage restrictions; email, with threat detection and data loss prevention; and documents, with classification, encryption, and access control.

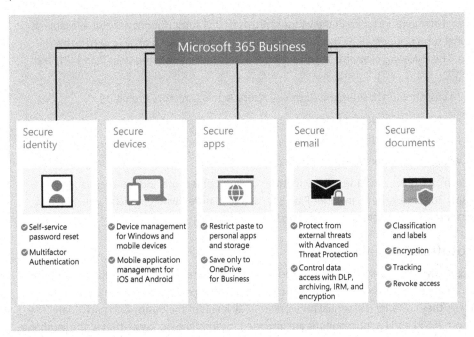

FIGURE 4-1 Security functions in Microsoft 365 Business Premium

Microsoft 365 Business allows up to 300 user subscriptions in one tenancy, but this does not mean an organization's network is limited to 300 users. Every user on the network does not need a Microsoft 365 Business license, although only the license-holders can utilize the cloud services included with the product. It is also possible to combine license types in a single tenancy, meaning if an organization running Microsoft 365 Business expands to more than 300 users, more users can be added with Microsoft 365 Enterprise licenses without upgrading the original 300 Business users.

Microsoft 365 Enterprise

For organizations with more than 300 users, there are two subscription options: Microsoft 365 Enterprise E3 and Microsoft 365 Enterprise E5. Both include Windows 11 Enterprise, Microsoft 365 productivity applications, and various cloud-based services. Both subscriptions support unlimited users, including networks with fewer than 300. The feature lists for the E3 and E5 subscriptions are largely identical, with Microsoft 365 Enterprise E5 including all the features of E3 plus more advanced security, threat protection, and analytics tools.

EXAM TIP

MS-900 exam candidates should understand that while Microsoft 365 Enterprise is targeted at larger organizations, more than 300 users are not required. Small- or medium-sized businesses requiring the additional security and analytical capabilities in the Enterprise E3 or E5 product can use it, too.

Several elements included in the various Microsoft 365 subscriptions are also available as individual subscriptions, allowing consumers to assemble a network on an à *la carte* basis if desired. The following elements are all available in two plans—referred to as Plan 1 (P1) and Plan 2 (P2):

- Microsoft Entra ID Premium (formerly Azure Active Directory Premium)
- Microsoft Defender for Endpoint
- Microsoft Defender for Office 365
- Azure Information Protection Premium

In each case, Plan 2 includes all the features of Plan 1 plus some additional capabilities. Microsoft 365 Enterprise E5 includes Plan 2 for all the features, whereas Plan 1 is included in one or more other subscriptions, as shown later in Table 4-1.

Microsoft 365 Frontline

Microsoft envisions the Microsoft 365 product as a crucial step in an organization's transition from traditional on-premises computing to cloud-based services. For that transition to be complete, they consider it essential for workers at all levels of the business to participate. The Microsoft 365 F1 and F3 subscriptions are intended for *frontline workers*—that is, the segment of an organization's work force that provides the first point of contact between the organization and the outside world. This refers specifically to workers in the field, call centers, shop floors, and customer service roles.

The Microsoft 365 F1 and F3 subscriptions provide a streamlined version of the same basic functionality as the other Microsoft 365 Enterprise subscriptions, including similar productivity, collaboration, and security tools but at a lower price and with limitations suitable to first-line workers' typical needs.

Compared to the Enterprise and Business subscriptions, the primary difference in the Frontline subscriptions is that users only receive access to the Microsoft 365 productivity applications in their web and mobile versions; the installable desktop applications are not included. The product includes access to the Microsoft 365 cloud-based services, including limited access to Exchange Online and SharePoint, plus OneDrive, Microsoft Teams, and Microsoft Intune, as well as access to some of the Microsoft Viva and Microsoft Defender services. Most of the applications and services in the Frontline subscriptions have limitations that suit the tasks they typically perform and the devices that these workers employ, including the following:

- Exchange Online mailboxes are limited to 2 GB.
- SharePoint access is included without personal sites, site mailboxes, or the ability to create forms.
- OneDrive is limited to 2 GB of cloud storage without desktop synchronization.
- Microsoft Teams is limited to one-to-one calls only; users can join but not create meetings.
- Stream is limited to consumption only; users cannot create or upload video streams.

The Microsoft 365 Frontline subscriptions also include many of the same threat protection and device management services as the Microsoft 365 Business and Enterprise E3 subscriptions. The end result is a package that enables frontline workers to fully participate in the culture and community of the organization, with access to the same productivity, collaboration, and security tools as users with Microsoft 365 Enterprise or Business subscriptions. At the same time, frontline workers can gain skills and experience with tools that can enable them to grow and develop within the work force.

Microsoft 365 Business and Enterprise feature comparison

The components and features included in the main Microsoft 365 subscriptions are shown in Table 4-1.

TABLE 4-1 Features and benefits of Microsoft 365 subscriptions

Features Included	Microsoft 365 Business Premium	Microsoft 365 Enterprise E3	Microsoft 365 Enterprise E5	Microsoft 365 F3
Windows 11	None	Enterprise	Enterprise	Enterprise
Microsoft 365 productivity applications	Desktop versions of Word, Excel, Power Point, Outlook, Access, and Publisher	Desktop versions of Word, Excel, Power Point, Outlook, Access, and Publisher	Desktop versions of Word, Excel, PowerPoint, Outlook, Access, and Publisher	Web and mobile versions of Word, Excel, PowerPoint, Outlook, Access, and Publisher
Exchange Online	Yes, with a 50 GB mailbox	Yes, with 50 GB mailbox	Yes, with a 50 GB mailbox	Yes, with a 2 GB mailbox
SharePoint	Yes	Yes	Yes	Yes (without personal site, site mailbox, or form creation)
Microsoft Teams	Yes	Yes	Yes	Yes (one-to-one calls only, meetings join only)
OneDrive	1 TB	5 TB (five or more users) 1 TB (less than five users)	5 TB (five or more users) 1 TB (less than five users)	2 GB (without desktop synchronization)

Features Included	Microsoft 365 Business Premium	Microsoft 365 Enterprise E3	Microsoft 365 Enterprise E5	Microsoft 365 F3
OneDrive for Business	No	Unlimited	Unlimited	No
Microsoft Stream	Yes	Yes	Yes	Yes (consume only)
Audio conferencing/ Phone System	No	No	Yes	No
Viva Engage (Yammer)	Yes	Yes	Yes	Yes
Planner	Yes	Yes	Yes	Yes
Windows Hello for Business	Yes	Yes	Yes	Yes
Microsoft Entra ID Premium (Azure Active Directory Premium)	Plan 1	Plan 1	Plan 2	Plan 1
Azure Active Directory Privileged Identity Management	No	No	Yes	No
Microsoft 365 admin center	Yes	Yes	Yes	Yes
Microsoft Intune	Yes	Yes	Yes	Yes
Windows Autopilot	Yes	Yes	Yes	Yes
Microsoft Advanced Threat Analytics	No	Yes	Yes	Yes
Microsoft Defender for Endpoint	No	Plan 1	Plan 2	No
Microsoft Defender for Office 365	Plan 1	No	Plan 2	No
Office 365 Threat Intelligence	No	No	Yes	No
Microsoft Defender for Identity	No	No	Yes	No
Microsoft Defender for Cloud Apps	No	No	Yes	No
Data Loss Prevention for emails and files	Yes	Yes	Yes	No

Features Included	Microsoft 365 Business Premium	Microsoft 365 Enterprise E3	Microsoft 365 Enterprise E5	Microsoft 365 F3
Microsoft Advanced Threat Analytics	Yes	Yes	Yes	Yes
Microsoft Purview	No	No	Yes	No
Azure Information Protection	Plan 1	Plan 1	Plan 2	Plan 1
Privileged Access Management	No	No	Yes	No
Power Platform	No	No	Yes	No

> **NOTE MICROSOFT 365 INTERNATIONAL USERS**
>
> The exact features included in the Microsoft 365 subscriptions and their pricing and licensing requirements can vary depending on the country or geographical region in which the subscription is purchased.

Microsoft 365 Government

In addition to the core Microsoft 365 subscriptions mentioned earlier, Microsoft has also created specialized packages for governmental and educational organizations designed to suit their specific needs. The Microsoft 365 Government G3 and G5 subscriptions contain the same tools and services found in their Enterprise E3 and E5 equivalents, but the packages are designed to adhere to the additional compliance regulations and requirements to which United States government entities are often subject.

For all the Microsoft 365 Government products, data is stored under special conditions, including the following:

- All Microsoft 365 Government user content, including Exchange Online mailboxes, SharePoint site content, Skype for Business conversations, and Microsoft Teams chat transcripts, is stored in datacenters located within the United States.

- The user content generated by Microsoft 365 Government subscribers is logically segregated from commercial Microsoft 365 user content within the Microsoft datacenters.

- Access to Microsoft 365 Government user content within the Microsoft datacenters is restricted to employees who have undergone additional security screening.

Access to Microsoft 365 Government products is restricted to United States federal, state, local, tribal, or territorial government entities and other entities required to handle government data in compliance with the same regulations and requirements as a government entity. Eligibility to purchase these products is subject to verification by Microsoft using various government resources, including those of law enforcement agencies and the Department of

State, as well as government standards, such as the International Traffic in Arms Regulations (ITAR) and the FBI's Criminal Justice Information Services (CJIS) Policy.

In addition to the Microsoft 365 Government G3 and G5 subscriptions, which define the products' feature sets, there are versions of Microsoft 365 Government that define various levels of security and compliance, including the following:

- **Microsoft 365 U.S. Government Community (GCC)**   Intended for Federal Risk and Authorization Management Program (FedRAMP) moderate risk impact situations; also complies with the Internal Revenue Service Publication 1075 standard, the U.S. Criminal Justice Information Services (CJIS) Security Policy, and the U.S. Department of Defense (DoD) Defense Information Systems Agency (DISA) Level 2 requirement for noncontrolled unclassified information

- **Microsoft 365 U.S. Government Community (GCC) High**   Intended for FedRAMP high-impact situations; complies with the International Traffic in Arms Regulations (ITAR) and the Defense Federal Acquisition Regulation Supplement (DFARS)

- **Microsoft 365 DoD**   Restricted to the exclusive use by U.S. Department of Defense agencies; complies with the U.S. DoD Defense Information Systems Agency (DISA) Level 5 requirement for controlled unclassified information and unclassified national security systems

In addition to the Microsoft 365 Government subscriptions, Microsoft also maintains an alternative means of accessing Microsoft 365 cloud services, called Azure Government ExpressRoute, which is a private, dedicated network connection to the Microsoft cloud services for eligible subscribers that have regulatory requirements that prevent them from using the public Internet.

Microsoft 365 Education

Microsoft 365 Education is another specialized version of Microsoft 365 that includes additional tools and services specifically targeted at teachers and students. There are two subscription levels—Microsoft 365 Education A3 and Microsoft Education A5—which correspond to the Enterprise E3 and E5 subscriptions in most of their features and services.

The Education subscriptions include the Windows 11 Education operating system. Some of the tools included in the Education subscriptions are also specially modified for classroom use, and additional educational tools are included.

> *NOTE* **MICROSOFT 365 EDUCATION A1**
>
> In addition to Microsoft Education A3 and A5, there is also a Microsoft Education A1 product, which is a one-time, per-device license that includes the Microsoft 365 web and mobile applications and cloud-based email, Microsoft Teams, video conferencing, and compliance and information-protection tools; it does not include the installable Microsoft 365 applications and also omits some of the educational, security, and analytics tools found in the A3 and A5 subscriptions.

The education-specific modifications in the Microsoft 365 Education A3 and A5 subscriptions include the following:

- **OneNote Class Notebook** A shared OneNote implementation that includes a collaboration space for class work, a content library for handout documents, and a personal notebook space for each student.

- **Yammer Academic** An implementation of the Yammer private social networking service that includes school branding and administration capabilities that provide content management and access control.

- **Minecraft Education Edition with Code Builder** An educational adaptation of the Minecraft game that teaches students how to code software by dragging and dropping visual code blocks.

- **Take A Test app** An application that enables teachers to deploy high-stakes or low-stakes tests to students in a distraction-free environment, as shown in Figure 4-2. Once students have begun taking a test, they cannot browse the web, print or share the screen, open other applications, use the Windows clipboard, or change system settings.

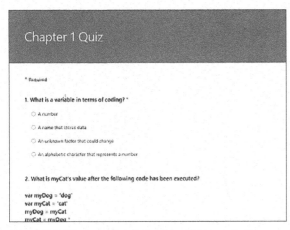

FIGURE 4-2 A test question in the Take A Test application

- **Set Up School PCs app** An application that enables administrators or teachers to easily set up computers running Windows 11 by joining them to an Azure Active Directory tenant, installing approved applications (as shown in Figure 4-3), removing unapproved applications, configuring Windows Update to install updates outside of class time, and locking down the system to prevent its use for anything other than educational purposes.

- **School Data Sync (SDS)** A service that uses data synchronized from a school's Student Information System (SIS) to create Microsoft 365 groups for Exchange Online and SharePoint, Microsoft Intune groups, class teams for Microsoft Teams, and class notebooks for OneNote, as shown in Figure 4-4. Also, SDS can populate many other third-party applications with student information.

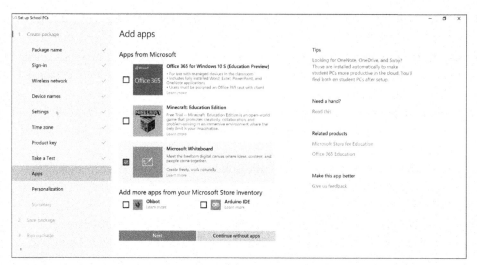

FIGURE 4-3 Adding applications in the Set Up School PCs application

FIGURE 4-4 School Information System data synchronization

- **Office Lens**   A tool that uses the camera of a smartphone or tablet to take pictures of printed pages or whiteboards. This tool crops, straightens, and sharpens them; converts them to PDF, Word, or PowerPoint files; and then saves them to a OneNote notebook, a OneDrive folder, or a local drive.

- **Intune for Education**   A streamlined version of Microsoft Intune that provides device management and application-deployment services for teacher and student devices through a web-based portal, as shown in Figure 4-5.

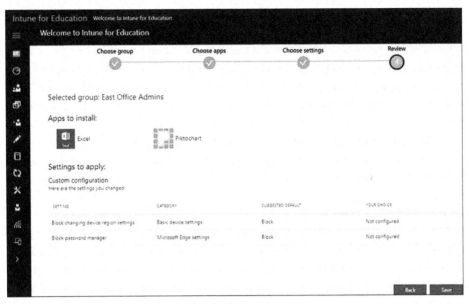

FIGURE 4-5 Intune for Education application deployment

Quick check

Which of the following is one of the features included in Microsoft 365 F1?

   a. Install Office 365 on up to five devices

   b. 50 GB Exchange Online mailboxes

   c. 2 GB of OneDrive cloud storage

   d. SharePoint personal sites

Quick check answer

C. Microsoft 365 F1 does not include the installable versions of the Office 365 applications, includes only 2 GB Exchange Online mailboxes, and does not include SharePoint personal sites.

Describe the pricing model for Microsoft cloud services, including enterprise agreements, cloud solution providers, and direct billing

It is possible for organizations to purchase Microsoft 365 subscriptions directly from Microsoft individually or by using a variety of volume licensing agreements, including the following:

- **Enterprise Agreement (EA)** A volume licensing agreement for organizations with at least 500 users or devices seeking to license software for at least three years, which provides discounts of 15 to 45 percent based on the number of users. Available with up-front or subscription payment terms, the agreement includes Software Assurance and the ability to add users and services during the life of the agreement.

- **Microsoft Products and Services Agreement (MPSA)** An ongoing, partner-based, transactional license agreement for organizations with 250 to 499 users or devices that optionally includes Software Assurance and requires no organization-wide commitment.

- **Cloud Solution Provider (CSP)** A partner-based licensing channel that enables orga-nizations of all sizes to obtain Microsoft 365 products through an ongoing relationship with a selected partner.

Cloud solution providers

The *Cloud Solution Provider (CSP)* program enables partners to establish ongoing relationships with end-user organizations of all sizes and provides them with sales and support for Windows 11 and all the Microsoft 365 Enterprise, Business, and Education products. Members of the Micro-soft Partner Network can become CSPs and play a more prominent part in their customers' cloud solutions.

Rather than simply reselling products, such as Windows 11 and Microsoft 365, a CSP can be a customer's single contact for everything from providing solutions to billing to technical support. CSP partners can enhance their customer relationships by adding value to Microsoft products by bundling industry-specific software products with Microsoft 365 or by offering managed services, such as data migrations and internal help desk support. CSP partners can also offer Microsoft products previously unavailable to smaller companies. For example, at one time, Windows 11 Enterprise was available only to customers with a Microsoft Volume Licens-ing Agreement; CSP partners can now offer the Enterprise edition of the operating system to small- and medium-sized companies.

Depending on the capabilities of the Microsoft partner, the CSP program operates in two ways—direct (Tier 1) and indirect (Tier 2)—as shown in Figure 4-6.

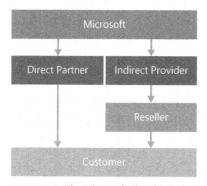

FIGURE 4-6 The Microsoft Cloud Solution Provider partner options

CSP DIRECT

The CSP direct model enables the partners to work directly with Microsoft and function as their customers' sole point of contact. The CSP direct partner is the only conduit between Microsoft's products and services and the customer. For a partner to participate in the CSP direct model, the partner's company must have existing billing and technical support infrastructures. The customer's entire relationship is with the partner; they have no direct contact with Microsoft at all. The CSP partner's relationship with Microsoft and with their customers proceeds as follows:

1. The CSP partner cultivates customers, sells them on Microsoft 365 and/or other Microsoft cloud-based subscription products, and sets them a price based on both the cost of the subscriptions and the added value the CSP partner provides.

2. The CSP partner sets up the customer's tenancy in Microsoft Entra ID and provides the necessary software, such as Windows 11 and any other products they might include in the customer's negotiated package.

3. The customer uses the supplied Microsoft products and contacts the CSP partner for any support issues.

4. Each month, Microsoft uses the Partner Center portal to bill the CSP partner for all the user subscriptions they have sold to their customers.

5. The CSP partner bills the customers at their negotiated rate for Microsoft subscriptions, technical support, and other services.

The upside of this model is that the relationship with the customers is wholly in the hands of the CSP partners. They are responsible for building and maintaining relationships with their customers and can establish whatever prices they feel are appropriate for their services. However, this responsibility also means that a CSP partner must have a company infrastructure that can fulfill all the customers' needs without any help from Microsoft.

CSP INDIRECT

For partners that do not have the infrastructure to handle all the billing and support issues that their customers might require, there is the CSP indirect model, which defines two levels of partners as follows:

- **Indirect provider** Typically, this is a larger company engaged by indirect resellers to be responsible for supplying products, customer service, billing, and technical support services to customers. Some indirect providers are also willing to provide indirect resellers with other types of assistance, such as technical training and marketing; some also provide financing and credit terms.

- **Indirect reseller** Typically, smaller companies or individuals concentrate on locating, cultivating, and signing customers for Windows 11, Microsoft 365, and other cloud-based products and services. To become an indirect reseller, an individual or firm must do the following:

  - Join the Microsoft Partner Network (MPN) and obtain an ID

- Enroll in the CSP program as an indirect reseller by supplying an MPN ID, business address, banking information, and a contact email address
- Establish a relationship with an indirect provider to obtain product, billing, and support services

The CSP indirect partner model enables individual consultants or small consulting companies to sign up as indirect resellers and concentrate on locating customers and developing relationships with them rather than on back-end services, such as billing and support.

Direct billing

Subscription-based products like Microsoft 365 require regular attention to billing to keep them current. If subscriptions are allowed to lapse, they become unusable. For example, if a Microsoft 365 subscription is allowed to lapse or if the computer does not connect to the cloud at least every 30 days, it deactivates and goes into reduced functionality mode. In this mode, users can view or print their existing documents, but they cannot create or edit new ones.

The **Billing** menu in the Microsoft 365 admin center is where administrators can manage all aspects of the billing process. The menu contains the following items:

- **Purchase Services**   Contains tiles with cloud-based subscription products that administrators can add to their tenancies
- **Your Products**   Lists the active subscriptions and specifies how many licenses have been assigned, as shown in Figure 4-7.

FIGURE 4-7 The Products & services page in the Microsoft 365 admin center

- **Licenses**   Contains a list of the tenancy's subscriptions and specifies how many licenses are assigned. Selecting a subscription displays a list of the users to which licenses have been assigned, enabling administrators to create new assignments.
- **Bills & Payments**   Displays a history of the invoices for the current subscriptions, the payment methods configured by the administrator, and the payment frequency (monthly or annual).

- **Billing Accounts**   Displays the account profile of the legal entity in the subscriber's organization responsible for signing software agreements and making purchases, as well as a list of the subscriber's partnerships.

- **Payment Methods**   Displays a list of the subscriber's current payment methods and enables the addition of new ones.

- **Billing Notifications**   Displays a list of the users who will receive billing notifications and renewal reminders from Microsoft, as shown in Figure 4-8.

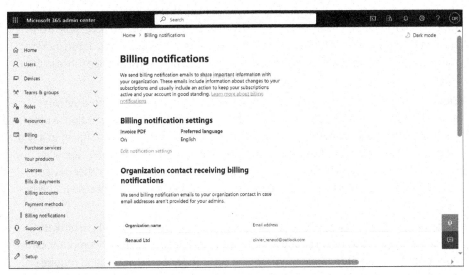

FIGURE 4-8   The Billing Notifications page in the Microsoft 365 admin center

For Microsoft partners, the **Billing** menu in the **Partner Center** console displays the Microsoft invoices for products the partners have resold to customers. Microsoft bills partners for their customers' licenses and usage fees 60 days in arrears so that the partners have time to collect. This **Billing** menu only handles the charges that partners remit to Microsoft. The partnership agreement has no conditions or requirements about how or when the partners invoice their customers and collect their payments.

Selling Microsoft 365

As noted elsewhere in this book, many IT professionals are hesitant to buy into the idea of cloud-based services, and the cloud is the first and biggest buzzword for the Microsoft 365 product. As a result, Microsoft has devoted a great deal of time, effort, and expense to developing a product and a campaign that can convince people like these to adopt—or at least consider—Microsoft 365 as a viable route for the development of their enterprise infrastructures. The following sections discuss the key selling points for Microsoft 365 in four major areas.

Productivity

Few IT professionals must be sold on Microsoft Office productivity applications, such as Word, Excel, PowerPoint, and Outlook; they are industry standards virtually without competition. However, some do need to be sold on a cloud-based, subscription-based implementation such as Microsoft 365, as opposed to perpetual versions like Office 2019 and 2021. The selling points that make an effective case for Microsoft 365 include the following:

- **Applications**   Some people might think that with Microsoft 365, the productivity applications are accessible only from the cloud and that an Internet connection is required to run them. While the productivity applications are indeed accessible from the cloud with a Microsoft 365 subscription, most versions of the product also include fully installable desktop versions of the productivity applications, just like those in Office 2021.

- **Devices**   A perpetual Office 2021 license enables a user to install the productivity applications on a single computer; however, with a Microsoft 365 subscription, a user can install the applications on up to five PC, Mac, or mobile devices and sign in to any or all them at the same time. This means that users can run the Microsoft 365 applications on an office computer, a home computer, and a smartphone, plus two other devices, with a single license, while an Office 2021 user would need a separate license for each device.

- **Installation**   A Microsoft 365 license includes access to a cloud-based portal, with which users can install the productivity applications themselves on any computer. Office 2021 and other perpetual versions include no self-service portal access and require administrators to install the applications on each device.

- **Activation**   When users install the Microsoft 365 productivity applications from the self-service portal, they are automatically activated. They remain activated as long as the computers connect to the Office Licensing Service in the cloud at least once every 30 days. If a device exceeds the 30-day requirement, Microsoft 365 goes into reduced functionality mode, which limits the user to viewing and printing existing documents. Office 2021 and other perpetual versions in an enterprise environment require administrators to keep track of each license's product key or utilize a network-based activation method, such as Key Management Service (KMS) or Multiple Activation Key (MAK). Once activated, Office 2021 installations do not require periodic reactivation.

- **Updates**   Microsoft 365 installations are automatically updated either monthly or semi-annually with the latest security, quality, and feature updates. Office 2021 and other on-premises versions receive security updates but no feature updates. There is also no upgrade path to Office's next major on-premises version. For example, Office 2019 users must pay full price for a new license to install Office 2021.

- **Support**   Office 2021 and other perpetual versions include free technical support for the installation process only. Microsoft 365 subscriptions include free technical support for the life of the subscription.

- **Storage**   A Microsoft 365 subscription includes 1 TB of OneDrive cloud storage. Office 2021 and other perpetual versions do not include cloud storage.

- **Mobile apps**   Access to the Office mobile apps on devices with screens smaller than 10.1 inches with core editing functionality is free to everyone. Microsoft 365 subscribers receive extra features on all mobile apps. Users of Office 2021 or other perpetual versions do not receive the extra features.

Collaboration

The nature of collaboration in the workplace has changed, so the tools that facilitate collaboration must change with it. One of the primary advantages of cloud-based computing is that it allows users to access enterprise resources from any location. Microsoft 365 takes advantage of that benefit by enabling access to the cloud using nearly any device with an Internet connection. Microsoft Entra ID (formerly known as Azure Active Directory) and Microsoft Intune are services based in the cloud, providing identity and device management functions that secure these user connections to the cloud. These components, along with the increased capabilities and emphasis on smartphones and other mobile devices in the business world, have made Microsoft 365 an unprecedented platform for collaboration.

With an infrastructure in place that can provide users with all but universal access to enterprise resources, the next step toward a collaboration platform is the applications and services that enable users to communicate and share data. Microsoft 365 includes four primary collaboration services—shown in Figure 4-9—that provide different types of communication for different situations. Additional services also provide more specific functions for the other services.

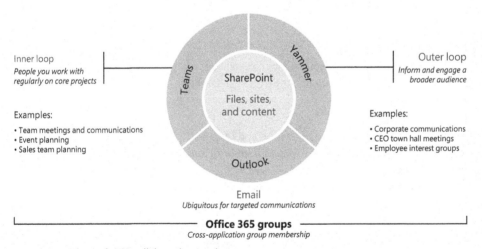

FIGURE 4-9 Microsoft 365 collaboration services

The services that contribute to the collaboration capabilities in Microsoft 365 are as follows:

- **SharePoint**   Provides content storage and publishing services for group and personal intranet websites and for all the other Microsoft 365 collaboration tools. A SharePoint site can be a collaboration platform, or its elements can be embedded in other service publications.

- **Exchange Online/Outlook**   Provides standard email communication and calendar and scheduling functions. Email is asynchronous communication that can be one-to-one or, with the aid of distribution lists, one-to-many. Scheduling functions can be embedded in other services.

- **Microsoft Teams**   Provides synchronous chat- and call-based communication among team members who must communicate quickly and frequently. By incorporating elements from other services, such as Exchange Online scheduling, SharePoint content, and Stream video, Teams can function as a comprehensive collaboration platform.

- **Yammer**   Provides a group-based or company-wide private social media service designed to accommodate larger groups than Microsoft Teams or foster a sense of community within the enterprise. Yammer also provides a platform for the functions provided by other services, such as content from SharePoint sites or scheduling with Exchange Online.

- **Stream**   Provides video storage and distribution services directly to users in web browsers or embedded in other Microsoft 365 collaboration services, including Exchange Online, SharePoint, Microsoft Teams, and Yammer.

- **Planner**   Provides project management services that enable users to create schedules containing tasks, files, events, and other content from Microsoft 365 services.

- **OneDrive**   Provides private file storage for individual users unless the user explicitly shares specific documents.

> ***NEED MORE REVIEW?***   **MICROSOFT 365 COLLABORATION TOOLS**
>
> For more information about the collaboration capabilities of the Microsoft 365 services, see the "Describe collaboration solutions of Microsoft 365" section in Chapter 2, "Describe Microsoft 365 apps and services."

Microsoft Entra ID (Azure Active Directory) and Microsoft 365 Groups provide the identity-management infrastructure for all the Microsoft 365 collaborative services. This enables users and administrators to set up and use these services any way they want. However, the content from the various services is combined; only one set of user accounts and group memberships applies to all. This turns the collection of Microsoft 365 collaboration services into a flexible and interoperable toolkit.

Figure 4-10 illustrates how workers and teams can use the Microsoft 365 collaboration services to work together by creating a digital daily plan containing specific tasks and the circumstances in which they might be performed.

FIGURE 4-10 A sample Microsoft 365 collaboration task schedule

Security

For many IT professionals who are hesitant to move their operations to the cloud, security is the biggest issue that concerns them. The idea of storing sensitive company data on Internet servers, over which they have no direct control— and for which they do not even know the exact location—can be frightening. However, Microsoft has invested an enormous amount of time, effort, and expense into securing its datacenters, and Microsoft 365 includes an array of security tools that subscribers can utilize to provide defense against outside intrusions.

Every security situation is a matter of judgment. Administrators must evaluate the organization's data and decide how much security it requires. In cases of highly sensitive data, the prospect of storing it in the cloud should rightly be frightening. In such cases, it might be necessary for an organization to maintain local storage and split the enterprise functionality between cloud-based and on-premises systems.

As noted elsewhere in this book, Microsoft maintains dozens of datacenters worldwide. The fact that Microsoft's cloud services are storing data for thousands of organizations means they have the incentive and the capital to build datacenters with equipment and physical security that only the largest corporations could conceivably duplicate. For most prospective Microsoft 365 subscribers, the cloud will provide greater physical security, higher availability, and more fault tolerance than they could provide themselves.

Therefore, if the Microsoft datacenters can be considered safe against physical theft and most natural disasters, the remaining security concerns are centered around protecting identities, devices, and documents. These concerns threaten any enterprise network, whether on-premises or in the cloud. Unauthorized users can conceivably gain access to sensitive data wherever it is stored, and IT professionals must always try to prevent that from happening.

Security is a continuously developing challenge, with threats growing as quickly as the means to protect against them. For administrators who want to use Microsoft products to keep up with the latest developing threats, there is no question that the latest and best security tools that Microsoft makes are to be found in cloud-based platforms, such as Microsoft 365. Perpetual products, such as Exchange Server and Office 2021, are being left behind in their security capabilities in favor of Software as a Service (SaaS) products like Microsoft 365, Exchange Online, and the cloud-based SharePoint.

The Microsoft 365 security components include the following:

- **Microsoft Intune**   Provides device and application management services that allow mobile devices to join the network only if they comply with security policies that ensure they are appropriately equipped and configured

- **Azure Information Protection**   Enables users and administrators to apply classification labels to documents and implement various types of protection based on the labels, such as access restrictions and data encryption

- **Data Loss Prevention**   Enables the automated discovery of documents that contain common data patterns, such as those of credit cards and Social Security numbers, using preconfigured sensitive information types

- **Microsoft Defender for Cloud Apps**   Analyzes traffic logs and proxy scripts to identify the cloud apps that users are accessing and enables administrators to analyze app security and sanction or unsanction individual apps

- **Microsoft Entra ID Protection**   Evaluates the sign-in activities of individual user accounts and assigns them risk levels that increment when multiple negative events occur

- **Microsoft Defender for Identity**   Uses machine intelligence to prevent, detect, and remediate security threats unique to the Azure environment by analyzing user behavior and comparing it to known attack patterns

- **Microsoft Advanced Threat Analytics**   Captures network traffic and log information and analyzes it to identify suspicious behaviors related to known phases of typical attack processes

Another aspect of Microsoft 365 that might help to convince traditionalists that a cloud platform can be secure is its use of intelligent analysis to identify behavior indicative of an attack. Tools like Microsoft 365 Defender gather information from Microsoft 365 devices, applications, and services and use endpoint behavioral sensors, cloud security analytics, and threat intelligence to prevent, discover, investigate, and remediate potential and actual threats.

Compliance

As the proliferation and value of data increases over time, businesses, agencies, and individuals are becoming increasingly concerned with the privacy and protection of their data. Hundreds of regulatory bodies—private and governmental—quantify the nature of this data protection and publish standards for data storage and handling.

Some of the most common data privacy standards in use today are as follows:

- **Federal Information Security Modernization Act (FISMA)**   Specifies how U.S. federal agencies must protect information

- **Health Insurance Portability and Accountability Act (HIPAA)**   Regulates the privacy of personal health information

- **Family Educational Rights and Privacy Act (FERPA)**   Regulates the disclosure of student education records

- **Personal Information Protection and Electronic Documents Act (PIPEDA)** Specifies how commercial business organizations can gather, retain, and share personal information

- **Gramm–Leach–Bliley Act (GLBA)**   Specifies how financial institutions must protect and share the personal information of their customers

- **General Data Protection Regulation (GDPR)**   Specifies data protection and privacy regulations for citizens of the European Union

These standards can define elements such as the following:

- The controls that organizations must exercise to protect the privacy of personal data

- How organizations can and cannot use personal data

- The rights of government and other official agencies to access personal data held by an organization

- The lengths of time an organization can and must retain individuals' personal data

- The rights of individuals to access and correct their personal data held by organizations

Whether adopting certain standards is mandatory or voluntary, many organizations are concerned with whether the tools and procedures they use for storing and handling data comply with these standards.

Every organization must assess its own data resources and determine what standards should apply to them. The nature of the business in which the organization is engaged can often dictate compliance with particular standards. For example, companies in the health care industry or those with government contracts might be legally required to store, handle, and protect their data in specific ways. Indeed, there are regulatory standards to which Microsoft 365 products on their own cannot possibly comply, such as those requiring data to be stored on devices and in locations wholly owned and controlled by the organization, precluding cloud storage entirely.

However, many of the hundreds of privacy standards in use do allow the possibility of compliance when data is stored in the cloud, and Microsoft is well aware of the importance of adherence to these standards for many organizations considering a migration to the cloud. For IT professionals who are hesitant to become Microsoft 365 adopters because they fear that changing the location and the data storage conditions will negatively affect their compliance with standards like these, Microsoft has tested their products' compliance with many different standards and published documents certifying the results.

Microsoft divides the compliance effort into three phases, as shown in Figure 4-11. The phases are described as follows:

- **Assess**   The organization gathers the information needed to assess its current compliance status and produce a plan to achieve or maintain compliance with specific standards. Microsoft's Service Trust Portal website contains a vast library of documents specifying information about the testing processes and the third parties involved in compliance testing. Also, Microsoft Purview includes Compliance Manager, a risk assessment tool organizations can use to record their actions to achieve compliance with specific standards.

- **Protect**   The organization implements a protection plan for its data, based on its sensitivity, using the tools provided in the Microsoft 365 services, including access control permissions, file encryption, Information Protection, and Data Loss Prevention.

- **Respond**   The organization develops protocols for responding to regulatory requests using artificial intelligence tools such as Microsoft 365 eDiscovery to perform complex searches of Exchange Online mailboxes, Microsoft 365 Groups, SharePoint and OneDrive sites, and Microsoft Teams conversations.

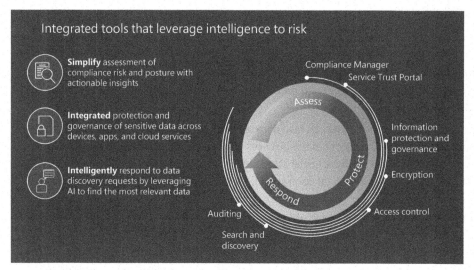

FIGURE 4-11 Microsoft compliance phases

NEED MORE REVIEW?   **MICROSOFT 365 COMPLIANCE**

For additional information on Microsoft 365's compliance efforts, see the "Describe trust, privacy, risk, and compliance solutions in Microsoft 365" section in Chapter 3, "Describe security, compliance, privacy, and trust in Microsoft 365."

Skill 4.2: Identify licensing options available in Microsoft 365

Cost is always a factor when introducing new technology into a business network. Deciding whether Microsoft 365 is an economically sound choice when compared to a traditional on-premises network infrastructure is complicated. Every organization contemplating an entry into cloud-based computing must factor the results of a *cost-benefit analysis (CBA)* into its decision. However, comparing Microsoft 365 to on-premises server products is not just a matter of how much the technologies cost but also when the costs are incurred.

Cost-benefit analysis for cloud vs. on-premises networks

Evaluating the total cost of ownership (TCO) for a Microsoft 365 implementation is the relatively simple part of a cost-benefit analysis. There is a monthly or annual fee for each Microsoft 365 user subscription, and those subscriber fees are predictable and ongoing. Contracts might be renewed with different prices at intervals, but those costs still remain predictable. It is possible that costs could rise precipitously in the future when the contracts are renewed, and the subscriber might feel locked into one provider, but that is a risk with any software product.

Predicting the cost of an on-premises network is more difficult. It is common for businesses to categorize their expenses by distinguishing between two types of expenditures, as follows:

- Capital expenditures (CapEx) are money spent on fixed assets, such as buildings, servers, and other hardware, deployment expenses, and purchased software.
- Operational expenditures (OpEx) are ongoing expenses, such as rent, utilities, staff, and maintenance.

The basic differences between CapEx and OpEx expenditures are shown in Table 4-2.

TABLE 4-2 Capital expenditures versus operational expenditures

	Capital Expenditures (CapEx)	Operational Expenditures (OpEx)
Purpose	Hardware and software assets with at least one year of usefulness	Ongoing business costs
Payment	Initial lump sum	Recurring monthly or annual
Accounting	Three or more years of asset depreciation	Current month or year
Description	Property, equipment, software	Operating costs
Taxes	Multiple years of deduction based on depreciation	Current year deduction

For a Microsoft 365 shop, nearly all the expenses are OpEx, including the subscription fees. There are virtually no CapEx expenses involved, except perhaps for things like initial administrator cloud training. Businesses like working with OpEx expenses because they enable them to create accurate budgets and forecasts.

For an on-premises network, the CapEx outlay required to set up the infrastructure can be enormous, including the cost of building and equipping datacenters and purchasing server software products. Depending on the nature of the business and the sensitivity of the data involved, these expenses can by multiplied by the need for redundant datacenters and equipment. These big expenses must be paid before the network can even go live. These CapEx costs can be amortized or depreciated in the company's accounts over a period of years, but the initial investment is substantial compared to that of a cloud-based network, which requires almost none.

An on-premises network also has OpEx expenses, including rent, power, and other utilities datacenters require, and the salaries of the staff needed to operate and maintain the datacenter equipment. There are also expensive software upgrades to consider every two to three years. The main cost benefit of an on-premises network is that hardware and software are purchased outright and do not require monthly subscription fees.

There are other factors to consider as well. When designing an on-premises network, the organization must consider the possibility of future growth, as well as seasonal business fluctuations. Therefore, the already substantial CapEx outlay can be increased by the cost of the additional datacenter space and equipment needed to support the busiest times of the year, as well as several years of predicted growth.

A cloud-based infrastructure like that of Microsoft 365 uses a pay-as-you-go model, which can accommodate virtually unlimited growth and occasional business fluctuations with no extra expenses other than the increased subscription fees for the extra services. The organization never pays for hardware and software that it isn't using. In addition, the growth and fluctuations can be accommodated almost immediately and downsized when necessary, while on-premises resources can require months to approve, obtain, and install.

The entire cost-benefit analysis can be further complicated if the organization has already invested substantially in on-premises infrastructure. For example, if the expanding company already has sufficient space in its datacenters and sufficient IT staff, the CapEx needed for a network expansion can be much less than it would be for an entirely new network installation. The question then becomes whether it is more economical to add to the existing on-premises infrastructure or expand into the cloud, creating a hybrid network that might require additional planning and training to bring personnel up to speed in cloud technologies.

Therefore, the result can only be that every organization must consider its own economic, personnel, and business situations and calculate the TCO of its network options. In a new deployment, a subscription-based, cloud-based option, such as Microsoft 365, can be faster and less expensive to implement, but there are many situations in which organizations might be compelled to consider an on-premises network instead.

EXAM TIP

Candidates for the MS-900 exam seeking greater familiarity with the characteristics of cloud-based services versus on-premises services should also consult the "Describe the benefits of and considerations for using cloud, hybrid, or on-premises services" section in Chapter 1, "Describe cloud concepts."

Describe license management

To install and run the Microsoft 365 components and access the Microsoft 365 cloud services, each user in an organization must have a Microsoft 365 *user subscription license (USL)*. Typically, an administrator for an organization deploying Microsoft 365 creates a tenancy in Microsoft Entra ID (Azure Active Directory), purchases a specific number of USLs, and then assigns them to users in the Microsoft 365 admin center console by selecting **Licenses** in the **Billing** menu, as shown in Figure 4-12.

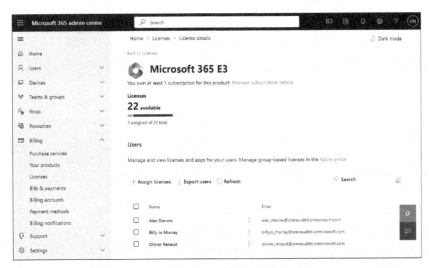

FIGURE 4-12 A License Details page in Microsoft 365 admin center

Global administrators or user management administrators can assign licenses to up to 20 users at once from this interface. It is also possible to assign licenses to hybrid user accounts created through Active Directory synchronization or federation or while creating new user accounts in the Microsoft 365 admin center.

Assigning a Microsoft 365 license to a user causes the following events to occur:

- Exchange Online creates a mailbox for the user
- SharePoint grants the user edit permissions for the default team site
- Microsoft 365 enables the user to download and install the Office productivity applications on up to five devices

From the **Purchase Services** page in the admin center, administrators can also purchase additional Microsoft 365 USLs or licenses for add-on products, as shown in Figure 4-13.

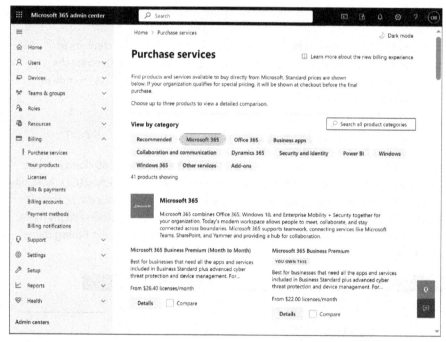

FIGURE 4-13 The Purchase Services page in Microsoft 365 admin center

Microsoft offers four different USL types for each of the Microsoft 365 products, depending on the purchaser's existing relationship with the company, as follows:

- **Full USL**   This is a complete Microsoft 365 license for new purchasers who do not have existing Microsoft product licenses or for owners of on-premises Microsoft product licenses that do not include Software Assurance—Microsoft's software maintenance agreement.

- **Add-on USL**   This is a license for purchasers with existing on-premises Microsoft product licenses, including Software Assurance, who want to maintain their infrastructure while adding Microsoft 365 cloud services in a pilot or hybrid deployment.

- **From SA USL**   This is a license for purchasers with existing perpetual Microsoft product licenses, including Software Assurance, who want to transition to a cloud-based infrastructure with continued Software Assurance for the Microsoft 365 product. Qualifying purchasers can only obtain From SA USLs at their contract renewal time and must maintain their existing Software Assurance agreement. A Microsoft 365 Software Assurance agreement includes cloud-oriented benefits, such as Deployment Planning Services, Home Use Program, online user training courses, and additional support incidents.

- **Step-up USL**   This is a license for current Microsoft customers who want to upgrade their subscriptions during an existing enrollment or agreement period, such as from Office 365 to Microsoft 365 or from Microsoft 365 Business to Microsoft 365 Enterprise E3.

Because the Add-on USLs, From SA USLs, and Step-up USLs are intended for existing Microsoft customers, their prices reflect significant discounts from the Full USL price.

Describe the differences between base licensing and add-on licensing

Many Microsoft 365 services are maintained as separate add-on products, often in two plans, which customers can purchase to augment the capabilities of their base licenses.

For example, the IT administrators for an organization might decide that the price of purchasing Microsoft 365 Enterprise E5 licenses for all of their users is just too high and that the users don't need all of the advanced features in the E5 product anyway. They choose the Microsoft 365 Enterprise E3 subscription instead, representing substantial cost savings.

Many administrators were attracted to the E5 product because it includes Microsoft Defender for Endpoint Plan 2, which provides endpoint detection and automated incident remediation. However, this feature alone was not enough to justify the difference in price between E3 and E5. Later, the administrators discovered they could purchase the Microsoft 365 E3 subscriptions as their users' base license and then purchase Microsoft Defender for Endpoint Plan 2 as an add-on license. For this organization, the total cost of the two subscriptions was far less than the price of Microsoft 365 E5.

Microsoft has many add-on products that allow administrators to assemble a working environment with a curated selection of features. Add-on licenses come in two types, as follows:

- **Traditional add-on**   An add-on license linked to a particular base subscription. The add-on subscription is also terminated if the base subscription lapses or is canceled.

- **Standalone add-on**   An add-on license that appears as a separate subscription on the Billing pages in the Microsoft 365 admin center, with its own expiration date, independent of the base subscription.

Implementing best practices

As mentioned throughout this book, the Microsoft 365 product is a bundle of services, many of which remain available as separate subscriptions. In addition, subscriptions are available for combinations of individual features within these products.

Finally, to further complicate the picture, combining different licenses in a single Microsoft Entra ID tenancy is possible. With all these options available, organizations contemplating a migration to a cloud-based infrastructure or thinking of adding cloud services to an on-premises infrastructure should design a licensing strategy fulfilling the following requirements:

- Provide the organization's users with the services they need
- Avoid providing users with unnecessary services that complicate the maintenance and support processes
- Minimize subscription costs

Generally speaking, a Microsoft 365 subscription will likely be significantly less expensive than purchasing subscriptions for each component separately. This might be true even if some users do not need all the Microsoft 365 components.

Obviously, the simplest solution is to choose one Microsoft 365 product and purchase the same subscription for all the organization's users. This can easily fulfill the first of the requirements but might not be a solution for the other two.

Depending on the nature of the business the organization is engaged in, an Enterprise E5 subscription might be suitable for some users, but there might also be many workers who do not need all the applications and services included in Enterprise E5. Depending on the number of users in each group, the expense of purchasing E5 subscriptions for everyone could be extremely wasteful and require additional administrative effort to provide customized environments for the different user groups. This is one of the primary reasons why Microsoft offers the Microsoft 365 F1 subscription for first-line workers.

> **NOTE MICROSOFT 365 F1**
>
> For more information on the Microsoft 365 F1 package, see the "Microsoft 365 Frontline" section earlier in this chapter.

Therefore, the best practice is to compare the features included in each of the Microsoft 365 licenses with the requirements of the various types of users in the organization. In a large enterprise, this can be a complicated process, but in the case of a major migration like this, prior planning is crucial and can save a great deal of expense and effort.

> **Quick check**
>
> Which of the following is not one of the three phases of the Microsoft compliance effort?
>
> a. Simplify
>
> b. Assess
>
> c. Protect
>
> d. Respond

Skill 4.3: Identify support options for Microsoft 365 services

For many IT professionals, there are important concerns about what happens after their organization commits itself to the use of cloud-based applications and services. These issues include concerns about downtime, monitoring the continuity of Microsoft services, and the product support provided by Microsoft and its partners.

Describe how to create a support request for Microsoft 365 services

The Microsoft 365 support subscribers receive depends on their subscription level and how they obtained it. Nearly every page in the Microsoft 365 admin center console has a **Help & Support** button in the bottom-right corner and a **Support** menu allowing administrators to search for help with specific problems and create support requests when a solution is unavailable in the existing help information. Telephone and email support are also available.

To prevent excessive use and abuse of its support services, Microsoft carefully defines the division of responsibilities between the Microsoft support team and the administrators at Microsoft 365 subscription sites. Table 4-3 lists some of the responsibilities of each entity.

TABLE 4-3 Responsibilities of Microsoft 365 administrators and Microsoft Support

Microsoft 365 Administrator Responsibilities	Microsoft Support Responsibilities
Service setup, configuration, and maintenance	Respond to support issues submitted by subscribers
User account creation, configuration, and maintenance	Gather information about technical support issues from subscribers
Primary support contact for enterprise users	Provide subscribers with technical guidance for submitted issues
Gather information from users about technical support issues	Troubleshoot subscriber issues and relay pertinent solution information
Address user software installation and configuration issues	Maintain communication with subscribers regarding ongoing service issues
Troubleshoot service availability issues within the bounds of the organization	Provide guidance for presales and trial-edition evaluators
Utilize Microsoft online resources to resolve support issues	Provide licensing, subscription, and billing support
Authorization and submission of support issues to Microsoft	Gather customer feedback for service improvement purposes

Microsoft 365 administrators are expected to do what they can to address a support issue before submitting a support request to Microsoft. There are considerable Microsoft online support, training, blog, and forum resources available for this purpose, including the following:

- Microsoft Support (*support.microsoft.com*)
- Microsoft Community (*answers.microsoft.com*)
- Microsoft 365 Tech Community (*techcommunity.microsoft.com/t5/Microsoft-365/ct-p/ microsoft365*)

When an administrator clicks the **Help & Support** button in the Microsoft 365 admin center console or opens the **Support** menu and selects **New Service Request**, a **How Can We Can We Help?** pane appears, prompting a description of the issue. Based on the furnished description, relevant material appears, such as step-by-step procedures and links to product documentation that might be helpful, as shown in Figure 4-14.

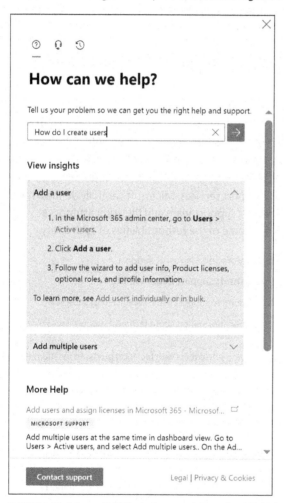

FIGURE 4-14 Microsoft 365 admin center's How Can We Help? pane

At the bottom of the **How Can We Help?** pane is a **Contact Support** link that opens the pane shown in Figure 4-15. In this pane, the administrator can provide a more detailed description of the issue, add contact information, specify time zone and language references, and attach documents pertinent to the issue.

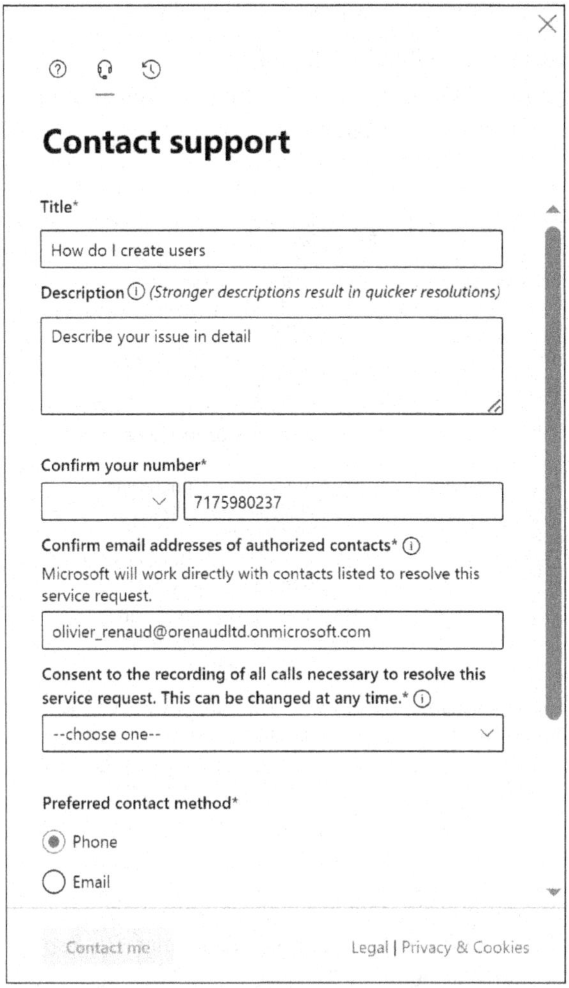

FIGURE 4-15 Microsoft 365 admin center's Contact Support pane

Support provided with the Microsoft 365 product is intended primarily to provide help with service installation and configuration issues, such as the following:

- **Microsoft Entra ID (Azure Active Directory)** Domain setup, synchronization with on-premises Active Directory, and single sign-on configuration
- **Microsoft 365** Service configuration issues
- **Exchange Online** Mailbox migration and configuration, autodiscover configuration, setting mailbox permissions, sharing mailboxes, and creating mail forwarding rules

- **SharePoint** Creation of user groups, assigning site permissions, and external user configuration
- **Microsoft 365 Apps for Business** Office application installation on various device platforms
- **Microsoft Teams** Setup of a Microsoft Teams environment and creating contacts
- **Microsoft Intune** Mobile device and application management setup

When subscribers submit support requests to Microsoft, they go through a triage process and are assigned a severity level using the values shown in Table 4-4.

TABLE 4-4 Microsoft Support severity levels

Severity Level	Description	Examples
Critical (Sev A)	<ul><li>One or more services are inaccessible or nonfunctional.</li><li>Productivity or profit is impacted. Multiple users are affected.</li><li>Immediate attention is required.</li></ul>	<ul><li>Problems sending or receiving email with Outlook/Exchange Online.</li><li>SharePoint or OneDrive sites are inaccessible.</li><li>Cannot send or receive messages or calls in Microsoft Teams.</li></ul>
High (Sev B)	<ul><li>One or more services are impaired but still usable.</li><li>A single user or customer is affected. Attention can wait until business hours.</li></ul>	<ul><li>Critical service functionality is delayed or partially impaired but operational.</li><li>Noncritical functions of a critical service are impaired.</li><li>A function is unusable in a graphical interface but accessible using PowerShell.</li></ul>
Non-critical (Sev C)	<ul><li>One or more functions with minimal productivity or profit impact are impaired.</li><li>One or more users are affected, but a workaround allows continued functionality.</li></ul>	<ul><li>Problems configuring password expiration options.</li><li>Problems archiving messages in Outlook/Exchange Online.</li><li>Problems editing SharePoint sites.</li></ul>

After submitting support requests, administrators can monitor their progress in the Microsoft 365 admin center by selecting **View Service Requests** from the **Support** menu to display a list of all the support tickets associated with the account.

Describe support options for Microsoft 365 services

All Microsoft 365 subscriptions include access to basic support services, but for some types of subscribers or subscribers with special needs, there are alternative methods for obtaining support, such as the following:

- **FastTrack** Microsoft's FastTrack program uses a specialized team of engineers and selected partners to provide subscribers transitioning to the cloud with assistance in the envisioning, onboarding, and ongoing administration processes. Subscribers participating in this program are provided with a contact for support issues during the FastTrack transition.

- **Volume Licensing** Subscribers with an Enterprise Agreement or a Microsoft Products and Services Agreement that includes Software Assurance receive a specified number of support incidents as part of their agreement. The Software Assurance program includes 24x7 telephone support for business-critical issues and business hours or email support for noncritical issues.

- **Cloud Solution Providers** For subscribers who obtain Microsoft 365 through a Cloud Solution Provider (CSP), the CSP should be their first point of contact for all service and support issues during the life of the subscription. The reseller agreement between CSPs and Microsoft calls for the CSP to take full responsibility for supporting their customers, although the CSP can still escalate issues to Microsoft when they cannot resolve them independently.

- **Microsoft Professional Support** Subscribers with support issues beyond the standard service provided with Microsoft 365 can use Microsoft Professional Support to open support requests on a pay-per-incident basis, as shown in Figure 4-16. Individual incidents are available, as are five packs of incidents.

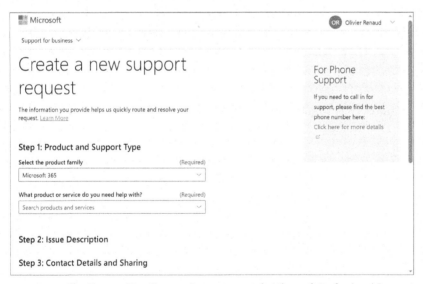

FIGURE 4-16 The Create a New Support Request screen in Microsoft Professional Support

- **Microsoft Unified Support** Subscribers can purchase a Microsoft Unified Support plan in addition to their Microsoft 365 subscriptions. Microsoft Unified Support is available at three levels: Core Support, Advanced Support, and Performance Support; each level provides increasing levels of included support hours, incident response times, and access to a technical account manager (TAM), along with increasing prices. Customers also receive access to the Microsoft Services Hub, a support portal that provides forms for submitting support requests, access to ongoing Microsoft support incidents, tools for assessing enterprise workloads, and on-demand education and training materials.

Software assurance

For Enterprise Agreement and, optionally, for Microsoft Products and Services Agreement customers, Software Assurance provides a variety of additional services, including the following, which can benefit Microsoft 365 licensees:

- **Planning Services**   Provides a number of partner service days, based on the number of users/devices licensed, to deploy Microsoft operating systems, applications, and services.

- **Microsoft Desktop Optimization Pack (MDOP)**   Provides a suite of virtualization, management, and restoration utilities, including Advanced Group Policy Management (AGPM), Microsoft Application Virtualization (App-V), Microsoft User Experience Virtualization (UE-V), Microsoft BitLocker Administration and Monitoring (MBAM), and Microsoft Diagnostics and Recovery Toolset (DaRT).

- **Windows Virtual Desktop Access Rights (VDA)**   Provides users with the rights needed to access virtualized Windows instances.

- **Windows to Go Use Rights**   Enables administrators to create and furnish users with USB storage devices containing bootable Windows images that include line-of-business applications and corporate data.

- **Windows Thin PC**   Enables administrators to repurpose older computers as Windows Virtual Desktop Interface (VDI) terminals.

- **Enterprise Source Licensing Program**   Provides organizations with at least 10,000 users or devices with access to the Windows source code for their own software development projects.

- **Training Vouchers**   Provides a number of training days based on the number of users/devices licensed for the technical training of IT professionals and software developers.

- **Step-up License Availability**   Allows licensees to migrate their licensed software products to a high-level edition.

- **Spread Payments**   Enables organizations to pay for three-year license agreements in three equal, annual payments.

> **NOTE   ADDITIONAL SOFTWARE ASSURANCE BENEFITS**
>
> There are additional Software Assurance benefits included that are intended for on-premises server software licensees, such as New Version Rights, which provides the latest versions of the licensed software released during the term of the agreement, and Server Disaster Recovery Rights and Fail-Over Rights, which provide licensees the right to maintain passive redundant servers for fault-tolerance purposes.

Describe service level agreements (SLAs), including service credits

When an enterprise uses on-premises servers, they know issues they experience that prevent the servers from functioning are their problem, and they must have the resources to resolve them. This is why organizations often use redundant components, servers, or even datacenters to keep business-critical services available. Many IT professionals prefer this self-reliance; they can be confident of their continued functionality by planning and implementing their services correctly. However, an enterprise that uses cloud-based services must rely on others to keep its services running.

For IT professionals, service outages are one of the potential showstopper issues for the adoption of Microsoft 365 and other cloud-based services. If the services suffer downtime, business stops. While it might not be the IT professionals' fault, it is their responsibility. What is worse, there is nothing they can do about it except call the provider and shout at them. Depending on the nature of the organization's business, service downtime can result in lost productivity, lost income, and—in extreme cases—even lost lives.

To address this issue, contracts with cloud service providers typically include a *service level agreement (SLA)*. The SLA guarantees a certain percentage of uptime for the services and specifies the consequences if that guarantee is not met. It is important to remember that an organization usually has more than one service provider that is needed to access the cloud. For example, an organization can contract with Microsoft for a certain number of Microsoft 365 subscriptions, but the reliability specified in Microsoft's SLA means nothing if the organization's Internet service provider (ISP) fails to provide them with access to the cloud. Therefore, an organization should have a contract with every cloud service provider they use that includes SLA terminology.

When negotiating an SLA with any cloud service provider or Internet service provider, there should be language included to address questions like the following:

- What formula is used to calculate the service levels that are actually achieved?
- Who is responsible for maintaining records of service levels?
- How and when is the subscriber provided with written reports of the service levels achieved?
- Are there exceptional circumstances specified in the SLA under which service outages are not classified as downtime?
- How much downtime is expected or allowable for the provider's scheduled and emergency maintenance?
- What are the terms of the agreement regarding service interruptions resulting from acts of war, extreme weather, or natural disasters?
- What are the terms of the agreement regarding service interruptions caused by third-party services, such as power outages?
- What are the terms of the agreement regarding service interruptions resulting from malicious cyberattacks against the provider?

- What are the terms of the agreement regarding service interruptions resulting from malicious cyberattacks against the subscriber?

- What remedy or penalty does the provider supply when they fail to meet the agreed-upon service levels?

- What is the liability to which the provider is subject when service interruptions cause a loss of business or productivity?

These questions are designed to quantify the nature of the SLA and how it can legally affect the relationship between the provider and the subscriber. For example, a provider can guarantee a 99 percent uptime rate. However, without specific language addressing the point, there is no way to determine exactly what constitutes uptime or downtime. What if a service is only partially operational, with some tasks functional and others not? Does that constitute downtime? There is also the question of what happens when downtime in excess of the guaranteed amount does occur. Is it the responsibility of the subscriber to make a claim? If excessive downtime occurs, is the provider responsible for the subscriber's lost business during that downtime or just for a prorated subscription fee? If issues like these are not discussed with specific language in the SLA, then they are potential arguments the provider can use to avoid supporting their uptime guarantee.

SLA Limitations

As an example of the terms that might appear in an SLA to limit the responsibility of the cloud service provider, consider the following excerpt from Microsoft's SLA for Microsoft Entra ID (Azure Active Directory):

This SLA and any applicable Service Levels do not apply to any performance or availability issues:

1. *Disaster, war, acts of terrorism, riots, government action, or a network or device failure external to our data centers, including at your site or between your site and our data center);*

2. *That result from the use of services, hardware, or software not provided by us, including, but not limited to, issues resulting from inadequate bandwidth or related to third-party software or services;*

3. *That results from failures in a single Microsoft Datacenter location, when your network connectivity is explicitly dependent on that location in a non-geo-resilient manner;*

4. *Caused by your use of a Service after we advised you to modify your use of the Service, if you did not modify your use as advised;*

5. *During or with respect to preview, pre-release, beta or trial versions of a Service, feature or software (as determined by us) or to purchases made using Microsoft subscription credits;*

---

6. *That result from your unauthorized action or lack of action when required, or from your employees, agents, contractors, or vendors, or anyone gaining access to our network by means of your passwords or equipment, or otherwise resulting from your failure to follow appropriate security practices;*

7. That result from your failure to adhere to any required configurations, use supported platforms, follow any policies for acceptable use, or your use of the Service in a manner inconsistent with the features and functionality of the Service (for example, attempts to perform operations that are not supported) or inconsistent with our published guidance;

8. *That result from faulty input, instructions, or arguments (for example, requests to access files that do not exist);*

9. *That result from your attempts to perform operations that exceed prescribed quotas or that resulted from our throttling of suspected abusive behavior;*

10. *Due to your use of Service features that are outside of associated Support Windows; or*

11. *For licenses reserved, but not paid for, at the time of the Incident.*

These limitations are not standard for all SLAs, but they are typical.

In the *Microsoft Volume Licensing Service Level Agreement for Microsoft Online Services* document, dated August 1, 2023, the terms for each of the individual cloud services are listed with the following information:

- **Downtime**   Specifies exactly what type or types of service interruption legally constitute downtime in the terms of the agreement. Some of the definitions of downtime for cloud services included in Microsoft 365 are shown in Table 4-5.

- **Monthly Uptime Percentage**   Specifies the formula by which the percentage of uptime is calculated for each month, considering the number of minutes the service was considered to be down and the number of user licenses affected by the outage. For example, the following formula subtracts the total number of downtime minutes for all the users from the total user minutes and calculates a percentage from that:

$$\frac{User\ Minutes - Downtime\ Minutes}{User\ Minutes}$$

- **Service Credit**   Specifies the percentage of the monthly subscription fee that will be credited to the subscriber's account based on the calculated monthly uptime percentage. For example, Microsoft's SLA for Microsoft 365 Apps for Enterprise guarantees 99.9 percent uptime, so the service credit for months that do not meet that percentage is calculated as shown in Table 4-6. Other Microsoft services can have different SLA guarantees, such as Azure Active Directory, which has a 99.99 percent guaranteed uptime.

- **Additional Terms** Identifies other parts of the document that might define other conditions constituting a refundable service outage. For example, a failure of Exchange Online to detect viruses or filter spam as agreed in the SLA can qualify for a service credit, even if no downtime occurs.

TABLE 4-5 Definitions of downtime in the Microsoft Volume Licensing Service Level Agreement for Microsoft Online Services

Cloud Service	Definition of downtime
Azure Active Directory Premium	Any period of time when users are unable to log in to the Azure Active Directory service, or Azure Active Directory fails to successfully emit the authentication and authorization tokens required for users to log into applications connected to the service.
Exchange Online	Any period of time when users are unable to send or receive email with Outlook Web Access.
Microsoft Teams	Any period of time when end users are unable to conduct instant messaging conversations or initiate online meetings.
Microsoft 365 Apps for Business	Any period of time when Office applications are put into reduced functionality mode due to an issue with Office 365 activation.
Office Online	Any period of time when users are unable to use the web applications to view and edit any Office document stored on a SharePoint Online site for which they have appropriate permissions.
OneDrive for Business	Any period of time when users are unable to view or edit files stored on their personal OneDrive for Business storage.
SharePoint Online	Any period of time when users are unable to read or write any portion of a SharePoint Online site collection for which they have appropriate permissions.
Yammer Enterprise	Any period of time greater than 10 minutes when more than 5 percent of end users are unable to post or read messages on any portion of the Yammer network for which they have appropriate permissions.
Microsoft Intune	Any period of time when the customer's IT administrator or users authorized by customer are unable to log on with proper credentials. Scheduled downtime will not exceed 10 hours per calendar year.
Microsoft Defender for Endpoint	The total accumulated minutes that are part of Maximum Available Minutes in which the Customer unable to access any portion of a Microsoft Defender for Endpoint portal site collections for which they have appropriate permissions and customer has a valid, active, license.

TABLE 4-6 Service credit for monthly uptime percentages in the Microsoft Volume Licensing Service Level Agreement for Microsoft 365 Apps for Enterprise

Monthly Uptime Percentage	Service Credit
Less than 99.9 percent	25 percent
Less than 99 percent	50 percent
Less than 95 percent	100 percent

Microsoft requires subscribers to file a claim for service credits containing evidence of the outages, as described in the following SLA excerpt:

In order for Microsoft to consider a claim, you must submit the claim to customer support at Microsoft Corporation including all information necessary for Microsoft to validate the claim, including but not limited to: (i) a detailed description of the Incident; (ii) information regarding the time and duration of the Downtime; (iii) the number and location(s) of affected users (if applicable); and (iv) descriptions of your attempts to resolve the Incident at the time of occurrence.

Generally speaking, it appears as though the SLA for Microsoft's online services is rarely even needed. For example, Table 4-7 lists the worldwide quarterly uptime percentages for the Microsoft 365 cloud services in recent years, and none of the figures even comes close to dropping below the 99.9 percent uptime guaranteed for most of the Microsoft 365 services. This is not to say that there weren't a few isolated outages resulting in service credits, but the overall record for the Microsoft 365 products is impressive.

TABLE 4-7 Quarterly Uptime Percentages for Microsoft 365, 2019 to 2023

Year	Quarter 1	Quarter 2	Quarter 3	Quarter 4
2023	99.98 percent	99.99 percent		
2022	99.98 percent	99.98 percent	99.99 percent	99.99 percent
2021	99.97 percent	99.98 percent	99.99 percent	99.98 percent
2020	99.98 percent	99.99 percent	99.97 percent	99.97 percent
2019	99.97 percent	99.97 percent	99.98 percent	99.98 percent

Determine service health status by using the Microsoft 365 admin center or the Microsoft Entra admin center

Monitoring the continuous operation of the Microsoft 365 services is a critical part of the administration process, and the Microsoft 365 admin center includes a **Health** menu that provides a real-time display of the status of the individual services when administrators select the **Service Health** option, as shown in Figure 4-17.

In addition to displaying the healthy services, the **Service Health** screen also lists other service status conditions:

- **Advisories** Indicates that the service is still available but that a known condition is inhibiting its performance. The condition might cause intermittent interruptions, affect only some users, or be limited in scope. In some cases, a workaround might be available.

- **Incidents** Indicates that a critical issue has been discovered that is rendering all or a significant part of the service unavailable or unusable. Typically, incidents are updated on their detail pages with information about the issue's investigation, mitigation, and resolution.

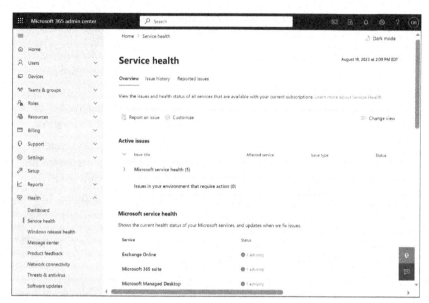

FIGURE 4-17 The Service Health page in the Microsoft 365 admin center

Selecting the **Issue History** tab on the **Service Health** page displays details about the resolved incidents and advisories, as shown in Figure 4-18, including the service affected, its current status, and the time the advisory was posted.

FIGURE 4-18 The Issue History tab of the Service Health page in the Microsoft 365 admin center

The **Status** indicators on the **Service Health** pages can have values such as the following:

- **Investigating**   Indicates that Microsoft is aware of the issue and is currently gathering information before taking action
- **Service Degradation**   Indicates that the service is experiencing intermittent interruptions, performance slowdowns, or failure of specific features

- **Service Interruption** Indicates that a significant, repeatable issue is occurring, which is preventing users from accessing the service

- **Restoring Service** Indicates that the cause of the issue has been determined and remediation is underway, which will result in service restoration

- **Extended Recovery** Indicates that remediation of the issue is in progress, but restoring service for all users may take some time or that an interim fix is in place that restores service until a permanent solution is applied

- **Investigation Suspended** Indicates that Microsoft is awaiting information from subscribers or other parties before the issue can be diagnosed or further action can be taken

- **Service Restored** Indicates that Microsoft has taken corrective action to address the issue and has successfully brought the service back to a healthy state

- **Post-Incident Report Published** Indicates that documentation on the issue has been published containing an explanation of the root cause and steps to prevent a reoccurrence

Each advisory or incident includes a detail page containing more information, as shown in Figure 4-19. This information may include a greater elaboration on the user impact of the advisory or incident and a log of its status as it proceeds through the process of being addressed, documented, and resolved.

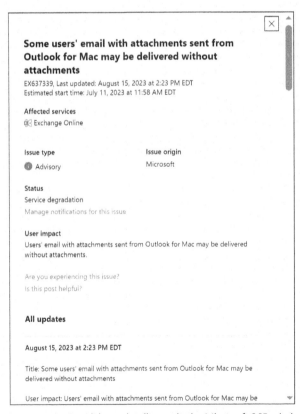

FIGURE 4-19 An advisory detail pane in the Microsoft 365 admin center

When an incident prevents administrators from signing in to the Microsoft 365 admin center console, a separate Microsoft 365 Service Health Status page (available at *status.office365.com*) indicates the health of the Microsoft 365 services, as shown in Figure 4-20.

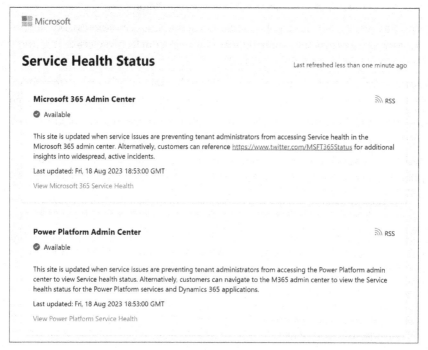

FIGURE 4-20 The Microsoft 365 Service Health Status page

It is also possible to monitor the health of the various Microsoft 365 services in the Microsoft Entra admin center and create new service requests, as shown in Figure 4-21.

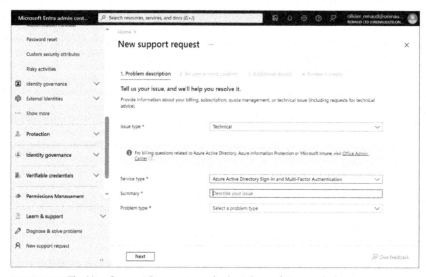

FIGURE 4-21 The New Support Request page in the Microsoft Entra admin center

Summary

- Microsoft 365 editions include various combinations of Office productivity applications and Microsoft 365 cloud services. Multiple subscription levels exist for the Microsoft 365 Business and Microsoft 365 Enterprise products.

- There are special editions of Microsoft 365 for frontline, government, and educational users. In addition, there are add-on subscriptions available that can enable administrators to create their own service combinations.

- The key selling points for Microsoft 365 are divided into four major areas: productivity, collaboration, security, and compliance.

- To install and run the Microsoft 365 components and access the Microsoft 365 cloud services, each user in an organization must have a Microsoft 365 *user subscription license (USL)*.

- Evaluating the total cost of ownership (TCO) for a Microsoft 365 implementation is relatively simple; there is a monthly or annual fee for each Microsoft 365 user subscription, and those subscriber fees are predictable and ongoing. Predicting the cost of an on-premises network requires businesses to categorize their expenses by distinguishing between capital expenditures (CapEx) and operational expenditures (OpEx).

- Organizations can purchase Microsoft 365 subscriptions directly from Microsoft individually or by using a variety of volume licensing agreements, including Enterprise Agreements (EA), Microsoft Products and Services Agreements (MPSA), or arrangements with Cloud Solution Providers (CSP).

- Typically, contracts with cloud service providers include a *service level agreement (SLA)*, which guarantees a certain percentage of uptime for the services and specifies the consequences if that guarantee is not met.

- Microsoft carefully defines the division of responsibilities between the Microsoft support team and the administrators at Microsoft 365 subscription sites.

- The **Service Health** page in the Microsoft 365 admin center displays a list of Microsoft 365 services with a status indicator for each.

Thought experiment

In this thought experiment, demonstrate your skills and knowledge of the topics covered in this chapter. You can find the answer to this thought experiment in the next section.

Ralph is responsible for planning the IT software deployment for his company's new branch office, which will have 50 users. He is currently trying to determine the more economically viable licensing choice: a cloud-based solution or on-premises servers. For the cloud-based solution, Ralph is considering Microsoft 365 Business, which costs $20 per user, per month. For an on-premises alternative providing the services his users need most, Ralph has searched through several online sources and found the software licensing prices shown in Table 4-8.

TABLE 4-8 Sample software licensing prices

Quantity needed	Product	Price each
2	Microsoft Windows Server 2019 Standard (16 core)	$976.00
1	Microsoft Windows Server 2019 Client Access Licenses (Pack of 50)	$1,869.99
50	Microsoft Office Home & Business 2019	$249.99
1	Microsoft Exchange Server 2019 Standard	$726.99
50	Microsoft Exchange Server 2019 Standard CAL	$75.99
1	Microsoft SharePoint Server	$5,523.99
50	Microsoft SharePoint Client Access License	$55.99

It is obvious to Ralph that the on-premises solution will require a much larger capital expenditure, but he is wondering whether it might be the more economical solution in the long term. Based on these prices and disregarding all other expenses (including hardware, facilities, and personnel), how long would it be before the ongoing Microsoft 365 Business subscription fees for 50 users become more expensive than the on-premises software licensing costs?

Thought experiment answer

Ralph has calculated the total software licensing costs for his proposed on-premises solution and has arrived at a total expenditure of $29,171.47, as shown in Table 4-9.

TABLE 4-9 Sample software licensing prices (with totals)

Quantity needed	Product	Price each	Total
2	Microsoft Windows Server 2019 Standard (16 core)	$976.00	$1,952.00
1	Microsoft Windows Server 2019 Client Access Licenses (Pack of 50)	$1,869.99	$1,869.99
50	Microsoft Office Home & Business 2019	$249.99	$12,499.50
1	Microsoft Exchange Server 2019 Standard	$726.99	$726.99
50	Microsoft Exchange Server 2019 Standard CAL	$75.99	$3,799.50
1	Microsoft SharePoint Server	$5,523.99	$5,523.99
50	Microsoft SharePoint Client Access License	$55.99	$2,799.50
	Grand Total		**$29,171.47**

- The Microsoft 365 Business subscription fees for 50 users amount to $1,000 per month. Therefore, Ralph has concluded that after 30 months, the subscription's ongoing cost will exceed the one-time cost for the on-premises server licensing fees. However, Ralph has been instructed not to consider an on-premises datacenter's hardware, utility, and administration costs. These expenses would vastly increase both the initial outlay and the ongoing costs of an on-premises solution.

CHAPTER 5

MS-900 Microsoft 365 Fundamentals, Second Edition exam updates

The purpose of this chapter

For all the other chapters, the content should remain unchanged throughout this edition of the book. Instead, this chapter will change over time, with an updated online PDF posted so you can see the latest version of the chapter, even after you purchase this book.

Why do we need a chapter that updates over time? For three reasons.

1. To add more technical content to the book before it is time to replace the current book edition with the next edition. This chapter will include additional technology content and possibly additional PDFs containing more content.

2. To communicate detail about the next version of the exam, to tell you about our publishing plans for that edition, and to help you understand what that means to you.

3. To accurately map the current exam objectives to existing chapter content. While exam objectives evolve and are updated and products are renamed, much of the content in this book will remain accurate and relevant. In addition to covering any content gaps that appear through additions to the objectives, this chapter will provide explanatory notes on how the new objectives map to the current text.

After the initial publication of this book, Microsoft Press will provide supplemental updates as digital downloads for minor exam updates. If an exam has major changes or accumulates enough minor changes, we will then announce a new edition. We will do our best to provide any updates to you free of charge before we release a new edition. However, if the updates are significant enough in between editions, we may release the updates as a low-priced standalone eBook.

If we do produce a free updated version of this chapter, you can access it on the book's companion website. Simply go to the companion website page and go to the "Exam Updates Chapter" section of the page.

If you have not yet accessed the companion website, follow this process below:

Step 1. Browse to *microsoftpressstore.com/register*.

Step 2. Enter the print book ISBN (even if you are using an eBook).

Step 3. After registering the book, go to your account page and select the Registered **Products** tab.

Step 4. Click on the Access **Bonus Content** link to access the companion website. Select the **Exam Updates Chapter** link or scroll down to that section to check for updates.

About possible exam updates

Microsoft reviews exam content periodically to ensure that it aligns with the technology and job role associated with the exam. This includes but is not limited to, incorporating functionality and features related to technology changes, changing skills needed for success within a job role, and revisions to product names. Microsoft updates the exam details page to notify candidates when changes occur. If you have registered this book and an update occurs to this chapter, Microsoft Press will notify you of the availability of this updated chapter.

Impact on you and your study plan

Microsoft's information helps you plan, but it also means that the exam might change before you pass the current exam. That impacts you, affecting how we deliver this book to you. This chapter gives us a way to communicate in detail about those changes as they occur. But you should watch other spaces as well.

For those other information sources to watch, bookmark and check these sites for news. In particular:

Microsoft Learn   Check the main source for up-to-date information: *microsoft.com/learn*. Make sure to sign up for automatic notifications from on that page.

Microsoft Press   Find information about products, offers, discounts, and free downloads: *microsoftpressstore.com*. Make sure to register your purchased products.

As changes arise, we will update this Chapter with more detail about exam and book content. At that point, we will publish an updated version of this Chapter, listing our content plans. That detail will likely include the following:

- Content removed, so if you plan to take the new exam version, you can ignore those when studying.

- New content planned per new exam topics, so you know what's coming.

The remainder of the Chapter shows the new content that may change over time.

News and commentary about the exam objective updates

The current official Microsoft Study Guide for the MS-900 Microsoft 365 Fundamentals exam is located at *https://learn.microsoft.com/en-us/certifications/resources/study-guides/MS-900*. This page has the most recent version of the exam objective domain.

This statement was last updated in August 2023, before Exam Ref MS-900 Microsoft 365 Fundamentals, Second Edition was published.

This version of this Chapter has no news to share about the next exam release.

In the most recent version of this Chapter, the MS-900 Microsoft 365 Fundamentals exam version number was Version 1.1.

Updated technical content

The current version of this Chapter has no additional technical content.

Objective mapping

This *Exam Ref* is structured by the author(s) based on the topics and technologies covered on the exam and is not structured based on the specific order of topics in the exam objectives. The table below maps the current version of the exam objectives to chapter content, allowing you to locate where a specific exam objective item has coverage without consulting the index.

TABLE 7-1 Exam Objectives mapped to chapters.

Exam Objective	Chapter
Describe cloud concepts	
Describe the different types of cloud services available ■ Describe Microsoft SaaS, IaaS, and PaaS concepts and use cases ■ Describe differences between Office 365 and Microsoft 365	1
Describe the benefits of and considerations for using cloud, hybrid, or on-premises services ■ Describe public, private, and hybrid cloud models ■ Compare costs and advantages of cloud, hybrid, and on-premises services ■ Describe the concept of hybrid work and flexible work	1
Describe Microsoft 365 apps and services	
Describe productivity solutions of Microsoft 365 ■ Describe the core productivity capabilities and benefits of Microsoft 365 including Microsoft Outlook and Microsoft Exchange, Microsoft 365 apps, and OneDrive ■ Describe core Microsoft 365 Apps including Microsoft Word, Excel, PowerPoint, Outlook, and OneNote ■ Describe work management capabilities of Microsoft 365 including Microsoft Project, Planner, Bookings, Forms, Lists, and To Do	2

Exam Objective	Chapter
Describe collaboration solutions of Microsoft 365	2
■ Describe the collaboration benefits and capabilities of Microsoft 365 including Microsoft Exchange, Outlook, Yammer, SharePoint, OneDrive, and Stream	
■ Describe the collaboration benefits and capabilities of Microsoft Teams and Teams Phone	
■ Describe the Microsoft Viva apps	
■ Describe the ways that you can extend Microsoft Teams by using collaborative apps	
Describe endpoint modernization, management concepts, and deployment options in Microsoft 365	2
■ Describe the endpoint management capabilities of Microsoft 365 including Microsoft Endpoint Manager (MEM), Intune, AutoPilot, and Configuration Manager with cloud attach	
■ Compare the differences between Windows 365 and Azure Virtual Desktop	
■ Describe the deployment and release models for Windows-as-a-Service (WaaS) including deployment rings	
■ Identify deployment and update channels for Microsoft 365 Apps	
Describe analytics capabilities of Microsoft 365	2
■ Describe the capabilities of Viva Insights	
■ Describe the capabilities of the Microsoft 365 Admin center and Microsoft 365 user portal	
■ Describe the reports available in the Microsoft 365 Admin center and other admin centers	
Describe security, compliance, privacy, and trust in Microsoft 365	
Describe identity and access management solutions of Microsoft 365	3
■ Describe the identity and access management capabilities of Microsoft Entra ID	
■ Describe cloud identity, on-premises identity, and hybrid identity concepts	
■ Describe how Microsoft uses methods such as multi-factor authentication (MFA), self-service password reset (SSPR), and conditional access to keep identities, access, and data secure	
Describe threat protection solutions of Microsoft 365	3
■ Describe Microsoft 365 Defender, Defender for Endpoint, Defender for Office 365, Defender for Identity, Defender for Cloud Apps, and the Microsoft 365 Defender Portal	
■ Describe Microsoft Secure Score benefits and capabilities	
■ Describe how Microsoft 365 addresses the most common types of threats against endpoints, applications, and identities	
Describe trust, privacy, risk, and compliance solutions of Microsoft 365	3
■ Describe the Zero Trust Model	
■ Describe Microsoft Purview and compliance solutions such as insider risk, auditing, and eDiscovery	
■ Describe how Microsoft supports data residency to ensure regulatory compliance	
■ Describe information protection features such as sensitivity labels and data loss prevention	
■ Describe the capabilities and benefits of Microsoft Priva	

Exam Objective	Chapter
Describe Microsoft 365 pricing, licensing, and support	
Identify Microsoft 365 pricing and billing management options	4
■ Describe the pricing model for Microsoft cloud services including enterprise agreements, cloud solution providers, and direct billing	
■ Describe available billing and bill management options including billing frequency and methods of payment	
Identify licensing options available in Microsoft 365	4
■ Describe license management	
■ Describe the differences between base licensing and add-on licensing	
Identify support options for Microsoft 365 services	4
■ Describe how to create a support request for Microsoft 365 services	
■ Describe support options for Microsoft 365 services	
■ Describe service level agreements (SLAs) including service credits	
■ Determine service health status by using the Microsoft 365 admin center or the Microsoft Entra admin center.	

Index

Symbols

@mentions, 65

A

ACL (access control list), 174
AD DS (Active Directory Domain Services), 45–47, 119,
121, 123, 168–169
    administration, 122–123
    container hierarchy, 121–122
    credential theft, 123
    domain controllers, 121, 123
    group policy, 134
    hybrid identity, 127
        authentication, 129–131
        passwords, 127–129
        SSO (single sign-on), 128–129
    multiple master replication, 124
    objects, 121–122, 124–125
    on-premises identity, 124–125
    role, 121, 124
add-on license, 230, 231
admin center
    Exchange Online, 28–29
    Microsoft 365, 32–33, 106–108
        Billing Notifications page, 219
        Contact Support pane, 235–236
        control categories, 33–34
        Home screen, 33
        Products & Services page, 218–219
        reports, 113–114
        Reports/Usage page, 111–113
        Service Health screen, 243–246
        Support menu, 233
administration
    AD DS (Active Directory Domain Services), 122–123
    comparing cloud-based versus on-premises services,
42–43
    Microsoft Teams, 70, 76

administrators, Microsoft 365, 233–234
Adoption Score, 109–111
advisories, 243–246
AIP (Azure Information Protection), 156–157, 186
analytics, 104
Application Proxy, Entra ID, 128
applications, 20. *See also* Microsoft 365; Office
productivity applications
    Microsoft 365, 37
    Office, 8
    productivity, 23–24
    threats, 153
    Zero Trust, 172–173
apps
    LOB (line of business), 75
    Microsoft Teams, 74–75
    Set Up School Pcs, 213
    Take a Test, 213
    Viva, 71–74
Apps page, Microsoft 365 portal, 35
App-V (Microsoft Application Virtualization), 26–27
architecture
    AVD (Azure Virtual Desktop), 91
    cloud
        hybrid, 13–14
        private, 11–13
        public, 9–11
artificial intelligence, 73
asset inventory, 192–194
ATA (Advanced Threat Analytics), 186–187
attacks, 142. *See also* threat protection
audit logging, 181–182
authentication, 132–133. *See also* identity
    Application Proxy, 128
    biometric
        facial recognition, 134–135
        fingerprint scans, 134
    hybrid identity

Q-R

S

Plug into learning at

MicrosoftPressStore.com

The Microsoft Press Store by Pearson offers:

- Free U.S. shipping

- Buy an eBook, get three formats – Includes PDF, EPUB, and MOBI to use with your computer, tablet, and mobile devices

- Print & eBook Best Value Packs

- eBook Deal of the Week – Save up to 50% on featured title

- Newsletter – Be the first to hear about new releases, announcements, special offers, and more

- Register your book – Find companion files, errata, and product updates, plus receive a special coupon* to save on your next purchase

 Pearson

Hear about
it first.

Since 1984, Microsoft Press has helped IT professionals, developers, and home office users advance their technical skills and knowledge with books and learning resources.

Sign up today to deliver exclusive offers directly to your inbox.

- New products and announcements

- Free sample chapters

- Special promotions and discounts

- ... and more!

MicrosoftPressStore.com/newsletters

 Pearson